Roosevelt and the Caribbean

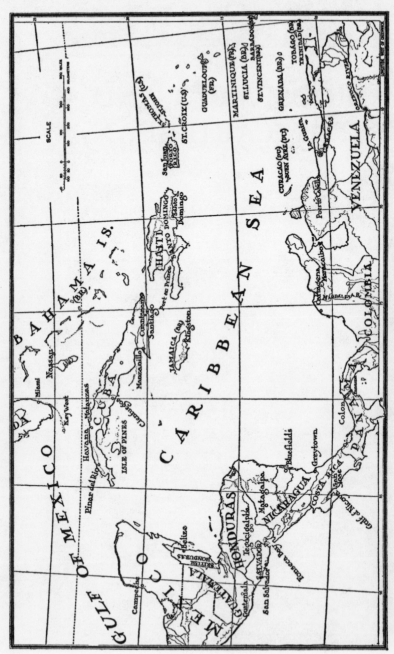

THE REGION OF THE CARIBBEAN

ROOSEVELT AND THE CARIBBEAN

By

HOWARD C. HILL, Ph.D.

New York

RUSSELL & RUSSELL

1965

TO
MY MOTHER

Preface

THEODORE ROOSEVELT came to the presidency at a significant moment in the history of the United States. The old era of isolation, initiated in a sense by Monroe, was giving way to a new period of expansion, foreseen by discriminating students and definitely launched by the unanticipated results of the war with Spain. In the development of the movement the young President, with his vigor, ambition, and fearlessness, occupies an important place. Although he cannot be regarded as the initiator of the new epoch, he played an influential part in determining its character.

Roosevelt's relations with foreign countries may be viewed conveniently as falling into three aspects, each influenced by and intricately related to the others, but each possessing characteristics and peculiarities of its own. The aspects referred to are as follows: first, relations with European countries; second, dealings with the Far East; and third, contacts in the New World, especially in the region of the Caribbean. It is to the last-named feature of Roosevelt's foreign policy that the present volume is devoted. I hope ultimately to treat the others also, especially the first.

The student of recent history faces serious problems. Working at close range to the subject with which he deals, he finds it difficult to see details in their true perspective and proper relationships. He also discovers that it is hard to attain the objective attitude that is characteristic of historical research at its best. In addition, the sources from which he draws and which alone can give validity to his conclusions and interpretations are in themselves causes of concern. On the one hand, he must sift a mass of material which, owing to modern stenography, typewriting, and printing, is enormous in extent and uneven in quality. On the other hand, he often faces serious, if not vital, gaps or omissions arising from an inability to gain access to important sources of information or from restrictions on the utilization of material during the lifetime of those concerned.

Notwithstanding such obstacles, historians must deal with contemporary movements as well as with periods more remote. Each generation is concerned in the history of its own personages and its own times. For obvious reasons it cannot wait for the clearer perspective and the more complete information of a later day. It cannot take advantage of the research of posterity.

Under the circumstances, therefore, the historical worker must do the best that conditions permit. He must investigate with diligence all available sources of information; he must sift material with an eye single for the truth; he must strive earnestly to interpret his findings with fidelity and impartiality. However imperfect the realization, such have been the ideals and purposes that have guided the preparation of the present volume.

In so far as the sources are concerned, I have been unusually fortunate. The writings and addresses of Roosevelt are voluminous. The correspondence, papers, and autobiographies of his contemporaries are extensive, and, for the most part, open to examination. The official records are exceptionally complete, the world-war having brought to light material, such as is contained in *Die grosse Politik*, which before the great conflict was inaccessible. Of greatest importance in the present study are the extensive *Roosevelt Papers* deposited in the Library of Congress. This invaluable body of material, to which I was given free and unrestricted access, includes, in addition to the great bulk of Roosevelt's public and private correspondence, copies of his speeches, significant memoranda, engagement books, confidential reports, and personal notes. But I need itemize no further; the Bibliography at the end of the volume shows the sources.

For stimulating criticism I am indebted, first of all, to Professor William E. Dodd, of the University of Chicago; under his guidance the study was undertaken and with his encouragement it has been brought to conclusion. I am also under heavy obligation to Professor Andrew C. McLaughlin, of the University of Chicago, for constructive suggestions and for invaluable assistance in securing essential material. I desire, further, to acknowledge my indebtedness to Professors Carl F. Huth and J. Fred Rippy, of the University of Chicago, for calling my attention to important sources of information, and for helpful comments growing out of a reading of the manuscript. Others from whose criticisms and suggestions I have profited are Professors Chauncey S. Boucher, Marcus W. Jernegan, and Rollo M. Tryon, of the University of Chicago. I wish to express my appreciation also for the courtesies shown me by the authorities and attendants of the Division of Manuscripts of the Library of Congress and of the Roosevelt House Library and Museum in New York City.

It is unnecessary to add that responsibility for statements and conclusions in the volume rests with me alone.

HOWARD C. HILL

UNIVERSITY OF CHICAGO
April 15, 1927

Contents

[xi]

Chapter I

THE PASSING OF NATIONAL ISOLATION

WE CANNOT sit huddled within our own borders and avow ourselves merely an assemblage of well-to-do hucksters who care nothing for what happens beyond. Such a policy would defeat even its own ends; for as the nations grow to have ever wider and wider interests and are brought into closer and closer contact, if we are to hold our own in the struggle for naval and commercial supremacy, we must build up our power without our own borders. We must build the Isthmian canal, and we must grasp the points of vantage which will enable us to have our say in deciding the destiny of the oceans of the east and the west."

The foregoing words were uttered by Theodore Roosevelt when governor of New York in an address in Chicago before the Hamilton Club, April 10, 1899.[1] The war with Spain, in which the speaker had played a dramatic part, had come to an end only a few months before. The pronouncement is significant for three reasons: first, it indicates Roosevelt's attitude toward the territories newly acquired from Spain; second, it expresses his view concerning the part that the United States should henceforth play in world-affairs; third, it reflects his realization of the truth that national isolation—the basic idea on which the foreign policy of America had hitherto rested—had passed,

[1] *Public Papers of Theodore Roosevelt, Governor*, p. 298.

or was passing, and that the world was fast coming to be an economic whole.[1]

As a matter of fact, isolation in any real sense had in large measure long since vanished, if indeed it had ever existed. United by both political and economic ties to the mother-country and affected by the tangled web of European diplomacy and policies during the Colonial period, the thirteen colonies had severed the political bond which joined them to Great Britain only to become involved in the intricacies of the French Alliance of 1778. When that union in turn was ended by the wisdom and courage of Washington and the elder Adams, the course of the new Republic remained vexed and troubled by the international difficulties growing out of the French Revolution, the billows of which, as Jefferson put it, reached "even this distant and peaceful shore."[2]

With the signing of the Treaty of Ghent and especially with the issuance of the Monroe Doctrine, an isolation from European politics and policies was in a sense inaugurated. But the separation was always more apparent than real. Involved for a century with Great Britain in a perplexing and complicated dispute over the Canadian boundary line and in an acrimonious discussion over the fisheries on the Grand Banks; affected in our economic life by the measures and policies of European governments; enlarged in population from decade to decade by an immigrant tide which with few exceptions seemed steadily on

[1] Roosevelt had repeatedly expressed views similar to those quoted above, although not in such succinct terms, prior to the Hamilton Club address. See his campaign speeches in the fall of 1898, when he was a candidate for the New York governorship (New York *Daily Tribune*, October 6, 19, 25) and his inaugural address as governor, January 22, 1899 (*Public Papers of Theodore Roosevelt, Governor*, p. 2). See also statements in other speeches (pp. 255 f., 289).

[2] J. D. Richardson, *Messages and Papers of the Presidents*, I, 322.

the rise, Americans were constantly reminded that they were not only on the earth, but of it. And all the time the shuttle of economic interests and social relationships—of commerce and business, telegraphs and cables, railways and steamships, trade and travel—was drawing the world closer and closer together.

That the tendency toward world-interdependence was realized by American leaders long before Roosevelt became prominent is clearly evident. As hard headed a man as General Grant said in 1873 in his second inaugural address:

> I do not share in the apprehension held by many as to the danger of governments becoming weakened and destroyed by reason of their extension of territory. Commerce, education, and rapid transit of thought and matter by telegraph and steam have changed all this. Rather do I believe that our Great Maker is preparing the world, in His own good time, to become one nation, speaking one language, and when armies and navies will be no longer required.[1]

Even in political matters the United States had not followed the rôle of the player of solitaire to the extent commonly supposed. In 1875 it had helped to found and maintain at Paris an International Bureau of Weights and Measures. Seven years later it ratified the Treaty of Geneva by which the contracting nations agreed to protect the relief societies of one another in war as well as in peace. In 1886 it was one of a number of nations which bound themselves to protect submarine cables. In 1890 it entered into an international agreement to suppress the African slave trade. And in 1899 it joined in an agreement to regulate the importation of spirituous liquors into Africa. More than five hundred pages of the bulky collections of *Treaties and Conventions between the United States*

[1] Richardson, *op. cit.*, VII, 222.

of America and Other Powers, 1776–1887, consist of similar international obligations incurred by the United States prior to 1888.[1]

In the realm of what may be regarded as world-activities and undertakings of a more purely political nature the United States had also played an important part before the Spanish-American War. The annexation of Alaska in 1867 marked in some respects a departure from the traditional policy of expansion which hitherto had led in no case to the acquisition of territory not contiguous to that already under the flag. But Alaska is situated in North America, and many Americans believed that it was only a matter of time until the region which separated the new purchase from the United States would also be acquired. In their eyes, therefore, the annexation of Alaska was only another step on a pathway which had long been trodden with success by the fathers.

The activities of the American government in the affairs of the Western Hemisphere were also numerous during the last half of the nineteenth century. In 1871 the United States ended the war between Spain and Peru, Chile, and Ecuador by mediation. In 1880 Chile and Colombia chose the President of the United States as perpetual arbitrator to settle disputes between the two countries in all cases in which other arbitrators were not selected by special agreements. The following year Secretary Blaine revived the idea of friendly conferences between the American powers, an idea which had been moribund for over a half-century. Nothing came of the proposal at the time,

---

[1] C. R. Fish, *The Path of Empire*, p. 284. See also P. B. Potter, *The Myth of American Isolation* (New York, 1921); A. B. Hart, *Foundations of American Foreign Policy*, pp. 2–4, 9–11; R. G. Adams, *The Foreign Policy of the United States*, pp. 21, 24.

owing to the death of Garfield, the resignation of Blaine, and the opposition of Secretary Frelinghuysen, Blaine's successor.[1] But upon Blaine's return to office in 1889, the plan was revived and the first International American Conference assembled that year at Washington at the invitation of Congress.[2]

It was in the Pacific, however, that the United States in the fifty years preceding the war with Spain showed most clearly its expansive tendencies. As early as the eighteenth century American merchantmen had plowed the waters first crossed by Magellan and had visited the ports of China and India. Hardly had the nineteenth century dawned before missionaries from New England braved the perils of the long voyage around the Horn in order to carry Christianity to the cannibal inhabitants of the islands of the Pacific.[3] In the thirties and forties treaties were negotiated with Borneo, Siam, and China. In 1853, after an unsuccessful effort by Commodore Biddle seven years before, Commodore M. C. Perry succeeded in establishing commercial relations with Japan. In 1863 the United States united with other powers in forcing an opening of the Shimonoseki Strait, and subsequently joined France, the Netherlands, and Great Britain in securing from Japan an indemnity to pay the cost of the expedition. In 1866 the United States co-operated with the same powers in obtaining a convention by which Japan agreed to adopt certain tariff regulations favorable to trade.

[1] The dropping of the plan brought a strong letter of protest from Blaine to President Arthur (*Arthur Papers* [Division of Manuscripts, Library of Congress, Washington, D.C.], Blaine to Arthur, February 3, 1882).

[2] Potter, *op. cit.*, p. 446.

[3] C. R. Fish, *American Diplomacy*, pp. 396, 402; G. Grosvenor, "The Hawaiian Islands," *National Geographic Magazine*, XLV (1924), 120-33.

More significant than the preceding commercial activities was the establishment of American authority over territory within the Pacific. In 1856, in order to protect American citizens who might engage in removing deposits of guano which they had discovered on islands not within the jurisdiction of any other government, Congress authorized the President to treat such regions as "appertaining to the United States," although no obligation to retain possession of them after the guano had been removed should be regarded as having been incurred. Under this statute the United States took possession of fifty islands in the Pacific and thirty in the Atlantic.

One of the most important and significant of the developments in the Pacific transpired in the Samoan Islands. As early as 1853 a commercial agent represented the United States at Apia. In 1872 an American naval officer entered into an agreement with the local chieftain of Tutuila, one of the most important of the Samoan group, by which the United States obtained the exclusive privilege of using as a naval station Pago-Pago, the finest harbor in that part of the Pacific. Six years later, as the result of closer relations with the inhabitants, a treaty was concluded by which the United States obtained permission from the Samoan king to use Pago-Pago as a coaling station, promising in return, in case of differences "between the Samoan government and any other government in amity with the United States, to . . . . employ its good offices for the purpose of adjusting those differences upon a satisfactory and solid foundation."[1]

Shortly afterward this arrangement threatened to end in international tragedy, for Germany and Great Britain,

[1] *Treaties and Conventions Concluded between the United States and Other Powers Since July 4, 1776*, pp. 972–73.

too, had long since acquired rights and interests in the islands. At Apia, the capital, the three foreign consuls intrigued and plotted against one another to secure advantages in trade and political influence for their respective countries, the British and the American representatives for the most part supporting each other as against the German agent. For a time the plots and counterplots bade fair to terminate in comic opera.[1] But the deposition of the native king by the German consul, the arrival of the German warship "Adler," and the ambushing by a native leader of a German landing party of which fifty members were killed precipitated a crisis.

The United States, Great Britain, and Germany immediately sent warships to Apia. During the spring of 1889 the public at large daily awaited news of bloodshed between the forces of the rival nations. Instead, there came at last the message that a hurricane had swept the islands and had wrecked all but one of the warships. In the midst of the common disaster the rivals forgot their differences and disputes; and stories of mutual help instead of tales of conflict filled the press. Later in the year (1889), in order to settle the difficulties which had brought the three countries to the brink of hostilities, a joint commission met in Berlin at Bismarck's invitation and compromised their differences by agreeing to guarantee the neutrality of the islands and to retain the native government in nominal power, but to place the real control of affairs in the hands of a chief justice and a president of the Municipal Council of Apia, all of whom were to be foreigners chosen by the joint action of the three powers.[2] By the treaty the United

[1] Hart, *op. cit.*, pp. 165 f.

[2] W. M. Malloy, "Treaties, Conventions, International Acts, Protocols and Agreements between the United States and Other Powers, 1776–1909," *Senate Document No. 357* (Sixty-first Congress, second session), II, 1576.

States for the first time, said Secretary Gresham (May 9, 1894), departed from its "traditional and well-established policy of avoiding entangling alliances with foreign powers in relation to objects remote from this hemisphere."[1]

Even more significant of the trend of American development in the Pacific than the Samoan episode was the course of events in the Hawaiian, or Sandwich Islands, as they were then called. Owing to their geographic proximity to North America, the islands, although discovered by the English navigator, Captain Cook, had always dealt chiefly with the United States. Early in the nineteenth century whaling vessels from New England visited the archipelago for supplies, frequently enlisting natives as sailors, while American missionaries Christianized the inhabitants and assisted the kings in conducting the government. In 1842 Daniel Webster extended the protection of the United States over the islands by declaring that European powers must not interfere with the established government. Seven years afterward a "treaty of friendship, commerce, and navigation and extradition" was entered into by the two countries.[2] In 1853 Secretary of State William L. Marcy drew up a treaty of annexation which the Senate failed to approve, while the Hawaiian government later withdrew its consent.

Twenty years later the mutual commercial interests of the two countries—Hawaii by this time had become the sugar bowl of California[3]—led to a treaty of reciprocity ratified in 1875 by which the lower grades of Hawaiian sugar obtained free entrance into the United States, American commodities were admitted free into Hawaii,

---

[1] *Foreign Relations of the United States*, Appendix I (1894), p. 504.

[2] Malloy, *op. cit.*, I, 908–15.

[3] Adams, *op. cit.*, p. 257.

and the islands became virtually an American protector-ate.[1] The treaty was renewed in 1884 with the grant to the United States of the right to establish a naval station in the Pearl River harbor.[2] So clear did the conviction become that the islands belonged to the American continent that in 1889 Secretary Blaine invited Hawaii to send delegates to the first Pan-American Congress.

The treaty of annexation, drawn up in 1893 at President Harrison's desire by Secretary of State John W. Foster upon the receipt of news of the Hawaiian revolution,[3] was therefore but the logical outcome of the events of the preceding half-century. Temporarily delayed by President Cleveland's action in withdrawing the treaty upon his accession to the presidency,[4] annexation was successfully consummated under President McKinley in 1898 by joint resolution of Congress.[5]

The next year saw the division of the Samoan Islands between the United States and Germany, the joint protectorate having proved acceptable to none of the three powers and resulting only in difficulty and friction. The United States received Tutuila, the rest of the group went to Germany, while Great Britain obtained compensation in the Gilbert and Solomon archipelagoes. The developments in Samoa and Hawaii have their chief significance in the light which they throw on the tendency of the United

[1] Malloy, *op. cit.*, I, 915-17.

[2] *Ibid.*, I, 919-20.

[3] J. W. Foster, *American Diplomacy in the Orient*, p. 376; *Diplomatic Memoirs*, II, 167 f.

[4] Concerning Cleveland's action Roosevelt wrote to his sister (January 7, 1894): "I think he has made a fearful mess of the Hawaiian affair" (*Letters from Theodore Roosevelt to Anna Roosevelt Cowles*, p. 134; see also p. 143).

[5] An excellent sketch of the reasons for annexation is given in J. W. Foster's *The Annexation of Hawaii.*

States, long before the annexation of the Philippines, to play a part in determining the fate of remote island groups in the Pacific.

Before the events which have been related reached the culmination described above, there had occurred the dramatic Venezuelan episode in which President Cleveland made the most vigorous application of the Monroe Doctrine that the world had yet seen. Regarding Great Britain's refusal to submit to arbitration all the points involved in her dispute with Venezuela over the boundary of British Guiana[1] as a violation of that dictum of Monroe which stated that "the American continents . . . . are henceforth not to be considered as subjects for future colonization by any European powers," Cleveland directed the secretary of state, Richard Olney, to present fully the attitude of the United States toward the controversy.[2]

This Secretary Olney proceeded to do (July 20, 1895) in one of the most amazing dispatches in the records of American diplomacy. After giving a historical sketch of the Venezuelan boundary dispute and repeating the familiar phrases of the Monroe Doctrine, Olney declared that "distance and three thousand miles of intervening ocean make any permanent political union between an European and an American state unnatural and inexpedient"; that "the United States is practically sovereign on this continent, and its fiat is law upon the subjects to which it confines its interposition"; that "its infinite resources combined with its isolated position render it master of the situation and practically invulnerable as against any

[1] Great Britain was willing to submit to arbitration the ownership of a portion of the territory in dispute with Venezuela, but not all of it. See R. M. McElroy, *Grover Cleveland*, II, 173–79.

[2] Grover Cleveland, *Presidential Problems*, pp. 256–59.

or all other powers." The communication ended with a request for "a definite decision upon the point whether Great Britain will consent or will decline to submit the Venezuelan boundary question in its entirety to impartial arbitration" and the statement that the President desired to be informed of the intentions of the British government before the next meeting of Congress.[1]

Months passed before Lord Salisbury made a response. In his reply dated November 26, 1895, the British Foreign and Prime Minister emphatically denied the American statements and implications, refused to admit the applicability of the Monroe Doctrine to the Venezuelan situation, and again declined to submit the boundary dispute to arbitration.[2] Three weeks later (December 17, 1895), President Cleveland astonished the world by the categorical character of his special message to Congress in which, after reviewing the controversy, he requested authority to appoint a special commission to investigate the facts and determine the true boundary. He concluded as follows:

In making these recommendations I am fully alive to the responsibility incurred and keenly realize all the consequences that may follow. I am, nevertheless, firm in my conviction that .... there is no calamity which a great nation can invite which equals that which follows a supine submission to wrong and injustice and consequent loss of national self-respect and honor, beneath which are shielded and defended a people's greatness.[3]

Cleveland's recommendations were promptly adopted by Congress. His message was warmly indorsed by Roosevelt who wrote the President that "it would be difficult to overestimate the good done in this country by the vigorous

[1] *Foreign Relations*, I (1895), 545–62.

[2] *Ibid.*, pp. 563–67; see also Cleveland, *op. cit.*, pp. 262–68.

[3] Richardson, *op. cit.*, IX, 655–58; see also Cleveland, *op. cit.*, pp. 269–72.

course taken by the National Executive and Legislature in this matter."[1] In a letter to Senator Lodge (December 20, 1895) Roosevelt says: "I am very much pleased with the President's or rather with Olney's message."[2] Two days later he writes to his brother-in-law: "I earnestly hope our government don't back down. If there is a muss I shall try to have a hand in it myself!"[3]

Fortunately for the cause of peace between the United States and Great Britain, the Kaiser's telegram congratulating President Krüger upon the failure of the Jameson raid was sent the following month (January, 1896). The telegram played an important part in causing the British people to demand that their diplomats find an amicable solution of the trouble with the United States.[4] Accordingly, Lord Salisbury indicated the willingness of the British government to aid the commission and also assented to the earlier request of the United States to have the boundary determined by an international tribunal. Hereupon the American investigation was dropped. Subsequently Lord Salisbury proposed that a treaty of general arbitration be entered into by the two countries, but the arrangement was rejected by the United States Senate.

Cleveland's victory in the Venezuelan affair marked the greatest recognition yet given by a foreign government of the peculiar interest of the United States in international

[1] J. B. Bishop, *Theodore Roosevelt and His Time*, I, 69.

[2] *Selections from the Correspondence of Theodore Roosevelt and Henry Cabot Lodge*, I, 200. See also pp. 204, 209. Roosevelt believed that Olney was "the mainspring of the administration in the Venezuelan matter" (see letter to his sister in *Letters to Anna Roosevelt Cowles*, p. 170); on the authorship of the message, see McElroy, *Grover Cleveland*, II, 188 f.

[3] *Letters to Anna Roosevelt Cowles*, p. 165. See also pp. 168 and 171.

[4] Lord Rosebery believed war on such an issue would be "the greatest crime on record." Balfour spoke of a conflict between the United States and Great Britain as having the "horrors of a civil war" (*Public Opinion*, XX [1896], 8, 106).

disputes affecting the welfare of the countries of the New World. In this respect it gave to the Monroe Doctrine the highest international recognition that that pronouncement had yet received.

The tendency toward expansion which has been pointed out in the preceding pages did not develop without encountering strong opposition. Rightly or wrongly, the experiences and memories of the forties and the fifties caused many Americans to look upon an extension of territory as undesirable if not actually evil. The scramble of European powers during the seventies and eighties for territories in Africa and Asia tended on the whole to confirm American suspicions. In all probability only a sense of obligation for what was interpreted as the friendly attitude of the Muscovite government during the Civil War and a feeling that the purchase of Alaska was a favor conferred upon Russia caused public opinion to support half-tolerantly the acquisition of that distant region in 1867.

Public sentiment at all events did not favor territorial additions elsewhere, for the same year that saw the extension of American authority over Alaska witnessed the Senate's rejection with popular approval of a treaty providing for the annexation of St. Thomas and St. John of the Danish West Indies.[1] Again in 1870 Grant's pet scheme for the acquisition of Santo Domingo was rejected by the Senate amid signs of public satisfaction. In view of such facts it is small wonder that in 1873 Hamilton Fish, the secretary of state, wrote that popular sentiment was opposed to all expansion. Indeed, during the next quarter of a century, the great majority of the American people, while keenly awakened to a new sense of national consciousness, seem on the whole to have had little if any desire to annex

[1] Hart, *op. cit.*, p. 45; J. F. Rhodes, *History of the United States*, VI, 213 f.

additional territory. They felt apparently no yearning for the acquisition of lands inhabited by peoples of an alien race possessing alien customs and alien ideals.

Nevertheless, the stars in their courses fought against national isolation. With the rapid disappearance of free land in the West that expansive tendency which, as Turner has pointed out, has characterized the American people almost from the beginning could hardly be expected to come to a sudden end.[1] If future expansion did not manifest itself in additional territorial acquisitions, it might be anticipated in the economic penetration of regions in other climes and under other auspices than that of the national flag.

The tendency to expansion was, indeed, stimulated by the amazing development of industrialism and the accompanying growth of urban population which marked the decades succeeding the Civil War. In 1860 agriculture occupied the leading position in American economic life, the value of farm property exceeding the value of manufactured products by more than 400 per cent; in 1900, on the other hand, the value of farm products, while still holding the premier rank, exceeded the value of manufactured products by barely 50 per cent.[2] Whereas in 1860 the cities of the United States contained barely 16 per cent of the population of the country, by 1900 they comprised more than 33 per cent of the population.[3] The economic revolution which ensued during the generation following Lee's surrender at Appomattox was fraught with

[1] F. J. Turner, *Frontier in American History*, pp. 37 f., 244–46.

[2] *A Century of Population Growth*, p. 145.

[3] The comparison is on the basis of places containing 8,000 or more population; *Census Reports, Population*, Vol. I (1901), Part I, p. xxxiii.

consequences the effects of which we are only now beginning to be aware.[1]

Not the least of the consequences was the effect upon the tradition of national isolation. Since the American people were producing in ever increasing quantities commodities of which at best they could consume only part, since they were forced more and more to seek markets in which to dispose of excess manufactured goods and in which to obtain raw materials, it was inevitable that in an economic sense at least isolation should vanish.

The disappearance of isolation was hastened by the accumulation of surplus capital that attended the progress of industrialism. At first, it is true, ample opportunities for profitable investments existed within the United States. Railroad-building, manufactures of all kinds, the development of natural resources in field, forest, and mine, utilized for decades the vast bulk of American capital and indeed enlisted in addition funds from foreign shores. With the ebbing of the century, however, the higher profits that were to be gained in the development of distant markets and in the exploitation of the resources of lands beyond the aegis of the American government proved an increasing lure to American bankers and capitalists.

The region of the Caribbean Sea proved one of the choicest fields for such expansion.[2] Situated at our very doors, endowed by nature so as to furnish or produce commodities for which our own soil and climate were in large measure unsuited, the islands and countries which bounded the shores of the American Mediterranean had served for centuries as sources for molasses, sugar, and cocoa and as markets for American flour, fish, barrel staves, hoops, and

[1] A. M. Schlesinger, *New Viewpoints in American History*, pp. 245–64.

[2] C. L. Jones, *Caribbean Interests of the United States*, pp. 9–13, 15–20, 23–29.

rum.[1] With the coming of industrialism in the United States, with the invention of the refrigerator car and the refrigerator ship, with improvements in communication, and with the accumulation of capital seeking profitable investment, the region assumed fresh and enlarged importance. As the years passed, bananas and cocoanuts, sugar plantations, coffee estates, oil concessions, and the fruit trade[2] received more and more attention from American business men and occupied more and more space in the consular and trade reports of foreign representatives in the region.[3]

Such was the character of the age when Theodore Roosevelt began to play an active part in national affairs. The expansion of American commerce[4]; the growing rivalry with other nations in economic matters; the realization by American manufacturers of the increasing necessity for foreign markets and by American financiers of the growing need of foreign fields for investment; the extension of American claims and interests in the Pacific; the development of telegraphs and railroads and cables; the Samoan, Hawaiian, and Venezuelan episodes—all combined to lessen or break down the American sense of isolation, both political and economic, from the rest of the world.

[1] W. B. Weeden, *Economic and Social History of New England*, II, 753–58, 780–83.

[2] Although they treat for the most part the developments after 1900, the following references also bear on the conclusions given above: C. L. Jones, "The Banana Trade," *Independent*, LXXV (1913), 77–80; "Bananas and Diplomacy," *North American Review*, CXCVIII (1913), 188–94; "Oil on the Caribbean and Elsewhere," *ibid.*, CCII (1915), 536–44.

[3] Cf., for example, *United States Consular Reports*, I (1880), No. 1, 60–64, with LXVII (1901), No. 252, 115–27, 131–33.

[4] Exports of manufactured goods rose from a value of $93,000,000 in 1880 to a value of $223,000,000 in 1898.

Chapter II

THE RISE OF ROOSEVELT

BORN in a well-to-do family in New York City (October 27, 1858), Theodore Roosevelt suffered from ill health and physical weakness during his boyhood days to an extent that caused his parents at times to despair of his life. By rigorous efforts in the home gymnasium provided by his father and by an active outdoor life, young Roosevelt gradually built up his body until in adult life he became a model of robustness and strength.

Too delicate as a lad to attend the public schools, Roosevelt received his early education from private tutors. He entered Harvard University in 1876. Here he continued to develop his body by "walking, boxing, vaulting, and gymnasium work."[1] He was popular among his mates and stood well toward the head of his class.[2] His four years of college were further distinguished by the beginning, apparently on his own initiative, of a study which resulted several years later in his first published work, *A Naval History of the War of 1812*.

The year following his graduation from Harvard

[1] *Letters from Theodore Roosevelt to Anna Roosevelt Cowles*, p. 16.

[2] On October 13, 1879, Roosevelt wrote his sister: "My studies have so far been tolerably difficult, but interesting. The other day I found out my average for the three years, 82%. I stand nineteenth in the class, which began with 230 fellows" (*ibid.*, p. 35). See also C. R. Robinson, *My Brother Theodore Roosevelt*, pp. 103, 107 f., 113; and Donald Wilhelm, *Theodore Roosevelt as an Undergraduate* (Boston, 1910), pp. 23–31.

witnessed the election of Roosevelt to the New York legislature, the youngest member of that body. Here he soon won a reputation as a vigorous advocate of reform measures. In the meantime his interest in foreign countries had been awakened and stimulated by trips abroad when still a boy—an interest which accounts, perhaps, in some degree for his study of the naval history of our second conflict with Great Britain.

Roosevelt was twice re-elected to the New York legislature. In 1884 he served as a delegate to the Republican National Convention where he worked earnestly but unsuccessfully for the nomination of Senator Edmunds, of Vermont. In the ensuing campaign he supported Blaine, taking the stump in Blaine's behalf and incurring thereby the denunciation of the Mugwumps. Following the death of his wife in 1884—he had married the year of his graduation—Roosevelt spent two years upon a ranch which he had purchased in the Dakota Bad Lands, herding cattle, engaging in the roundups, reading, and writing.

On his return to New York he became the Republican candidate for mayor, but was defeated in the three-cornered fight which ensued, Abram S. Hewitt, the Tammany nominee, being victorious over Roosevelt and Henry George, the Single Tax leader. In 1886, when in London, Roosevelt married Edith Carow Kermit, a playmate of his childhood days. Cecil Spring-Rice, subsequently British ambassador at Washington and a lifelong friend, served as best man in the ceremony. During these formative years Roosevelt wrote steadily, most of his writings dealing with hunting, politics, and history. Occasional trips to Europe, as well as hunting expeditions in the West, gave variety and zest to the days.

In 1889 President Harrison appointed Roosevelt to

membership on the United States Civil Service Commission. He served on this body for six years, the greater part of the time as its president. Here he won a national reputation by his fearless campaign for civil-service reform and by the originality and effectiveness of his attacks on spoilsmen both high and low. When W. L. Strong was elected mayor of New York on a fusion ticket, Roosevelt, after declining the headship of the Street-cleaning Department on the ground of lack of knowledge of such work, accepted a position as police commissioner, a post which he held for the next two years, 1895–97. He greatly improved the New York police system, but was seriously handicapped by the intrigues and opposition of local politicians. Against the protests of many of his admirers he resigned his office in 1897 to become assistant secretary of the navy.

Roosevelt owed his new position largely to the influence of Senator Henry Cabot Lodge, his most intimate friend for many years.[1] Lodge worked diligently in Roosevelt's behalf, conferring with President McKinley, Secretary of the Navy John D. Long, Senator Hanna, Secretary Bliss, John Hay, and Vice-President Hobart.[2] McKinley appar-

[1] "You got me the chance to be Civil Service Commissioner and Assistant Secretary of the Navy, and it was by your advice that I went into the police department" (Roosevelt to Lodge [February 2, 1900], *Roosevelt-Lodge Correspondence*, I, 447); see also pp. 241, 244, 246, 253, 260, 266 f., and *Letters to Anna Roosevelt Cowles*, p. 207.

[2] J. B. Bishop, *Theodore Roosevelt and His Times*, I, 71 f.; Theodore Roosevelt, *Autobiography*, pp. 204 f. In the *New American Navy*, II, 173, Secretary Long gives the impression that he had an entirely free hand in the appointment and selected Roosevelt from among several candidates. But Long is often inaccurate. For example, in the citation mentioned above, he says, "In May, 1897, ... I selected Roosevelt"; in his *Journal*, on the other hand, he writes under date of April 9, 1897, "Roosevelt calls. Just appointed Assistant Secretary of the Navy. Best man for the place" (see L. S. Mayo, *America of Yesterday . . . . Journal of John Davis Long*, p. 147).

ently had some misgivings over the appointment, for on one occasion he remarked to Lodge: "I hope he [Roosevelt] has no preconceived notions which he would wish to drive through the moment he got in."[1] Lodge assured the President that he knew Roosevelt's views upon the Navy and that "they were only to push on the policies which had been in operation for the last two or three administrations." That the Massachusetts Senator felt some uncertainty about the success of his mission to McKinley appears in the following comment in a letter he wrote at the time to Roosevelt: "The hitch, if there be one, is not with Long but with the White House. Whether there is any real resistance I cannot tell, and absolutely the only thing I can hear adverse is that there is a fear that you will want to fight somebody at once."[2]

No doubt the "somebody" in the case was Spain while the "fear," in all probability, was the result of the numerous emphatic declarations of Roosevelt during the preceding months that it was the duty of the United States to intervene in Cuba and drive the Spaniard from the New World.[3] At all events, from the moment when Roosevelt entered the national service he worked zealously to bring about American intervention and to put the Navy in the highest state of efficiency. From his viewpoint action in Cuba was called for on two grounds: first, national interest; second, humanity. Here are his words:

Our own direct interests were great, because of the Cuban tobacco and sugar, and especially because of Cuba's relation to the projected Isthmian canal. But even greater were our interests from the standpoint of humanity. Cuba was at our very doors. It was a dreadful

[1] Bishop, *op. cit.,* I, 71.

[2] *Ibid.*

[3] Theodore Roosevelt, *The Rough Riders,* p. 5.

thing for us to sit supinely and watch her death agony. It was our duty, even more from the standpoint of National honor than from the standpoint of National interest, to stop the devastation and destruction.[1]

After the destruction of the "Maine" (February 15, 1898), Roosevelt worked more energetically than ever for war with Spain. But almost to a man the leaders of the administration—President McKinley, Judge Day, Secretary Gage, Senator Hanna, Speaker of the House Reed, and Senator Hale—were opposed to hostilities.[2] Roosevelt seems to have been indefatigable in his efforts to bring about a conflict, seeing the President privately, going with him on drives, dining with him at the White House. Roosevelt also conferred with Judge Day (the real head of the Department of State, owing to the growing incapacity of John Sherman, the titular head of the Department), with his official superior Secretary Long, and with Senator Hanna, who was generally regarded as the real head of the Republican party, urging in season and out of season decisive action by the administration.[3] In a letter to his friend Brooks Adams (March 21, 1898), Roosevelt writes:

In the name of humanity and of national interest alike, we should have interfered in Cuba two years ago, a year and a half ago last April, and again last December. . . . . The blood of the murdered men of the "Maine" calls not for indemnity but for the full measure of atonement which can only come by driving the Spaniard from the New World. I have said this to the President before his Cabinet; I have said it to

[1] *Autobiography*, p. 209. Roosevelt had long favored American intervention in Cuba; see especially his letter to his sister, dated March 30, 1896 (*Letters to Anna Roosevelt Cowles*, p. 178).

[2] According to Roosevelt, Secretary of War Alger "was almost the only member of the Administration who felt all along that we would have to go to war with Spain over Cuba" (*ibid.*, p. 218); see also H. D. Croly, *Marcus Alonzo Hanna: His Life and Work*, pp. 310, 317.

[3] Bishop, *op. cit.*, I, 81, 82 f., 85, 86, 88 f.

Judge Day, the real head of the State Department, and to my own chief. I cannot say it publicly, for I am of course merely a minor official in the Administration. At least, however, I have borne testimony where I thought it would do good.[1]

How influential Roosevelt's exhortations were it is impossible to determine. Nothing in the published letters or diaries of McKinley, Hay, Hanna, or Long indicates that the pleadings of the Assistant Secretary had weight with those in authority.

Some of the actions of Roosevelt during these months were definitely disapproved by Secretary Long. The latter at one time records in his *Journal:* "He [Roosevelt] is so enthusiastic and loyal that he is in certain respects invaluable; yet I lack confidence in his good judgment and discretion. He goes off very impulsively."[2] At another time Long writes: "His ardor sometimes went faster than the President or the department approved."[3]

McKinley's objection to Roosevelt for the vice-presidency in 1900 reveals a lack of enthusiasm in the President for his former Assistant Secretary of the Navy as running mate. But the two men stand in marked contrast to each other in outlook and disposition, and a disinclination on McKinley's part for Roosevelt's name on the ticket in no sense proves that the President objected to Roosevelt's course when assistant secretary of the navy. In the end, moreover, McKinley did not oppose Roosevelt's nomination as vice-president.

Roosevelt's letters of this period do not indicate that he had an accurate knowledge of what was going on behind the scenes. On April 7, four days before McKinley sent his war message to Congress, Roosevelt writes a friend: "The

[1] *Ibid.*, p. 86.

[2] Mayo, *op. cit.*, p. 168. [3] *Ibid.*, p. 173.

President doesn't know what message he will send in or what he will do if we have war."[1] As a matter of fact, at the moment when Roosevelt penned this note the President's message had been ready for three days, but was being held back primarily at the suggestion of Fitzhugh Lee, the American consul-general in Havana, who reported that if the message went in at that time Americans in Cuba would be endangered.[2] Accordingly, a delay was decided upon, and it was not until April 11 that the long-deferred message was sent to Congress.[3] Fourteen days later that assembly passed a resolution which declared that war had existed with Spain since the twenty-first day of April.

During the preceding months, as pointed out above, Roosevelt did everything in his power to prepare the Navy for war. As a member of Secretary Long's Naval War Board he contributed to the making of plans.[4] In addition he pushed the gathering of material, the purchase of vessels, the completion of warships, and the recruiting of men. He also exerted influence in the selection of naval

[1] Bishop, *op. cit.*, I, 91.

[2] C. S. Olcott, *Life of William McKinley*, II, 26–29; Mayo, *op. cit.*, pp. 176–78; *House Document No. 1* (Fifty-fifth Congress, third session), I, 743.

[3] Olcott, *op. cit.*, II, 29 f. To what extent the delay was caused by a lingering hope on the President's part that the negotiations still in progress might result in peace cannot be determined. The character of the communications sent at the time to General Woodford, the American minister to Spain, indicates that the administration had determined on war. Nothing in Long's *Journal* points to a change of consequence in the President's message between April 4 and 11. Concerning the message Long writes under date of April 4, 1898: "This evening at eight o'clock there is a Cabinet meeting at the White House. The President read us his message on the Cuban situation. I suppose it is the best he can do; yet it seems to me the narrative which he makes the basis of his conclusion leads to a very different result from that which he reaches . . . . (Mayo, *op. cit.*, p. 176). The message is in *House Document No. 1*, I, 750–60.

[4] Mayo, *op. cit.*, p. 184; Long, *op. cit.*, I, 162.

commanders.[1] Most notable in the last respect was his part in the appointment of Commodore George Dewey to the command of the Asiatic squadron.[2]

According to Secretary Long, the value of Roosevelt's work in pushing preparations for war has been overrated; for, says Long, although Roosevelt's "typewriters had no rest," most of his suggestions, "so far as applicable, [had]

---

[1] Roosevelt, *Autobiography*, p. 210; Long, *op. cit.*, I, 152 f.

[2] The evidence concerning Dewey's appointment is conflicting. Secretary Long, in the *New American Navy*, I, 177, states: "I decided to give Dewey the Asiatic and Howell the European Station and this arrangement, on my submitting it to President McKinley, who had made no suggestion in the matter, and who always left such matters to the Secretary, was approved by him. I remember his simply saying to me, in his characteristically pleasant way, 'Are you satisfied that Dewey is a good man for the place and that his head is level?' to which I affirmatively answered. Political or personal influence had nothing to do with his selection, which was entirely my own." But Roosevelt, in his *Autobiography*, pp. 210–12, describes at length the cause for his own confidence in Dewey and his suggestion to the Commodore to enlist the support of some influential person in order to secure the Asiatic post. Roosevelt's account, on the whole, agrees with that of Dewey who tells of securing the support of Senator Proctor, of Vermont, after a talk with Roosevelt and of obtaining the appointment shortly afterward (G. Dewey, *Autobiography of George Dewey*, pp. 167–69). The evidence, however, hardly justifies the claim of Bishop (*op. cit.*, I, 96) that "the famous battle of Manila [was] fought and won by a commander whose appointment had been secured by Roosevelt against the wishes of Secretary Long"; for in a letter to John Hay (July 1, 1899), Roosevelt himself states (Bishop, *op. cit.*, I, 98): "In last year's fighting, as the President knows, there was a good deal of hesitation in sending Dewey to the Asiatic Squadron. It was urged very strongly by the Bureau of Navigation that Howell was entitled to go. Finally, and most wisely, the Secretary decided to disregard the argument of seniority and to send Dewey." In like manner, Dewey's statement (*op. cit.*, p. 178) that he began to assemble the fleet at Hongkong "entirely on his own initiative, without any hint whatsoever from the department that hostilities might be expected" is misleading. Before Dewey sailed to take command of the Asiatic squadron, he was told what course to follow in case of war with Spain; see Olcott, *op. cit.*, II, 38; Roosevelt, *Autobiography*, pp. 212 f.; Bishop, *op. cit.*, I, 92; Long, *op. cit.*, I, 178; Theodore Roosevelt, "Admiral Dewey," *McClure's Magazine*, Vol. XIII (1899), also *The Strenuous Life* (Homeward Bound ed.), pp. 161–65, and *Roosevelt-Lodge Correspondence*, I, 349, 408 f.

been already adopted by the various bureau chiefs."[1] Long seemed to find Roosevelt's custom of "frequently incorporating his views in memoranda which he would place every morning" on the desk of the Secretary a bit irritating. "I suggested to him," writes Long, "that some future historian reading his memoranda, if they were put on record, would get the impression that the bureaus were inefficient."

Perhaps, as Howland suggests, the truth is that some of the bureaus "were inefficient," and that Secretary Long with his easy-going nature assumed that actions and precautions had been taken by his subordinates in instances

[1] Long, *op. cit.*, II, 174. Looseness of language and inaccuracy of statement again mark Long's account. His original narrative of these days, published in the *Outlook*, LXXV (1903), 361, contains this statement: "Just before the war he [Roosevelt], as well as some naval officers, was anxious to send a squadron across the ocean to sink the ships and torpedo boat destroyers of the Spanish fleet while we were yet at peace with Spain." Regarding the statement as a serious charge, Roosevelt, who was serving as President at the time of the publication (Long had resigned as secretary of the navy the previous year), immediately wrote to Long denying the correctness of the account. When Long replied that he saw no difference between his statement and Roosevelt's explanation Roosevelt wrote a second time (October 15, 1903): "It is perfectly true that I wished a declaration of war long before we did declare it; and I also desired notice to be sent to the Spanish Government that we should treat the sailing of the fleet as an act of war, and then meet the fleet on the seas and smash it before it could act on the defensive [offensive?]. It was to my mind obvious that armed cruisers and torpedo-boats could not be used against the insurgents, and could only be intended for use against us. . . . . I am sure that you will recall that I had been urging a declaration of war for some time—that is, urging a declaration that we should take certain acts, or failures to act, as warranting such declaration after notice had been given. In the case of the sailing of the torpedo-boats, I did wish us to notify the Spanish Government that we should treat their being sent as an act of war. In the form in which the statement is made in the *Outlook*, I cannot admit that either I or any naval officer whom I was associated with made it—indeed I do not recall such a suggestion made by anyone, and certainly I never made any such suggestion myself, as that we should send a squadron across the ocean to sink the ships and torpedo-boat destroyers while we were

where little or nothing had been done.[1] That Long found the Assistant Secretary a stimulating influence appears in his statement that Roosevelt's "spirited and forceful habit is a good tonic for one who is disposed to be as conservative and careful as I am."[2]

When left in charge of affairs—a not infrequent occurrence, owing to Long's indifferent health and frequent absences from the office[3]—Roosevelt occasionally acted on matters in a manner most unusual for a minor official and in a way both irritating and embarrassing to his chief. On one instance in particular (February 25, 1898), according to Long, "the very devil seemed to possess him."

Having the authority for that time of Acting-Secretary, he immediately began to launch peremptory orders: distributing ships: ordering ammunition, which there is no means to move, to places where there is no means to store it; sending for Captain Barker to come on about the guns of *Vesuvius*, which is a matter that might have been

yet at peace with Spain. As I recall it and all that I remember any naval officer urging, was that we should notify the Spanish Government that we should treat their sailing as an act of war and that we should then conduct ourselves accordingly" (Bishop, *op. cit.*, I, 99 f.). Roosevelt's statement seems to be supported by a passage in a letter he wrote on March 16, 1898, to Captain Robley D. Evans, just after the news came that the Spanish torpedo flotilla had sailed from the Canaries for Porto Rico: "We ought to treat the sailing of the flotilla exactly as a European power would the mobilizing of a hostile army on its frontier" (*ibid.*, I, 87; see also Roosevelt's letter of March 24 to Captain A. T. Mahan, *ibid.*, and his letter to Lodge, dated September 21, 1897, in *Roosevelt-Lodge Correspondence*, I, 278 f.). It is worth noting that, although Long wrote that he saw no difference between Roosevelt's explanation and his own statement in the *Outlook*, he altered his phrasing in the final form of his history, but did not change the passage so as to meet fully Roosevelt's contention (cf. *Outlook*, *loc. cit.*, and J. D. Long, *op. cit.*, II, 173; see also J. D. Long to T. Roosevelt, October 17, 1903, *Roosevelt Papers*).

[1] Harold Howland, *Theodore Roosevelt and His Times*, pp. 243 f.

[2] Mayo, *op. cit.*, p. 168.

[3] *Roosevelt-Lodge Correspondence*, I, 267, 271 f., 279 f.

perfectly arranged by correspondence; sending messages to Congress for immediate legislation, authorizing the enlistment of an unlimited number of seamen; and ordering guns from the Navy Yard at Washington to New York, with a view to arming auxiliary cruisers which are now in peaceful commercial pursuit. The only effect of this last order would be to take guns which are now carefully stored, ready for shipment any moment . . . . and dump them in the open weather in the New York Navy Yard, where they would be only in the way and under no proper care.

He has gone at things like a bull in a china shop, and with the best purposes in the world has really taken what, if he could have thought, he would not for a moment have taken; and that is the one course which is most discourteous to me, because it suggests that there had been a lack of attention which he was supplying. It shows how the best fellow in the world—and with splendid capacities—is worse than no use if he lack a cool head and careful discretion.[1]

That the Assistant Secretary by such activities should have seemed to his superior "very near causing more of an explosion than happened to the 'Maine' "[2] is but natural, especially since Long had directed Roosevelt that same day to revoke an order which Roosevelt had issued for putting naval vessels in shape for action and had instructed him to take no step affecting the policy of the administration "without consulting the President or me."[3] The letter in which the foregoing instructions were given continues: "I am not away from town and my intention was to have you look after the routine of the office while I get a quiet day off. I write to you because I am anxious to have no

[1] Mayo, *op. cit.*, pp. 168 f.; see also *Roosevelt-Lodge Correspondence*, I, 279 f., 281.

[2] Mayo, *op. cit.*, pp. 168 f.

[3] Bishop, *op. cit.*, I, 86. Judging from the date, Long's letter was written prior to the stirring events of February 25, the day on which, among other activities, Roosevelt sent the notable dispatch to Dewey at Hongkong, directing him to be ready for immediate action in case of war with Spain (*ibid.*, I, 95; Roosevelt, *Autobiography*, p. 213).

unnecessary occasion for a sensation in the papers." Several weeks later Roosevelt wrote to his sister (April 1, 1898): "As for matters here, I'd give all I'm worth to be just two days in supreme command. I'd be perfectly willing then to resign, for I'd have things going so that nobody could stop them."[1]

In view of Long's easy-going nature one cannot but wonder if there may not have been in the Department of the Navy a lack of attention which Roosevelt supplied and if, in spite of Long's efforts to dissuade his impetuous assistant from resigning, something akin to relief was not felt by the Secretary when upon the outbreak of war Roosevelt announced his determination to join the colors. Even if such were his feeling, Long seems to have done everything in his power to cause Roosevelt to refrain from what he (Long) regarded as a foolish step. There is genuine and unmistakable appreciation of Roosevelt's personality and services in the passage in Long's *Journal* in which he records the outcome:

> Roosevelt has been of great use; a man of unbounded energy and force, and thoroughly honest—which is the main thing. He has lost his head to this unutterable folly of deserting the post where he is of the most service and running off to ride a horse and, probably, brush mosquitoes from his neck on the Florida sands. . . . . And yet how absurd all this will sound, if by some turn of fortune he should accomplish some great thing and strike a very high mark![2]

[1] *Letters to Anna Roosevelt Cowles*, p. 212.

[2] Mayo, *op. cit.*, pp. 186 f. At a later date Long wrote at the bottom of the page of his diary on which the statement quoted above occurs: "P.S.—Roosevelt was right, and we, his friends, were all wrong." Long's views of Roosevelt's action are echoed by John Hay, then in London, in a letter to C. F. Adams (May 9, 1898): "T— R—, that *wilder verwegener*, has left his Navy Department where he had the chance of his life, and joined a cowboy regiment" (*Letters and Diaries*, III, 123).

THE RISE OF ROOSEVELT

The story of the Spanish-American War and of Roosevelt's part in the conflict does not lie within the scope of this volume. In the words of Secretary Long, "His going into the army led straight to the Presidency."[1] Within two weeks after the Rough Riders were mustered out of the service, Roosevelt received the Republican nomination for governor of New York and was elected by a majority of seventeen thousand votes. Somewhat against his own inclination, he was nominated a year and a half later for the vice-presidency by the Republican National Convention, and was triumphantly elected the following November.[2] Six months after the inauguration, as a result of the assassination of McKinley, Roosevelt succeeded to the presidency (September 14, 1901). He was then in the prime of life, a man but forty-two years of age, the youngest in the history by the nation to occupy the office of chief magistrate. For the next eight years he was to be an outstanding figure on the world-stage.

[1] *New American Navy*, II, 175.

[2] From the account of Roosevelt's attitude at the Convention of 1900 in Olcott's *Life of William McKinley*, it is evident that, while Roosevelt preferred another term as governor of New York to the vice-presidency, the nomination for the latter office was not distasteful to him. Certainly, as Senator Hanna said to Roosevelt and as Silas Wright and Frank O. Lowden both demonstrated when they were nominated for the same office—the one in 1844, the other in 1924— "there is nothing in this country which can compel a man to run for an office who doesn't want it" (*ibid.*, II, 275). Roosevelt's course at the time is one of the instances when he does not seem to have made up his mind in advance with that finality which was his boast. Barely a week before the Convention he wrote to F. V. Greene: "I will not accept the Vice-Presidency under any circumstances and that is all there is about it" (cf. Howland, *op. cit.*, p. 23, and M. Sullivan, *Our Times*, I, 93). Concerning the vice-presidential nomination, see Olcott, *op. cit.*, II, 267–83; Croly, *op. cit.*, pp. 309–18; Howland, *op. cit.*, p. 23; Sullivan, *op. cit.*, I, 85–98; *Roosevelt-Lodge Correspondence*, I, 404, 426 f., 442, 447 f., 461, 465; *Letters to Anna Roosevelt Cowles*, pp. 225, 233, 235, 240–45; Robinson, *My Brother Theodore Roosevelt*, pp. 196 f.

Chapter III
THE TAKING OF PANAMA

NOTHING in his public career seems to have given Roosevelt more gratification or have been regarded by him as of greater importance than the construction of the Panama Canal.[1] He always felt that the one act for which he deserved most credit in his entire administration lay in his seizing the psychological moment to get complete control of the Isthmus.[2] In an article published over two years after the expiration of his term of office he wrote:

It must be a matter of pride to every honest American, proud of the good name of his country, that the acquisition of the canal and the building of the canal, in all their details, were as free from scandal as the public acts of George Washington and Abraham Lincoln. . . . . Every action taken was not merely proper, but was carried out in accordance with the highest, finest, and nicest standards of public and governmental ethics. . . . . Not only was the course followed as regards Panama right in every detail and at every point, but there could have been no variation from this course except for the worse. . . . . The United States has many honorable chapters in its history, but no

[1] J. B. Bishop, *Theodore Roosevelt and His Time*, I, 270. In a letter dated December 29, 1903, Roosevelt writes: "To my mind this building of the canal through Panama will rank in kind, though of course not in degree, with the Louisiana Purchase and the acquisition of Texas" (*ibid.*, p. 295); see also his *Autobiography*, pp. 512, 526. Roosevelt's gratification seems to have been shared by Secretary Hay; see W. R. Thayer, *Life and Letters of John Hay*, II, 325.

[2] T. Roosevelt to W. H. Taft, December 6, 1910, *Roosevelt Papers*.

more honorable chapter than that which tells of the way in which our right to dig the Panama Canal was secured.[1]]

None of Roosevelt's acts, in so far at least as his conduct of foreign affairs is concerned, proved so far reaching in its influence upon his later foreign policy as his course in Panama. At the same time nothing that he did has been the object of such severe denunciation by his critics.

Roosevelt's interest in a canal which would join the Atlantic and Pacific oceans dates from before the Spanish-American War. In a letter to Senator Lodge (October 27, 1894) Roosevelt says: "I do wish our Republicans would go in avowedly to annex Hawaii and build an oceanic canal."[2] Keenly interested in the Navy from early manhood, he was deeply concerned as assistant secretary of the navy during the months that preceded the struggle with Spain in the efficiency of that arm of the national defense. The long, doubtful voyage of the "Oregon" around the Horn on the eve of the war impressed him, as it did other thoughtful Americans, with the need of an interoceanic canal which would be not only of notable value to commerce but which would also virtually double the strength of American naval forces. Convinced of the nation's duty to expand, he believed that it was a natural corollary of the annexation of Hawaii and the Philippines to open the way for the Navy to operate with equal facility in either of the oceans which washed our eastern and our western shores.

Roosevelt's first important public expression concerning

[1] "How the United States Acquired the Right to Dig the Panama Canal," *Outlook*, XCIX (1911), 314–18.

[2] *Roosevelt-Lodge Correspondence*, I, 139. Six months previously (May 20, 1894) Roosevelt wrote his sister: "It is a great mistake that we have not started an interoceanic canal at Nicaragua" (*Letters to Anna Roosevelt Cowles*, p. 143).

the canal was an adverse comment upon the first Hay-
Pauncefote Treaty negotiated in 1900 by his friend John
Hay for the purpose of abrogating the Clayton-Bulwer
Treaty of 1850. For a score of years and more the Clayton-
Bulwer Convention with Great Britain, with its provision
for joint control, non-fortification, and neutrality,[1] had
been looked upon by most Americans as an anachronism
and as an impossible obstacle to the construction of an
interoceanic canal.[2] Public opinion was insistent that the
passage be built by the United States, owned by the United
States, controlled by the United States, and governed by
the United States.[3] The door to such results was not
opened by the treaty which Hay negotiated with Lord
Pauncefote in 1900. In the eyes of Roosevelt and others,
the proposed arrangement was fundamentally defective in
failing to authorize the United States to build, control, and
fortify the canal.

After some hesitation Roosevelt, then governor of New
York, expressed his dissatisfaction in a statement to the
press. In reply to Hay's "confidential letter of grieved protest,"[4] Roosevelt explained his position as follows:

My objections are twofold. First, as to naval policy. If the proposed canal had been in existence in '98, the *Oregon* could have come
more quickly through to the Atlantic; but this fact would have been
far outweighed by the fact that Cervera's fleet would have had open to
it the chance of itself going through the canal, and thence sailing to
attack Dewey or to menace our stripped Pacific Coast. If that canal

[1] W. M. Malloy, *Treaties, Conventions, International Acts, Protocols and
Agreements*, I, 660 f.

[2] Concerning the agreement of 1850 between the United States and Great
Britain, see I. D. Travis, *The Clayton-Bulwer Treaty*, "University of Michigan
Political Science Association Publications," Vol. III, No. 8.

[3] *Senate Document No. 474* (Sixty-third Congress, second session), XV, 1 f.,
53 f.; G. H. Stuart, *Latin America and the United States*, pp. 65–69.

[4] Roosevelt's description of Hay's letter (Bishop, *op. cit.*, I, 144).

is open to the warships of an enemy, it is a menace to us in time of war; it is an added burden, an additional strategic point to be guarded by our fleet. If fortified by us, it becomes one of the most potent sources of our possible sea strength. Unless so fortified it strengthens against us every nation whose fleet is larger than ours. One prime reason for fortifying our great seaports is to unfetter our fleet, to release it for offensive purposes; and the proposed canal would fetter it again, for our fleet would have to watch it, and therefore do the work which a fort should do; and what it could do much better.

Secondly, as to the Monroe Doctrine. If we invite foreign powers to a joint ownership, a joint guarantee, of what so vitally concerns us but a little way from our borders, how can we possibly object to similar joint action say in Southern Brazil or Argentine, where our interests are so much less evident? If Germany has the same right that we have in the canal across Central America, why not in the partition of any part of Southern America? To my mind, we should consistently refuse to all European powers the right to control, in any shape, any territory in the Western Hemisphere which they do not already hold.

As for existing treaties—I do not admit the "dead hand" of the treaty-making power in the past. A treaty can always be honorably abrogated—though it must never be abrogated in dishonest fashion.[1]

The first Hay-Pauncefote Treaty proved so objectionable to the Senate that, in accordance with a not uncommon practice, that body made three amendments in the document before consenting to its ratification. In the amended form the treaty proved unacceptable to Great Britain, and for a short time the matter was dropped. Before Roosevelt came to the presidency, however, negotiations had been renewed (April 25, 1901),[2] and were rapidly approaching a conclusion at the time of McKinley's death (September 14, 1901).

The influence of the new chief magistrate in the conduct

---

[1] *Ibid.;* the letter is dated February 18, 1900. See also Roosevelt's letters to Captain A. T. Mahan and to Dr. Albert Shaw, *loc. cit.,* and to his brother-in-law, Captain Cowles, in *Letters to Anna Roosevelt Cowles,* p. 236.

[2] *Senate Document No. 474,* XV, 19.

of foreign affairs is apparent almost from the first. Unlike McKinley who, according to John Hay, did not send for him on business once a month, Roosevelt saw the Secretary of State every day.[1] In a very real sense the new President was his own minister of foreign affairs, and at times consulted no member of his cabinet when making important decisions.[2] Upon his shoulders rests very definitely the responsibility for all acts of consequence during his administration.

The change in the management of foreign relations can be discerned by the change in Hay's dispatches. In the negotiations attending the first Hay-Pauncefote Treaty and in those connected with the second treaty of the same name prior to the assassination of McKinley, reference to the President's desires or orders is unusual;[3] after Roosevelt's accession Hay's communications frequently contain such expressions as "The President cordially approves draft of canal treaty and your instructions," "I am authorized by the President to say this," and "The Treaty . . . . has been submitted to the President, who approves of the conclusions reached."[4]

The second Hay-Pauncefote Treaty (ratified by the Senate, December 16, 1901) removed the obstacles in the

[1] Thayer, *op. cit.*, II, 297.

[2] *Ibid.*, II, 321; T. Roosevelt, *Autobiography*, p. 526; T. Dennett, *Roosevelt and the Russo-Japanese War*, pp. 22 f., 336.

[3] In the dispatches relating to the abrogation of the Clayton-Bulwer Treaty, I find but four references to consultation with or the directions of President McKinley. In most instances the consultation seems to have been sought by Hay and the decisions to have been largely of his making (see *Senate Document No. 474*, XV, 19, 36, 37).

[4] *Ibid.*, pp. 42, 45, 52, 58, 61, 65-68. See also Hay's reports to Roosevelt in the autumn of 1901, dated September 30, October 2, October 4, October 8, October 11, and October 24, *Roosevelt Papers*.

Clayton-Bulwer Convention for the construction of an interoceanic canal by the United States.[1] With the exchange of ratifications (February 21, 1902) the first diplomatic barrier to the undertaking disappeared, the United States having won all points in contest.[2] The way was clear, so far as the Old World was concerned, for the commencement of the gigantic enterprise.

The scene now shifts to the Western Hemisphere and to the efforts of the United States to conclude arrangements for constructing the canal with a New World power, the United States of Colombia. Here, too, as in our relations with Great Britain, the course of events was deeply influenced by a treaty which had been in effect for more than a half-century. An understanding of the diplomacy which ensued and of the policy which was adopted by Roosevelt requires therefore, first, an examination of the action of the American Congress in the selection of the canal route; second, a brief survey of the history of Panama; and third, an account of the previous relations between the United States and Colombia in so far as these relations concerned the isthmus.

Of the numerous routes which had been suggested for the building of the canal, both expert and popular opinion in the United States favored either Nicaragua or Panama. For a number of years the United States had investigated the cost of constructing an interoceanic canal. In its report dated November 16, 1901, the Walker Commission, which had been appointed in 1899, estimated the cost of constructing a Nicaragua Canal at $189,864,062, and the cost of building a Panama Canal at $144,233,358. To the cost of the latter, however, the Commission reported, must

[1] The text of the treaty is in Malloy, *op. cit.*, I, 782–84.

[2] Hay to Roosevelt, October 4, 1901, *Roosevelt Papers*.

be added $109,141,500 to pay for the rights and property of the New Panama Canal Company, a French corporation which years before had secured concessions on the isthmus, making the total cost by the Panama route $253,374,858. Since the value of the interests of the French company did not exceed $40,000,000, according to the Commission, it declared that "the most practicable and feasible route for an isthmian canal, to be under the control, management, and ownership of the United States, was that known as the Nicaragua route."[1]

The recommendation caused a crisis in the affairs of the French company, changes took place in the management, and on January 4, 1902, an offer to sell at $40,-000,000 was cabled to the Commission. By this time Roosevelt, who at first had favored the Nicaragua Canal,[2] seems to have become thoroughly convinced of the superiority of the Panama route. Calling the Commission together, he induced the members to reverse their decision and recommend Panama.[3] Nine days before the reversal (January 9, 1902) the House had passed a bill providing for a canal through Nicaragua.[4] When the bill came before the Senate, Senator Spooner offered as an amendment what was in reality a substitute measure. His proposal was adopted by a vote of 42 to 34, was finally accepted by the

[1] "Report of the Isthmian Canal Commission," *Senate Document No. 54* (Fifty-seventh Congress, first session), p. 263.

[2] "Hearings on the Rainey Resolution before the Committee on Foreign Affairs of the House of Representatives," *Story of Panama*, p. 243. See also p. 31, no. 2, above.

[3] *Senate Document No. 123* (Fifty-seventh Congress, first session), Vol. XII; *Congressional Record* (Sixty-second Congress, second session), p. 2653. Hay states that Roosevelt preferred that the route be decided by Congress (Thayer, *op. cit.*, II, 302).

[4] *Congressional Record* (Fifty-seventh Congress, first session), Part I, pp. 481, 513, 540, 557, 558.

House, and on June 25, 1902, received the signature of the President.

The Spooner Act, as the law is commonly known, authorized the President to purchase the concessions and property of the New Panama Canal Company at a cost not to exceed $40,000,000 and to acquire from Colombia, upon such terms as he might deem reasonable, perpetual control of, and jurisdiction over, a strip of land, not less than six miles in width, across the Isthmus of Panama; should he be unable to obtain a satisfactory title to the property of the French company and the control of the necessary strip of land from Colombia within a reasonable time and upon reasonable terms, the act directed him to secure control of the necessary territory from Costa Rica and Nicaragua and to proceed to construct a canal by the Nicaragua route.[1]

Before considering the diplomatic negotiations, which had been initiated by Colombia while the debate on the Spooner bill was still in progress, it will be necessary, as pointed out above, to sketch hurriedly the history of Panama and the early relations between the United States and Colombia.

As early as 1739 the Isthmus of Panama was joined as a province to the viceroyalty of New Granada. During the wars of liberation from Spain in the early nineteenth century Panama was one of the last provinces to declare its independence. Realizing their weakness as a separate state, the Panamanians declared that their territory belonged to the more powerful republic of Colombia, which at that time included the territory embraced in the present countries of Venezuela, Colombia, and Ecuador. After the withdrawal of Venezuela in 1829 and of Ecuador in 1830,

[1] *United States Statutes at Large*, Vol. XXXII, Part I, pp. 481–84.

the republic of New Granada was created (1831), Panama being one of the eighteen provinces comprising the new state.[1] The constitution recognized Panama's right to secede, a right she exercised in 1840, and for the next two years the isthmus was an independent republic.

In the constitution as revised in 1853 the right of each province to assume independence at any time was again recognized. Under this provision Panama four years later (1857) entered on a second period of independence, a period which lasted until 1863, when a new constitution was adopted and the present republic of Colombia came into being. As in the preceding constitutions the right of secession was recognized in the document of 1863.

For the next score of years Panama enjoyed practical autonomy. In 1885 she joined other provinces in an unsuccessful uprising against the tyrannical and unconstitutional rule of President Nunez. Victorious over the insurrectionists, Nunez declared the constitution of 1863 a nullity and assembled a convention controlled by himself to draft a new fundamental law. By the new constitution Panama lost her legislature and was made subject in all matters of consequence to the government of Bogotá. The discontent of the Panamanians at the situation cropped out from time to time in local insurrections and in participation in uprisings which affected the republic as a whole. Of this last nature was the revolt of 1899, an uprising which continued for three years.

Meantime, the American government had shown its interest repeatedly in an interoceanic canal. As early as Jackson's administration the Senate had adopted a resolution (1835) authorizing the President to enter into negotiations

[1] F. J. Urrutia, *Commentary on the Declaration of the Rights of Nations*, pp. 37–40.

with other countries, particularly with New Granada and the governments of Central America, with a view to giving protection to individuals or corporations which might undertake to open communication between the Atlantic and the Pacific.[1] But the efforts of Jackson and, later, of Van Buren to further this purpose proved abortive. Nothing definite was accomplished until President Polk's administration, when in 1846 a treaty of amity and commerce was concluded with New Granada.[2]

The thirty-fifth article of the treaty contains a stipulation which was to serve in the future on numerous occasions as the basis for important action by the American government. This article was also to play a most significant part a half-century later in President Roosevelt's policy in regard to Colombia and Panama. The vital features of the stipulation are as follows:

The Government of New Granada guarantees to the Government of the United States that the right of way or transit across the Isthmus of Panama upon any modes of communication that now exist, or that may be hereafter constructed, shall be open and free to the Government and citizens of the United States; . . . . And, in order to secure to themselves the tranquil and constant enjoyment of these advantages, ... the United States guarantee, positively and efficaciously, to New Granada, by the present stipulation, the perfect neutrality of the before-mentioned isthmus, with the view that the free transit from the one to the other sea may not be interrupted or embarrassed in any future time while this treaty exists; and, in consequence, the United States also guarantee, in the same manner, the rights of sovereignty and property which New Granada has and possesses over the said territory.[3]

[1] *Senate Journal* (Twenty-third Congress, second session), p. 238. In 1839 the House of Representatives adopted by a unanimous vote a resolution of the same general tenor. See *Congressional Globe* (Thirty-second Congress, third session), Appendix, xxvii, 251.

[2] Malloy, *op. cit.*, I, 302–14. The treaty was ratified in 1848.

[3] *Ibid.*, p. 312.

What did the foregoing stipulation mean? What did it involve? Did it guarantee to New Granada the possession of the isthmus against all attack, domestic as well as foreign? In the case of internal disorder on the isthmus menacing the lines of communication, did the treaty give the right to and place the obligation upon the United States to maintain peace? If transit were endangered, did the treaty authorize or require the use of military force on the isthmus by the United States without the request or permission of New Granada? Did the treaty give the United States the right to prevent New Granada from employing military force in the isthmus to reduce a riot or an insurrection?

The answers to such questions determine in large measure the legal justification or condemnation of the policy of Roosevelt in his dealings with Colombia and Panama, for on the meaning of the treaty of 1846 much of the merit of the controversy depends. An examination of the circumstances attending the negotiation of the treaty of 1846 together with a study of its subsequent interpretation and application will throw light on the issues involved.

The guaranties quoted above, according to President Polk, were included in the treaty by the American *chargé d'affaires* at Bogotá, Benjamin A. Bidlack, "upon his own responsibility and without instructions."[1] The activities of Great Britain in the region of the Caribbean at the time seem to have been the impelling cause of Bidlack's action. Without a guaranty to New Granada of the possession of the isthmus, Bidlack states that he could not secure the abolition of all differential duties stipulated in the treaty—a concession which had been urged unsuccessfully by the

---

[1] *Senate Document No. 17* (Fifty-eighth Congress, first session), II, 13; confirmed in Bidlack's dispatch of December 9, 1846 (*ibid.*, p. 23).

United States for twenty years—nor the right of transit and free passage over the isthmus which the treaty provided; moreover, he believed that a failure to agree to the wishes of the New Granadan Minister of Foreign Affairs would probably mean the securing of the same privileges by Great Britain.[1] The correspondence between the negotiators shows clearly that both men believed the United States obligated by the treaty to guarantee the integral possession of the isthmus to New Granada; nothing indicates that the obligations of the American government in case of domestic disorder were discussed.[2]

In his message transmitting the treaty, President Polk, in accordance with his practice in the Oregon Treaty (1846), made no direct recommendation to the Senate, but asked instead "for their advice with regard to its ratification." His communication shows that he held the same interpretation of American obligations under the treaty as was expressed by the American negotiator. One passage, which bears indirectly on subsequent events, is worth quoting:

> The guaranty of the sovereignty of New Granada over the isthmus is a natural consequence of the guaranty of its neutrality, and there does not seem to be any other practicable mode of securing the neutrality of this territory. New Granada would not consent to yield up this province in order that it might become a neutral State; and if she should, it is not sufficiently populous or wealthy to establish and maintain an independent sovereignty.[3]

During the decades which followed the ratification of the treaty of 1846 numerous occasions arose in which the interpretation of the document was involved. From these incidents it appears, in the first place, that the United

[1] *Senate Document No. 17*, II, 22.   [2] *Ibid.*, pp. 16–25.
[3] J. D. Richardson, *Messages and Papers of the Presidents*, IV, 513.

States, prior to 1903, invariably regarded the obligation of keeping the transit open and free as resting primarily on New Granada. In 1857, for example, the two countries entered into a convention for the settlement by arbitration of American claims growing out of a riot at Panama the previous year. In the convention the South American Republic "acknowledges its liability, arising out of its privilege and obligation to preserve peace and good order along the transit route."[1] In the commission which was established to carry out the terms of the convention the arbitrator ruled that the question of the liability of New Granada, so far as the purposes of the commission were concerned, was not open to argument.[2] In a dispatch dated October 29, 1873, Secretary Fish, in speaking of our obligations under the treaty of 1846, states:

> This engagement, however, has never been acknowledged to embrace the duty of protecting the road across it [the isthmus] from the violence of local factions, but it is regarded as the undoubted duty of the Colombian Government to protect it against attacks from local insurgents.[3]

On a number of occasions the United States went so far as to refuse its aid in protecting the transit against attacks by insurgents on the ground that the treaty provided for assistance only when a foreign power threatened the isthmus. Such was the position taken by Secretary Seward in 1865 in an instruction to the American Minister at Bogotá. In this communication Seward states that the opinion of the Attorney-General of the United States is that

[1] *Treaties and Conventions Concluded between the United States of America and Other Powers*, p. 211.

[2] *Ibid.*, 1275. The obligation is again specifically recognized by the Colombian Minister at Washington in an official note to the United States dated September 22, 1902. See *Senate Document No. 474*, XV, 254 f.

[3] *Senate Document No. 143* (Fifty-eighth Congress, second session), IV, 46.

neither the text nor the spirit of the stipulation in that article [Art. 35] .... imposes an obligation on this Government to comply with a requisition like that referred to. The purpose of the stipulation was to guarantee the isthmus against seizure or invasion by a foreign power only. It could not have been contemplated that we were to become a party to any civil war in that country by defending the isthmus against another party.[1]

On November 7, 1865, Attorney-General Speed also maintained that

it cannot be supposed that New Granada invited the United States to become a party to the intestine troubles of that Government, nor did the United States become bound to take sides in the domestic broils of New Granada. The acceptance of such a guarantee would amount to a surrender of sovereignty on the part of New Granada.[2]

On October 9, 1866, Secretary Seward sums up the American policy in the following words:

The United States have always abstained from any connection with questions of internal revolution in the State of Panama, or any other of the States of the United States of Colombia, and will continue to maintain a perfect neutrality in such domestic controversies. In the case, however, that the transit trade across the isthmus should suffer from an invasion from either domestic or foreign disturbances of the peace in the State of Panama, the United States will hold themselves ready to protect the same.[3]

Prior to 1903, there are a number of instances in which American forces were used on the isthmus. The circumstances are significant in view of Roosevelt's later course at the time of the Panama revolution.

[1] *Ibid.*, p. 27. The rest of the dispatch implies that conditions might arise on the isthmus which would make it expedient to use force to prevent the freedom of transit from danger or obstruction.

[2] *Treaties and Conventions between the United States and Other Powers*, pp. 1275 f. See also *House Document No. 1* (Fifty-eighth Congress, second session), I, 304; *ibid.* (third session), p. 210; J. B. Moore, *Digest of International Law*, III, 24–34.

[3] *Senate Document No. 143*, IV, 43 f.

In September, 1856, at the request of the Acting Governor of Panama, about one hundred and fifty men were landed for three days to protect American citizens from danger due to local disorder.[1] Four years later American and British forces were used in Panama for several days in response to the written request of the authorities to protect the lives and property of the foreign residents during an attack by insurgents.[2] On March 9, 1865, danger from local disorder caused the landing of sailors and marines for several hours, after permission had been given by the local officials.[3] In September, 1873, naval forces were used at the request of the government and citizens of Panama to protect the railroad and property of American citizens and to keep the transit open.[4] In January, 1885, at the request of the President of Panama, twelve marines were used as a guard for twelve and one-half hours to protect the safes and vaults of the Panama Railroad office.[5] Later in 1885 troops were kept on the isthmus for several weeks with the apparent approval of the Colombian government to maintain the freedom of transit and to protect American lives and property during the revolution of that year.[6] In 1901 the right of way was protected, at the suggestion of the Governor of Panama, by American forces.[7]

In the instances cited it will be noticed that American intervention was always attended by the consent of the Colombian authorities. An exception occurred in 1902. In September and October of that year, armed forces were used without the request of Colombian officials by Admiral

[1] *Ibid.*, pp. 4, 89.
[2] *Ibid.*, pp. 5 f., 91.
[3] *Ibid.*, pp. 25 f.
[4] *Ibid.*, pp. 44 f., 97 ff.
[5] *Ibid.*, pp. 53-58, 106-13.
[6] *Ibid.*, pp. 67-69.
[7] *Ibid.*, pp. 71 f.

[44]

Casey, of the American Navy, to prevent the transportation of Colombian troops on the Panama Railroad during
an insurrection. His action brought forth a strong protest
against any restriction of the use of the road by the Colombian government "as an invasion of sovereign and
treaty rights," a protest in which the American government acquiesced. In a communication to the American
Minister at Bogotá (October 16, 1902) Hay expressed regret at the misunderstanding which had arisen in Panama,
declaring that there had been "no intention to infringe
sovereignty or wound dignity of Colombia."[1]

To summarize: The record shows that during the entire period between the drafting of the treaty of 1846 and
the Panama revolution of 1903 American troops were employed on the isthmus in connection with seven insurrections. In every instance, prior to 1902, the forces were
used only with the approval or consent of the Colombian
authorities. On but one occasion, according to the evidence,[2] did the Americans interfere with the movement of
Colombian troops; and in this instance (September-
October, 1902), as noted above, the Colombian protest was
accepted and regret was expressed by the United States.
Prior to the Panama revolution of 1903, to quote the
words of the Colombian Minister at Washington (April 12,

[1] *Ibid.*, pp. 73–76; see also pp. 285–97.

[2] *Senate Document No. 143* is devoted entirely to the use by the United
States of military forces in the internal affairs of New Granada, or Colombia,
under the treaty of 1846. In the memorandum submitted by J. B. Moore in
August, 1903 (see pp. 57 f. below), the statement appears that in July, 1852, the
United States sent several hundred troops across Panama without asking permission of the Colombian government. No reference to such action is found in
the Senate document just cited. The latter purports to be a complete record of
the employment of American military forces in Panama down to September,
1902 (*ibid.*, p. 2).

1904), the United States "had never in previous disturbances prevented the landing of troops of the Colombian Government, nor their transport on the railroad."[1]

Events from 1846 to 1903 seem to indicate, then, that the United States by the provisions of the treaty of 1846 bound itself as follows: first, to protect the neutrality of Panama against foreign attack; second, to maintain the sovereignty of Colombia over the isthmus from foreign aggression; third, with the approval of the Colombian government, to preserve freedom of transit from interruption or embarrassment due to internal disorder beyond the power of the Colombian authorities to control; fourth, to avoid interference with the movement of Colombian armed forces. In no way did the treaty bind the United States, in case of insurrection, to support either the insurrectionists or the government; in such a contingency the obligations of the United States seem to have been limited to the maintenance of freedom of transit from interference or danger from any source. In the light of such conclusions let us examine the course of events as guided and determined by President Roosevelt.

Negotiations for the Panama route were begun on March 31, 1902, with Dr. Concha, the Colombian minister

---

[1] *House Document No. 1* (Fifty-eighth Congress, third session), I, 214. On February 19, 1887, Secretary Bayard responded to a resolution of the House of Representatives by a report in which he stated: "On several occasions the Government of the United States, at the instance and always with the assent of Colombia, has, in times of civil tumult, sent its armed forces to the Isthmus of Panama to preserve American citizens and property along the transit from injuries which the Government of Colombia might at the time be unable to prevent. But, in taking such steps, this Government has always recognized the sovereignty and obligation of Colombia in the premises, and has never acknowledged, but, on the contrary, has expressly disclaimed, the duty of protecting the transit against domestic disturbance" (*House Executive Document No. 183* [Forty-ninth Congress, second session], p. 2).

at Washington, while the debate in Congress upon the relative merits of the Nicaragua and Panama routes was still in progress. The demands of the United States were so repugnant to the Colombian representative that he finally left Washington unceremoniously rather than put his name to the treaty. Negotiations continued, however, with the Colombian *chargé d'affaires,* Thomas Herran, and were brought to a conclusion on January 22, 1903, with the signing of the Hay-Herran Convention. This arrangement authorized the New Panama Canal Company to sell its properties to the United States and granted the United States full control over a strip of land six miles wide across the isthmus for the construction of a ship canal. The arrangement was to continue for ninety-nine years, and was to be renewable for similar periods at the option of the United States. In return the United States promised to pay in cash to Colombia $10,000,000 in gold and an annuity of $250,000 in gold beginning nine years after the exchange of ratifications.[1] The convention was ratified by the American Senate on March 17, 1903.

During the negotiations the draft of the convention originally proposed by Colombia was changed by the United States in important particulars, some of which were highly objectionable to the South American Republic.[2] Among the most obnoxious of the provisions of the convention in its final form were the following: first, the apparent renunciation by Colombia of sovereignty over the canal zone; second, the stipulation which (according to the

[1] *Senate Document No. 474,* XV, 277–88.

[2] Hay and Roosevelt maintained that few modifications were made in the original draft and that the changes incorporated were of slight consequence. If their assertion be correct, one cannot but wonder at their insistence upon modifying the original document (*ibid.,* pp. 261–63, 385, 392, 399, 497–500, 508); see also *Story of Panama,* pp. 175–92, and Urrutia, *op. cit.,* p. 46.

United States) prohibited negotiations between Colombia, on the one hand, and the New Panama Canal Company and the Panama Railroad Company, on the other; third, the establishment in the canal zone of courts uncontrolled by the Colombian government; fourth, the compensation to be paid for the privileges conceded. So objectionable were the foregoing provisions that Dr. Herran, Concha's successor, refused his consent until Secretary Hay delivered an ultimatum to the effect that the United States would adopt the Nicaragua route unless the proposed terms were accepted. Then, and then only, did the Colombian representative affix his name to the document.[1]

Throughout the correspondence, especially after the passage of the Spooner Act, the United States gave frequent evidence of insistence and impatience at any delay caused by Colombia.[2] The American government also manifested at times an aggressiveness rarely found in friendly diplomatic intercourse. The bluntness of the American communications is in marked contrast to the tone of consideration and moderation which characterizes its correspondence with the British government in connection with the Hay-Pauncefote Treaty. Ultimately, a few concessions were made to Colombia, but in general pressure was employed to bring the negotiations to the desired end. In the light of the action of the United States in 1921[3] the terms

[1] *Senate Document No. 474*, XV, 399; Hay's ultimatum to Herran, January 22, 1903, in *Story of Panama*, p. 322. Cf. Roosevelt, *Autobiography*, pp. 513-20.

[2] In view of the charge, often made by Roosevelt and Hay, that Colombia was guilty of indefinite delays, it is only fair to point out that during the negotiations delays were frequently caused by the United States. Later, when the treaty was submitted for ratification, the Colombian Congress was dilatory, but not to an extreme degree. See on this point *Senate Document No. 474*, XV, 263.

[3] In 1921 the United States paid Colombia $25,000,000. See also p. 51.

of the convention fall far short of "extraordinary liberality," as Hay characterized them.

The Colombian government at the time of the drafting of the Hay-Herran Convention was in the hands of Vice-President Marroquin. In 1898 Marroquin by a *coup de main* had imprisoned the President and seized the reins of authority. Like most usurpers gaining power by violence, Marroquin felt none too firm in his position. His insecurity undoubtedly influenced his attitude and policy toward the new treaty. Had he entertained any illusions concerning the popular feeling toward the document, they must have quickly vanished in the emphatic manifestations of public hostility which soon appeared.

The dispatches of Beaupré, the American minister at Bogotá, contain repeatedly such descriptions of popular sentiments in Colombia as these:

Without question public opinion is strongly against ratification, [March 30]; if the proposed convention were to be submitted to the free opinion of the people it would not pass [April 15]; the opposition to the ratification of the canal convention is intensifying [May 4]; the tremendous tide of public opinion against the canal treaty is appalling to the Government [May 7]; opposition to the ratifications of the canal conventions is very strong [June 17].[1]

The chief causes of the hostility to the treaty have already been indicated (see pp. 47 f). The Colombian government insisted upon its right to negotiate with agents of the companies for the cancellation of concessions; the United States insisted that the treaty covered the whole matter and that negotiations between Colombia and the companies would be contrary to the provisions of the treaty. The hope of securing additional compensation from the companies doubtless influenced the attitude of the Co-

[1] *Ibid.*, pp. 379, 380, 388, 390, 397.

lombian officials.[1] In the second place, Colombia objected to the provisions which related to the alienation of territory, maintaining that such stipulations brought her sovereignty over the canal zone in doubt and that they were in violation of her constitution;[2] the United States contended that Colombia was amply protected by the stipulation in the convention that "the rights and privileges granted to the United States . . . . should not affect the sovereignty of the Republic of Colombia over the territory within whose boundaries such rights and privileges were to be exercised."[3] Closely related to the last issue was the question of the constitutionality of the courts which were to be set up in the canal zone. Finally, although little is said about the subject in the diplomatic correspondence, the compensation was a source of difficulty, most Colombians regarding the sum offered as utterly inadequate to the benefits granted.[4]

[1] The agent of the Panama Canal Co. informed Beaupré that he had been notified that ratification could be secured if the company would pay Colombia $10,000,000. The American Minister reported that he was told that the treaty could not be ratified without two amendments: first, a payment of $10,000,000 by the company; and, second, an increase of $5,000,000 in the cash payment of the United States (*Senate Document No. 474*, XV, 396, 410; also *Senate Document No. 133* [Fifty-eighth Congress, second session], IV, 4).

[2] Isidro Fabela, *Los Estados Unidos contra la Libertad*, p. 150.

[3] *Senate Document No. 474*, XV, 380, 399, 416, 468–71; see also Fabela, *op. cit.*, pp. 153 f.

[4] There were, of course, other grounds for hostility to the treaty besides those enumerated above. In his dispatch of August 15, Beaupré states: "The coffee planters and exporters, who think their business would be ruined by low foreign exchange, have been unpatriotic enough to place personal interests above national good, and have been against the treaty because the $10,000,000 once paid Colombia would send exchange so low that coffee could not be exported from the interior" (*Senate Document No. 474*, XV, 431). Bunau-Varilla maintains that the rejection of the treaty by Colombia was due to German influence; see his *Great Adventure of Panama*, pp. 143–53.

THE TAKING OF PANAMA

That there were grounds for dissatisfaction in regard to the compensation appears in the fact that in the first ten years of operation the canal brought the United States more than $100,000,000. In the year ending June 30, 1924, "the gross receipts . . . . exceeded the expenditures by $17,000,000." In 1921 Senator Lodge, who from first to last defended the course of Roosevelt, estimated the value of the Colombian claims in Panama at $50,146,942.75.[1]

But to return to events in Colombia. For five years the Colombian Congress had not assembled. Not venturing to act on the treaty alone in direct violation of the Colombian constitution, Vice-President Marroquin called a special session of the national legislature for June 20. The elections made it evident that the treaty would encounter strong opposition in the Congress, due partly to a desire to discredit the government but chiefly to hostility to the measure itself.[2]

The situation which had been foreseen by the American Minister was fully realized when the Congress assembled. Typical comments from Beaupré's reports follow:

If Congress, as now constituted, were allowed to give a free vote I feel convinced the Convention would not be ratified [April 15, 1903]; Members of Congress arriving. Opposition . . . . is very strong [June 17]; It is now apparent that the treaty will not be ratified without amendment. . . . . There are but eight Senators of the twenty-four in favor of it [August 5]; The treaty, as such, has had no active friends or supporters, and if it is ratified at all it will be because of the strong attitude taken by the United States [August 12].[3]

[1] *Congressional Record* (Fifty-seventh Congress, first session), Vol. LXI, Part I, p. 160. See also letters from Roosevelt to Taft, August 21, 1907, *Roosevelt Papers*.

[2] *Senate Document No. 474*, XV, 379, 380, 390, 432, 442 f.

[3] *Ibid.*, 380, 397, 419, 432. Notwithstanding the hostility of the Colombian representatives to the treaty, Roosevelt declared that the Congress was made up of "mere puppets" and that "the President had entire power to confirm his

The spirit of the Roosevelt diplomacy, in so far as it concerns the more backward nations, is revealed clearly in the communications between Washington and Bogotá. The American dispatches show, in the first place, utter disregard of the attitude of the Colombian people or their representatives. The correspondence displays, in the second place, a fixed determination to secure the ratification of the treaty—to quote the American Minister— "exactly in its present form, without any modifications whatever."[1] Indeed, the Colombian government was informed that the United States would be fully warranted "in considering any modification whatever of the terms of the treaty as practically a breach of faith on the part of the Government of Colombia."[2] The contrast between this attitude of inflexibility and the action only two years before of the United States Senate in drastically amending the first Hay-Pauncefote Treaty needs no comment.

Imputations of ill faith form a third theme running through the American communications. Ill faith is charged if changes, no matter how minute, are incorporated in the convention by the Colombian Congress. Ill faith is charged if Colombia persists in its efforts to negotiate with the companies for the cancellation of contracts.[3] Ill faith is charged

own treaty and act on it if he desired" (*Autobiography*, pp. 520 f.). So bitter was the feeling against the United States that when another Colombian administration, six years after the Hay-Herran Convention, submitted a treaty for the settlement of existing controversies between Colombia, Panama, and the United States, the government was overthrown and the Colombian representative who signed the treaty was forced to flee from the country to save his life (*Senate Executive Document No. 1* [Sixty-fifth Congress, special session], p. 35). See also E. Root's letters to H. Hagedorn, July 1, 1925, *Roosevelt Papers* (Roosevelt Memorial House, New York).

[1] *Senate Document No. 474*, XV, 423; see also pp. 379, 381, 415, 423, 426, 483.

[2] *Ibid.*, p. 424; see also Fabela, *op. cit.*, p. 153.

[3] *Ibid.*, pp. 388, 395, 424, 498.

if Colombia fails to ratify the convention.[1] The correspondence contains, in the fourth place, veiled threats of retaliation in case the treaty is rejected. On June 9, for example, Secretary Hay sent the American Minister at Bogotá the following telegram:

The Colombian Government apparently does not appreciate the gravity of the situation. The canal negotiations were initiated by Colombia, and were energetically pressed upon this Government for several years. The propositions presented by Colombia, with slight modifications, were finally accepted by us. In virtue of this agreement our Congress reversed its previous judgment and decided upon the Panama route. If Colombia should now reject the treaty or unduly delay its ratification, the friendly understanding between the two countries would be so seriously compromised that action might be taken by the Congress next winter which every friend of Colombia would regret. Confidential. Communicate substance of this verbally to the minister of foreign affairs. If he desires it, give him a copy in the form of memorandum.[2]

This communication, to quote Beaupré's report of its reception in the Colombian Senate, was "construed by many as a threat of direct retaliation against Colombia in case the treaty is not ratified."[3]

What "action" Roosevelt had in mind when the foregoing dispatch was sent has eluded search. He may have contemplated the seizure of the isthmus by force, in accordance with a later plan, or he may have considered the adoption of the Nicaragua route. Efforts of the Colombian Minister of Foreign Affairs for further information concerning the intentions of the American government proved

[1] *Ibid.*, p. 496.

[2] *Ibid.*, p. 392. In view of the third and fourth sentences in Hay's telegram it should be noted that the Spooner Act became law on June 25, 1902, while the Hay-Herran Convention was not signed until January 22, 1903; *supra*, pp. 36 f., 47.

[3] *Senate Document No. 474*, XV, 405; see also pp. 424, 463, 484.

unavailing.[1] In due time the treaty was rejected (August 12), the Colombian Congress adjourned (October 31), the people of Panama revolted (November 3), the independence of the isthmus was recognized (November 11), and a treaty satisfactory to the United States in every respect was concluded with the new republic of Panama (November 18).

The relation of Roosevelt to the revolution in Panama now calls for consideration. The subject involves two important matters: first, Roosevelt's connection, if any, with the uprising; second, his employment of American forces on the isthmus.

The charge that the Washington government was, in a direct sense, responsible for the uprising in Panama is not sustained by the evidence. Roosevelt, Hay, and Root repeatedly denied that the government, or any responsible member of it, had a part in fomenting or inciting the insurrection or in giving assurances of assistance to the Panamanians in case of a revolt.[2] The private correspondence between the three men supports their assertions. But in view of the conversations that Bunau-Varilla had with Roosevelt, Hay, and Loomis, the facts hardly warrant Hay's statement to the Colombian representative that "any charge that this Government, or any responsible

[1] *Ibid.*, p. 397.

[2] *Ibid.*, pp. 492, 584; *House Document No. 1* (Fifty-eighth Congress, second session), I, 272; Bishop, *op. cit.*, I, 288, 296, 299; Thayer, *op. cit.*, II, 325 f.; Roosevelt, *Autobiography*, pp. 522 f.; P. Bunau-Varilla, *Panama*, pp. 289–91, 336 f. In a letter to Dr. Albert Shaw, editor of the *American Review of Reviews*, dated October 10, 1903, Roosevelt states: "I cast aside the proposition made at this time to foment the secession of Panama. Whatever other governments can do, the United States can not go into the securing by such underhand means, the cession. Privately, I freely say to you that I should be delighted if Panama were an independent State, or if it made itself so at this moment; but for me to say so publicly would amount to an instigation of a revolt, and therefore I can not say it" (Bishop, *op. cit.*, I, 279).

member of it, held intercourse, whether official or unofficial, with agents of revolution in Colombia, is utterly without justification."[1] There is no question that both the attitude and the actions of the administration during the weeks which followed the rejection of the treaty gave encouragement, at least indirectly, to the leaders of the insurrection.

While the treaty was before the Colombian government, threats were made repeatedly that the rejection of the arrangement would be followed by the secession of Panama. This likelihood was commented upon with some frequency in the press. It is mentioned again and again in the correspondence between Roosevelt and his advisers. The newly appointed Governor of Panama frankly told the Colombian President that, in case the department found it necessary to revolt to secure the canal, he would stand by Panama.[2]

Upon the defeat of the treaty, investors who were financially interested in the Panama route as well as individuals who had other reasons for wishing to see the isthmus independent began to push their plans for an insurrection. Most active in the movement were William Nelson Cromwell, attorney for the New Panama Canal Company of New York; Philippe Bunau-Varilla, formerly chief engineer for the company; and Dr. Manuel Amador,[3] one of the conspirators on the isthmus and subsequently the first president of the republic of Panama.

[1] Cf. *Senate Document No. 474*, XV, 492, with Bunau-Varilla, *Panama*, pp. 316–18, and with the letter of Loomis to Roosevelt, January 5, 1904, *Roosevelt Papers*.

[2] *Senate Document No. 474*, XV, 438; see also Bunau-Varilla, *op. cit.*, pp. 267 f.

[3] Although the last name of Amador was Guerrero, he is ordinarily referred to as Dr. Amador.

When the treaty was rejected by Colombia, Bunau-Varilla was in Paris. In an article published in *Le matin*, September 2, 1903, a marked copy of which he says he sent to President Roosevelt, Bunau-Varilla foretold with startling accuracy what later occurred on the isthmus.[1] In the article he maintained that, in view of the rejection of the treaty, the President had only two alternatives in Panama: either he could wait until the isthmus declared itself independent and then "make a treaty with the new State" or he could under the treaty of 1846 legally coerce Colombia to obtain "control over the territory required for the operation of the Canal."[2] Shortly after the publication of the article Bunau-Varilla left for New York.

Meanwhile, Captain Beers, an employee of the Panama Railroad Company, came to the United States to obtain funds and military assistance for a revolution. Receiving assurances from Cromwell that financial and military aid would be provided when needed, Beers returned with high hopes to the isthmus. Encouraged by Beers's report, Dr. Amador immediately sailed for the United States. On reaching Washington he was greatly disappointed to learn that no assurance of help had come from any official source; with Colombia in command of the sea the prospect of a successful revolution seemed remote. In this moment of discouragement Bunau-Varilla arrived in New York and shortly afterward met Dr. Amador.

In the meantime, Roosevelt was in a quandary. When the word came that Colombia had rejected the treaty, Hay was in Newbury, New Hampshire. He immediately wrote

[1] According to Loomis, Bunau-Varilla asked the President, during a visit at the White House, for permission to send him a copy of the article (Loomis to Roosevelt, January 5, 1904, *Roosevelt Papers*).

[2] Bunau-Varilla, *Panama*, p. 287; see also Bishop, *op. cit.*, I, 296 f.

to Roosevelt, pointing out two possible courses of action: first, the adoption of the Nicaragua route; second, the building of the Panama Canal in spite of Bogotá. He urged, however, that nothing be done for a few weeks, adding that the President might conclude that it would be best to lay the question before Congress.[1] To Hay's communication Roosevelt responded as follows: "The one thing evident is to do nothing at present. If under the treaty of 1846 we have a color of right to start in and build a canal, my off-hand judgment would favor such proceeding."[2]

A month later Hay wrote that there was every likelihood of an uprising on the isthmus and suggested that the President decide whether he would (1) wait for the result of that movement, or (2) take a hand in saving Panama from chaos, or (3) begin negotiations with Nicaragua.[3] Two days later Roosevelt replied, mentioning two possible alternatives:[4] "First, to take up Nicaragua; second, in some shape or way to interfere when it becomes necessary so as to secure the Panama route without further dealing with the foolish and homicidal corruptionists in Bogotá."[5]

During this period of uncertainty other influences were also making themselves felt. About the seventh or eighth of August, F. B. Loomis, acting secretary of state during Hay's absence, had a long conversation over the Panama situation with John Bassett Moore. Impressed with the latter's suggestions, Loomis requested Moore to put his

[1] Hay to Roosevelt, August 16, 1903, *Roosevelt Papers.*

[2] Bishop, *op. cit.*, I, 276.

[3] Hay to Roosevelt, September 3, 1903, *Roosevelt Papers.*

[4] According to Bunau-Varilla, the marked copy of *Le matin* probably reached Roosevelt September 13 (*op. cit.*, p. 297).

[5] Bishop, *op. cit.*, I, 278. See also comments of Roosevelt as reported in W. D. Foulke, *Hoosier Autobiography*, pp. 123 f.

views in writing for the use of the President. Moore accordingly summed up his ideas in a ten- or twelve-page memorandum, writing, he says, with a view to further correspondence with Colombia, in case Congress should decide to modify the Spooner Act, and not with the possibility of action in case an insurrection occurred on the isthmus. Loomis immediately forwarded Moore's statement to the President, who in turn sent it on to Hay.[1]

So impressed was Roosevelt with the memorandum that early in September he invited Moore to dine and spend the night at Oyster Bay in order to provide opportunity to go over the whole matter. The conference seems to have been decisive, for, in a subsequent letter to Moore, Roosevelt states that it was after the conversation at Sagamore Hill that he first definitely, or tentatively, formulated even to himself the course of action he afterward adopted although he had been thinking over the problem during the preceding six weeks.[2]

Shortly after the conference at Oyster Bay, Bunau-Varilla became the most active figure on the stage. Late in September or early in October he was introduced to Moore. As a result of their conversation, Bunau-Varilla came to the conclusion that Moore had advised Roosevelt

[1] F. B. Loomis to B. F. Barnes, August 15, 1903; T. Roosevelt to J. Hay, August 19, 1903; J. B. Moore to T. Roosevelt, January 7, 1903 (1904?), *Roosevelt Papers.*

[2] Roosevelt to Moore, September 5, 1903; Roosevelt's memorandum of engagements, September 15, 1903; Moore to Roosevelt, January 7, 1903 (1904?), *ibid.* In this connection it should be added that the arguments defending the policy of the administration in Panama as given in Roosevelt's special message to Congress of the following January, to be commented on later, were contributed by Moore to such an extent that the President refers to the document as their joint product. According to Roosevelt, Moore had about as much to do with the message as he did. Roosevelt also gives credit, however, to suggestions he received from Root, Hay, Loomis, Moody, and Lodge (Roosevelt to Moore, December 28, 1903, and January 6, 1904, *ibid*).

that "the treaty of 1846 with New Granada gave the United States the right of carrying out the works necessary for the canal," regardless of the attitude of Colombia.

Such, at all events, was the decision that the President finally reached; for in the first draft of his message to Congress, written before the revolution occurred, he recommended that "we should purchase all the rights of the Panama company and, without any further parley with Colombia, enter upon the completion of the canal which the French company has begun."[1]

Meanwhile, Bunau-Varilla had learned the results of Amador's unsuccessful mission to Washington, had conversed again with John Bassett Moore, had met President Roosevelt, Secretary Hay, and Assistant Secretary Loomis, and had come to the conclusion that, although no funds or assurances of military aid could be obtained from official sources, the American government in case of a revolution on the isthmus would not permit Colombia to use coercion to reduce the uprising. He had also formed the impression that the United States would have naval vessels at Panama within forty-eight hours of the revolt. In conjunction with Amador, Bunau-Varilla now perfected the final plans for the uprising.[2]

[1] Bishop, *op. cit.*, I, 289; Thayer, *op. cit.*, II, 328; Roosevelt, *Autobiography*, pp. 521, 530 f. Hay characterized the alternative action—the taking of the isthmus by force of arms—as a "defiance of the Constitution, the law, and the treaties, rather than the perfectly regular course" subsequently followed (Thayer, *op. cit.*, II, 324). Cf. with Roosevelt's statement in his special message of January 4, 1904, in Roosevelt's *Presidential Addresses and State Papers*, II, 718 f.

[2] Bunau-Varilla, *op. cit.*, pp. 289–331; Bunau-Varilla, *Great Adventure of Panama*, pp. 179–85, 202–5, 212–25. Bunau-Varilla's account of his conferences differ in numerous details from that given by Moore and Loomis; see Loomis to Roosevelt, January 5, 1904, and Moore to Roosevelt, January 7, 1903 (1904?), *Roosevelt Papers*.

In the latter part of October, Amador returned to Panama. Doubt being expressed by his associates concerning the intentions of the United States, Amador cabled Bunau-Varilla that it would be necessary to provide reassurance by having an American naval vessel sent to Colon. Concluding from a remark of Loomis that the Navy would act at once, and calculating the time necessary for the "Nashville," then at Kingston, to reach Panama, Bunau-Varilla sent a dispatch to Amador stating that an American warship would arrive at the isthmus within two days and a half.[1]

In this dispatch Bunau-Varilla may have expressed as a certainty what he felt as a hope. If so he had grounds for his expectation. Although he does not seem to have received direct assurance from the administration that American naval vessels would be sent to the isthmus if disturbances occurred, he would have been "a very dull man," as Roosevelt says, had he been unable to make "a very accurate guess" concerning what "our Government would do."[2]

As early as October 16, from which date Roosevelt seems to have taken complete charge of the situation,[3] the President had ordered the Navy Department to hold warships within striking distance of the Isthmus of Panama on both the Atlantic and Pacific sides.[4] On October 30, the gunboat "Nashville" was ordered to Colon. On November 2, the following instructions were sent to the commanders of the "Marblehead" and the "Boston":

[1] Bunau-Varilla, *Panama*, pp. 325–31; Bunau-Varilla, *Great Adventure*, pp. 234–36.

[2] Bishop, *op. cit.*, I, 295; see also Roosevelt's letter to Lodge, *ibid.*, pp. 296 f.

[3] Thayer, *op. cit.*, II, 316 f.

[4] *Congressional Record* (Sixty-second Congress, second session), Part III, p. 2655; Bishop, *op. cit.*, I, 281.

Proceed with all possible dispatch to Panama. Telegraph in cipher your departure. Maintain free and uninterrupted transit. If interruption is threatened by armed force, occupy the line of railroad. Prevent landing of any armed force, either Government or insurgent, with hostile intent at any point within fifty miles of Panama. If doubtful as to the intention of any armed force, occupy Ancon Hill strongly with artillery. . . . . Government force reported approaching isthmus in vessels. Prevent their landing if in your judgment landing would precipitate a conflict.[1]

Instructions of a similar character were sent to the commanders of the "Nashville" and the "Dixie."[2]

The "Nashville" arrived at Colon on the afternoon of November 2. On the following morning Commander Hubbard learned that the Colombian gunboat "Cartagena" had come in during the night, having on board some four or five hundred soldiers. He immediately boarded the boat and was informed that the troops were on their way to join the garrison at Panama. Not having received the Washington dispatch of November 2 quoted above, Hubbard took no steps to prevent their disembarkment. Two hours later (10:30 A.M.) he received the cablegram and immediately went ashore. Meanwhile, the commanding officers of the Colombian troops had left by train for Panama accompanied by members of their staff. At this time Hubbard reported to Washington: "No revolution has been declared on the isthmus and no disturbances have occurred."[3]

The intentions of the conspirators may have been known to the authorities at Washington. The plans may even have received their approval, although this seems improbable. Whatever the truth in the foregoing respect may

[1] *Senate Document No. 474*, XV, 363.

[2] *Ibid.*, p. 362.

[3] *House Document No. 1* (Fifty-eighth Congress, second session), I, 249.

be, the Department of State, aroused at the delay of the Panama leaders or stirred by a report published in the press, sent at 3:40 P.M., on November 3, the following dispatch to the American consuls at Colon and Panama: "Uprising on isthmus reported. Keep department promptly and fully informed.—LOOMIS, *Acting*."[1] At 8:15 P.M., a reply came from the American Consul at Panama: "No uprising yet. Reported will be in the night. Situation is critical.—EHRMAN."[2] An hour and a half later (9:50 P.M.) a second cablegram was received from Ehrman: "Uprising occurred tonight, six; no bloodshed. Army and navy officials taken prisoners. Government will be organized tonight. . . . . Soldiers changed. Supposed same movement will be effected in Colon. Order prevails so far. . . . ."[3]

Meanwhile, Hubbard had learned that a revolution had occurred in Panama; that the Colombian officers who had crossed the isthmus were prisoners; that a provisional government had been established and a military force organized; and that the provisional government desired that the Colombian troops at Colon be sent to Panama. On the following morning, November 4, Hubbard refused to allow troops to be transported in either direction.[4]

Although a critical situation obtained during the next twenty-four hours, no shots were fired by either side and no blood was shed. On the afternoon of November 5 representatives of the provisional government succeeded, by bribery it is said, in persuading Colonel Torres to embark his troops on the "Orinoco," a Royal Mail steamer, and return to the city of Cartagena. The gunboat on which the Colombian troops had come had sailed away the preceding

---

[1] *Senate Document No. 474*, XV, 345.

[2] *Ibid.*, p. 346.   [3] *Ibid.*

[4] *House Document No. 1* (Fifty-eighth Congress, second session), I, 250.

day.[1] On November 6 the United States recognized the *de facto* government of Panama,[2] and within a week seven American war vessels had arrived at Colon and at Panama.

On November 7 the American Minister at Bogotá telegraphed Secretary Hay that the Colombian government had inquired whether it would be permitted "to land troops at those ports [Colon and Panama] to fight there and on the line of railway."[3] On November 11 Hay replied that it was "not thought desirable to permit landing of Colombian troops on isthmus, as such a course would precipitate civil war and disturb for an indefinite period the free transit which we are pledged to protect."[4] From November 2, when orders were sent to the commanders of the "Marblehead" and the "Boston" instructing them to "prevent the landing of any armed force . . . . with hostile intent at any point within fifty miles of Panama,"[5] and throughout the entire insurrection the United States prevented every attempt of Colombia to reduce the uprising by military operations. Commenting on his Panama policy several years later in a letter to W. R. Thayer, Roosevelt said:

The people of Panama were a unit in desiring the Canal and in wishing to overthrow the rule of Colombia. If they had not revolted, I should have recommended Congress to take possession of the Isthmus by force of arms; and, as you will see, I had actually written the first draft of my Message to this effect. When they revolted, I promptly used the Navy to prevent the bandits, who had tried to hold us up, from spending months of futile bloodshed in conquering or endeavoring to conquer the Isthmus, to the lasting damage of the Isthmus, of us, and of the world. I did not consult Hay, or Root, or any one else as to what I did, because a council of war does not fight; and I intended to do the job once for all.[6]

[1] *Ibid.*, pp. 248, 269–72.

[2] *Senate Document No. 474*, XV, 348, 358.

[3] *Ibid.*, p. 357.

[4] *Ibid.*, p. 358.

[5] See p. 61 above.

[6] Thayer, *op. cit.*, II, 328.

In a special message to Congress, January 4, 1904,[1] Roosevelt justified his course in Panama in the first place on treaty rights. The primary object of the treaty of 1846, he declared, was to assure the construction of an interoceanic canal; under this treaty Colombia was obliged by implication to permit the United States to build such a passageway; the rejection by Colombia of the Hay-Herran Convention was therefore a virtual repudiation of treaty obligations to the United States. Upon recognizing the independence of Panama the United States, he maintained, was bound under international law by the treaty of 1846 to protect against external attack the new republic as the lawful successor of Colombia in sovereignty over the isthmus.

In the second place, Roosevelt declared that national interests and safety necessitated the policy which he adopted. The indefinite delays inevitable after the rejection of the treaty by the Colombian Congress would have endangered national self-defense by postponing the construction of an interoceanic canal. In all probability further delay, he insisted, would have involved the United States in serious difficulties with France. Colombia's effort to deprive the New Panama Canal Company of its property and rights on the isthmus by postponing action until she could declare that the concessions to the company had expired (1904), he maintained, would have resulted in war. On the first appearance of such danger, Colombia would have summoned the United States to interpose in order to maintain the guaranties of the treaty of 1846.[2]

[1] *House Document No. 1* (Fifty-eighth Congress, second session), I, 260–278; see also p. 58, n. 2 above.

[2] *House Document No. 1* (Fifty-eighth Congres, ssecond session), I, 275. It should be noted that more than twenty years before the Panama revolution the French government had assured the United States that it was in no way concerned in the De Lesseps enterprise and did not intend to give it any support, direct or indirect (E. E. Sparks, *National Development*, pp. 217 f.).

In the third place, Roosevelt held that the policy pursued in Panama was demanded by the interests of civilization. The construction of the canal was an enterprise for the benefit of the entire world and one for which the United States had received a virtual mandate from civilization. In order that no obstacle might hinder the undertaking Great Britain had consented to the abrogation of the Clay-ton-Bulwer Treaty and the purpose of the United States had been approved and encouraged in all quarters of the globe.

In justifying his policy Roosevelt seems to have ignored or overlooked a number of pertinent points. If the primary purpose of the United States in ratifying the treaty of 1846 was to assure the construction of an interoceanic canal—an assertion which the circumstances attending the negotiation of the treaty do not support[1]—the principal object of the South American Republic, on the other hand, was to provide for the continuance of its sovereignty over the isthmus. As the Minister of Colombia stated in 1906:

> Colombia never agreed by the treaty of 1846 that the United States, while complying with its terms, might lawfully cause the loss to Colombia of the very thing for which Colombia entered into that treaty. . . . . Is it possible to believe that any national entity would ever enter into an agreement with another for the preservation of a member of its own body and by the very terms of the agreement authorize the severance of that member by the act of the party that was binding itself to preserve said member?[2]

[1] See pp. 40 f. above.

[2] *House Document No. 1* (Fifty-eighth Congress, second session), I, 591. If Roosevelt's contention be correct, it is difficult to justify the action of the United States in rejecting the treaty of 1869 or that of 1870 under both of which the United States was to construct a canal across the isthmus (*op. cit.*, p. 586). See also *Senate Executive Department No. 112* (Forty-sixth Congress, second session), pp. 34–84, and *House Report No. 224* (Forty-sixth Congress, third session), p. 24. Only by the broadest interpretation, in fact, can the assertion be maintained that the treaty of 1846 gave the United States by implication the right to construct a canal.

The argument that national interests and safety required the action taken at Panama rests on the theory that "necessity knows no law." It is even doubtful that delay would have endangered such interests. Among its stipulations the Hay-Herran Convention provided for possible delays in the completion of the work totaling thirty-six years, an arrangement which suggests that a delay of a few years for further negotiations with Colombia would not have been a matter of major consequence. At all events the point was not made or the issue raised when Great Britain refused to accept the amended form of the first Hay-Pauncefote Treaty.

The truth is that Colombia's rejection of the treaty necessitated no delay whatever in the building of an interoceanic canal. If the need for speed were as urgent as Roosevelt maintains, steps could have been taken at once to provide a canal by way of Nicaragua in accordance with the Spooner Act. Indeed, under the provisions of this Act, it is at least open to question whether the President was not legally obligated, upon the rejection of the Hay-Herran Convention, to go to Nicaragua.

Furthermore, the construction of a canal through Nicaragua would have amply protected "the interests of collective civilization." Whether the United States could claim to have received a mandate from civilization for the construction of a canal may indeed be questioned; the method of determining the accuracy of the claim would in itself be a most difficult problem. But in any case, the obligations of the United States, if such existed, would have been met as fully by the Nicaragua route as by the Panama route.

But for almost a year Roosevelt's mind had apparently been made up: The canal must be built across the isthmus.[1] To accomplish the end in view, it is asserted, he brought pressure upon the members of the Walker Commission in order to secure a reversal of the recommendation in their first report. Little in his correspondence, either before or after the rejection of the Hay-Herran Convention (August 12), indicates serious consideration of the Nicaragua route. With the regular session of Congress only a few weeks off, when demands for construction by way of Nicaragua were certain to be made, Roosevelt seems to have seized upon the Panama revolution as a way out of the dilemma. Acting with a haste unparalleled in American history and unwarranted in international law, he immediately recognized the new republic and promptly concluded a treaty with it on terms most favorable to the United States.

Roosevelt may not have incited the insurrection, but he greeted it with delight; for it relieved him of all necessity of dealing with the "cut-throats of Bogotá" and enabled him to face Congress with an accomplished fact. So far as he was concerned, there was to be no backward step. In his special message to Congress (January 4, 1904)—a message devoted entirely to the canal situation—he said:

The only question now before us is that of the ratification of the treaty [with Panama]. For it is to be remembered that a failure to ratify the treaty will not undo what has been done, will not restore Panama to Colombia. . . . . The question actually before this Government is not that of the recognition of Panama as an independent republic. That is already an accomplished fact. The question, and the only question, is whether or not we shall build an Isthmian canal.[2]

Many years later Roosevelt summed up his action in Panama in an address at Berkeley, California, March 11, 1911, in these words:

[1] A Latin-American interpretation is given in Fabela, *op. cit.*, pp. 160–63.
[2] *House Document No. 1* (Fifty-eighth Congress, second session), I, 277 f.

I am interested in the Panama Canal because I started it. If I had followed traditional, conservative methods I should have submitted a dignified state paper of probably two hundred pages to Congress, and the debate on it would be going on yet; but I took the Canal Zone and let Congress debate and while the debate goes on the canal does too.[1]

Panama is the first instance of the swinging of the Big Stick in international affairs. The effect of the policy upon Latin-Americans and upon the friendly relations which the United States had hitherto sustained with Colombia was later described by Mr. du Bois, the American minister to Bogotá, in a statement submitted to Secretary of State Knox, December 30, 1912, containing these words:

Nine years ago this [friendly attitude] was changed suddenly and unexpectedly when President Roosevelt denied to Colombia the right to land her troops upon her own soil to suppress a threatened revolt and maintain a sovereignty guaranteed by treaty stipulations. The breach came and it has been growing wider since that hour. By refusing to allow Colombia to uphold her sovereign rights over a territory where she had held dominion for eighty years, the friendship of nearly a century disappeared, the indignation of every Colombian, and millions of other Latin-Americans, was aroused and is still most intensely active. The confidence and trust in the justice and fairness of the United States, so long manifested, has completely vanished, and the maleficent influence of this condition is permeating public opinion in all Latin-American countries, a condition which, if remedial measures are not invoked, will work inestimable harm throughout the Western Hemisphere.[2]

[1] Bishop, *op. cit.*, I, 307.

[2] *Senate Executive Document No. 1* (Sixty-fifth Congress, special session), p. 35.

Chapter IV

CUBA AND INTERVENTION

IN STRIKING and pleasing contrast to Roosevelt's dealings with Colombia are his relations with Cuba. Moved by the recollection of his part in the winning of Cuban independence, or rendered cautious by the severe criticism which his Panama policy received, or regarding the problem as quite dissimilar from that on the isthmus, he assumed toward the island republic an attitude which on the whole resembles that of a father who takes pride in the achievements of his child but who does not hesitate, if need arises, to admonish and discipline his offspring.

The foundation for such parental oversight, as well as for the independence of Cuba, was laid during President McKinley's administration. The joint resolutions of Congress (April 19, 1898), which initiated the Spanish War, contained the following self-denying clause:

> The United States hereby disclaims any disposition or intention to exercise sovereignty, jurisdiction, or control over said island except for the pacification thereof, and asserts its determination, when that is accomplished, to leave the government and control of the island to its people.[1]

The obligation arising from the foregoing resolution was strengthened by the treaty of peace concluded at Paris, December 10, 1898. The first article of the treaty provides that

[1] *United States Statutes at Large*, XXX, 738.

as the island is, upon its evacuation by Spain, to be occupied by the United States, the United States will, so long as such occupation shall last, assume and discharge the obligations that may under international law result from the fact of its occupation, for the protection of life and property.[1]

In accordance with the resolution and the treaty the United States occupied Cuba upon its evacuation by Spain. The American military administration under the direction of General Leonard Wood gave the island the best government it had ever known. Order was maintained, hospitals and charitable institutions were organized, extensive public works were undertaken, the public-school system was reorganized and enlarged, business and agriculture were encouraged, sanitation was promoted, and public health safeguarded as never before.

The first steps toward the introduction of self-government in Cuba were the taking of a census of the population, the determination of the proper basis for suffrage, and the holding of municipal elections for the establishment of local governments. Such measures having been accomplished, a general election was held (September, 1900) for the selection of delegates to a Constitutional Convention

to frame and adopt a constitution for the people of Cuba, and, as a part thereof, to provide for and agree with the Government of the United States upon the relations to exist between that Government and the Government of Cuba, and to provide for the election by the people of officers under such constitution and the transfer of government to the officers so elected.[2]

The Constitutional Convention assembled in Havana, November 5, 1900. The assembly was called to order by General Wood. In his opening address, General Wood

[1] W. M. Malloy, *Treaties, Conventions, International Acts, Protocols and Agreements*, II, 1691.

[2] *House Document No. 1* (Fifty-seventh Congress, second session), I, 359.

called the attention of the delegates to their obligation to formulate the relations which, in their opinion, "ought to exist between Cuba and the United States." He added that the government of the United States would "doubtless take such action on its part as shall lead to a final and authoritative agreement between the people of the two countries."[1]

Before the end of February, 1901, the Convention agreed upon a constitution resembling that of the United States.[2] But the delegates seem to have had no intention of defining the future relations between Cuba and the United States in any way which might imply that the island was under the tutelage or oversight of its powerful neighbor to the north. In the original form the constitution was silent upon the subject while the Committee appointed to report upon the matter voiced what were probably the true sentiments of the Convention in these words:

> The commission to which such an honorable duty was intrusted imagined the first time it met that its task would be as easy as it would be brief. The sentiment of gratitude toward the people of the United States for the powerful and decisive aid they rendered our people in their struggle to separate themselves from Spain, to the end that they might establish themselves in an independent and sovereign State, is so alive in all Cuban patriots that in order to express the opinion requested it seemed to all that we could simply declare we thought the United States and Cuba should eternally maintain ties of the most intimate and fraternal friendship, inasmuch as there is not a glimmer of the slightest opposition between their legitimate interests, nor possible the least disparity in their reasonable aspirations.[3]

But the government of the United States had no thought of withdrawing from the island without establishing a binding relationship between the two countries.

[1] *Ibid.*, pp. 359 f.

[2] Secretary of War, *Annual Reports*, Vol. I (1902), Part I, p. 84.

[3] *House Document No. 1*, I, 361.

Shortly after the Committee was appointed by the Convention, General Wood requested a private conference in which he communicated to the Committee the views of the American executive.[1] These views, with some modifications and additions, were later embodied in what is known as the Platt Amendment to the Army Appropriation Act of March 2, 1901. The Platt Amendment authorized the President to leave the government and control of Cuba to its people as soon as a government should be established under a constitution defining the future relations of the island with the United States as follows:

I. That the government of Cuba shall never enter into any treaty or other compact with any foreign power or powers which will impair or tend to impair the independence of Cuba, nor in any manner authorize or permit any foreign power or powers to obtain by colonization or for military or naval purposes or otherwise, lodgment in or control over any portion of said island.

II. That said government shall not assume or contract any public debt, to pay the interest upon which, and to make reasonable sinking fund provision for the ultimate discharge of which, the ordinary revenues of the island, after defraying the current expenses of government, shall be inadequate.

III. That the government of Cuba consents that the United States may exercise the right to intervene for the preservation of Cuban independence, the maintenance of a government adequate for the protection of life, property, and individual liberty and for discharging the obligations with respect to Cuba imposed by the treaty of Paris on the United States, now to be assumed and undertaken by the government of Cuba.

IV. That all acts of the United States in Cuba during its military occupancy thereof are ratified and validated, and all lawful rights acquired thereunder shall be maintained and protected.

V. That the government of Cuba will execute, and as far as necessary extend, the plans already devised or other plans to be mutually agreed upon, for the sanitation of the cities of the island, to the end that a recurrence of epidemic and infectious diseases may be prevented,

[1] Secretary of War, *op. cit.*, p. 46.

thereby assuring protection to the people and commerce of Cuba, as well as to the commerce of the Southern ports of the United States and the people residing therein.

VI. That the Isle of Pines shall be omitted from the proposed constitutional boundaries of Cuba, the title thereto being left to future adjustment by treaty.

VII. That to enable the United States to maintain the independence of Cuba, and to protect the people thereof, as well as for its own defense, the government of Cuba will sell or lease to the United States lands necessary for coaling or naval stations at certain specified points, to be agreed upon with the President of the United States.

VIII. That by way of further assurance the government of Cuba will embody the foregoing provisions in a permanent treaty with the United States.[1]

The foregoing articles seem to have originated with General James H. Wilson who in 1899 was in command of one of the departments of Cuba and who in a report made in the summer of that year substantially stated "every proposition embodied in the Platt amendment except only the requirement that the definition of our relations should be embodied in the Cuban Constitution."[2] Some time later Senator Orville H. Platt, of Connecticut, submitted a draft of four propositions to President McKinley and Secretary Root. The articles were discussed in full with President McKinley, Secretary Root, Senator Spooner, and other

[1] *United States Statutes at Large*, Vol. XXXI, Part I, pp. 897-98. The provisions originally submitted to the Cubans are in *House Document No. 2* (Fifty-seventh Congress, first session), II, 46. Articles 5, 6, and 8 were not included in the original stipulations, nor was the phraseology of the articles as given above.

[2] J. B. Foraker, *Notes of a Busy Life*, II, 59-61. The authorship of the various provisions of the Platt Amendment is a matter of controversy. Senator Platt claims that they originated with him (L. A. Coolidge, *An Old-Fashioned Senator: Orville H. Platt*, pp. 337-56). Elsewhere it is asserted that Secretary Root and General Wood were the authors (J. B. Scott, *Robert Bacon, Life and Letters*, p. 113 n.; editorial, "The Origin and Purpose of the Platt Amendment," *American Journal of International Law*, VIII, 585-87).

Republican members of the Senate Committee on Cuban Relations, of which Senator Platt was the chairman. In order to secure action by Congress before the end of the short session, Senator Platt proposed the adoption of the resolutions as an amendment to the Army appropriation bill, and in that manner the measures were enacted into law.

The Platt Amendment was heartily disliked by the Cuban Constitutional Convention and by the Cuban people. In the report, which was adopted by the Convention, the Committee appointed to draw up recommendations concerning the future relations of Cuba and the United States[1] objected vigorously to the proposals of the American government, insisting that the stipulations violated the very object that they were supposed to guarantee, namely, the independence of Cuba. After reviewing the powers and obligations of the Convention, the character of the new Cuban constitution, and the propositions of the American Secretary of War, the Committee states:

The undersigned commission, taking the American Executive's departing point that it is important that the independence of Cuba be absolutely guaranteed, considers that some of these stipulations are not acceptable, exactly because they impair the independence and sovereignty of Cuba. Our duty consists in making Cuba independent of every other nation, the great and noble American nation included, and, if we bind ourselves to ask the governments of the United States for *their consent* to our international dealings, if we admit that they shall reserve and retain the right to intervene in our country to maintain or precipitate conditions and fulfill duties pertaining solely to Cuban governments, and, lastly, if we grant them the right to acquire and preserve titles to lands for naval stations and maintain these in determined places along our coast, it is clear that we could seem independent of the rest of the world although we were not in reality, but never would we be independent with reference to the United States.[2]

[1] See pp. 71f. above.   [2] *House Document No. 1*, I, 362.

The argument is then advanced that the new constitution provides a solid and ample basis for the accomplishment of the desires of the American executive. In order to strengthen the confidence of the United States, however, the Committee recommended that the Convention express itself as "*of the opinion* that the constitutional powers of the Republic of Cuba, if they deem proper,"[1] should adopt the following provisions:

First, that the Government of Cuba will enter into no convention or no treaty limiting the independence of Cuba or alienating in any manner Cuban soil.

Second, that the Government of Cuba will not permit its soil to be used as a basis for war operations against the United States or any other foreign nation.

Third, that the Government of Cuba will accept in full the treaty of Paris, of December 10, 1898, and all international obligations imposed by it.

Fourth, that the Government of Cuba will recognize the legal validity of all acts of the American military government.

Fifth, that the Governments of the United States and of Cuba should regulate their commercial relations by means of a convention based on reciprocity.[2]

The proposals of the Committee proved unacceptable to the United States. Within less than a month the American Congress adopted the Platt Amendment, but the provisions were so objectionable to the Cubans that in April a delegation of five members of the Convention were sent to Washington to enter a protest.[3] President McKinley and Secretary Root received the delegation in a friendly manner, but informed it that no changes could be made. The

[1] Italics are in the document (*ibid.*, p. 364).

[2] *Ibid.* Most Latin-Americans viewed the Platt Amendment as contrary to Cuban liberty and of advantage chiefly to the selfish interests of the United States; see I. Fabela, *Los Estados Unidos contra la Libertad*, pp. 106–15.

[3] Coolidge, *op. cit.*, pp. 344, 371.

administration promised, however, to use its influence with Congress to establish commercial relations favorable to Cuba, an assurance highly gratifying to the delegates. The American government subsequently allayed in large part the dissatisfaction aroused among the Cubans by the third clause of the Platt Amendment (that relating to intervention) by the following official statement conveyed to a committee of the Convention by General Wood by order of the President:

> You are authorized to state officially that in the view of the President the intervention described in the third clause of the Platt Amendment is not synonymous with intermeddling or interference with the affairs of the Cuban Government, but the formal action of the government of the United States, based upon just and substantial grounds, for the preservation of Cuban independence, and the maintenance of a government adequate for the protection of life, property, and individual liberty, and adequate for discharging the obligations with respect to Cuba imposed by the treaty of Paris on the United States.[1]

After receiving the preceding assurance, the Convention adopted the Platt Amendment (June 12, 1901) as an appendix to the new Cuban constitution. Two years later the Amendment was incorporated in a convention (proclaimed July 2, 1904) entered into by Cuba and the United States.[2] On February 23, 1903, the provision relating to coaling or naval stations was fulfilled, the United States receiving Guantanamo in eastern Cuba and Bahia Honda in the northwestern part of the island.[3] By the arrangement the sovereignty of Cuba over the two harbors was

---

[1] *House Document No. 2*, II, 48; see also editorial, "The Origin and Purpose of the Platt Amendment," *op. cit.*, pp. 585-91.

[2] Malloy, *op. cit.*, I, 362-64.

[3] *Ibid.*, pp. 358 f.; Roosevelt comments vigorously on the delay of the Cubans in granting the naval stations in a letter to Hay, October 23, 1902, *Roosevelt Papers*.

recognized and, by later agreement, the United States promised to pay an annual rental of $2,000 so long as it occupied the places named.[1]

In accordance with the Cuban constitution elections were held by the people on December 31, 1901, and by the electoral college on February 24, 1902, to choose a president, vice-president, senate, and house of representatives. On May 20, 1902, Tomas Estrada Palma was inaugurated as first president of the republic of Cuba, the government of the island was handed over to the newly constituted authorities, and General Wood, his staff, and the American forces embarked for the United States.[2] A cash balance of $689,191.02 in the Cuban treasury was transferred by the American military government to the Cuban officials.[3]

The withdrawal of the American forces, according to Secretary Root, was made an occasion for "universal expressions of gratitude, esteem, and affection" by the Cuban people.[4] In the report describing the evacuation of the island General Wood states:

It would have been impossible for any people to have shown more friendship and cordiality to the representatives of another nation than was shown by the people of Havana of all classes to the representatives of the late military government of the United States in Cuba. It is safe to say that at least 100,000, probably 150,000, people were assembled along the water front . . . . to see the troops off.[5]

[1] *Ibid.*, pp. 360 f.

[2] *House Document No. 2* (Fifty-seventh Congress, second session), IV, 8–9, 69–77, 81–83, 121–26. A small force of artillery remained temporarily in the coast fortifications in order to provide a defense for the island until the new government could organize an adequate military organization to assume the obligation (*ibid.*, pp. 69, 71 f., 77 f., 79 f.).

[3] *Ibid.*, pp. 123 f. A consolidated financial statement of Cuban affairs during the American occupation (1898–1902) is given in *ibid.*, pp. 127–36.

[4] *Ibid.*, p. 9.

[5] *Ibid.*, p. 126.

The Cubans had good reason for gratitude to the United States. During the four years of the American occupation order had been maintained, public revenues had been honestly collected and wisely expended, public health had been improved through medical research and sanitation, capital had been attracted, free schools had been established, public works had been constructed, and the Cubans had received training in administration and self-government.[1]

President Roosevelt summed up the results of the first occupation and administration of Cuba in his annual message to Congress in the following words:

For three years our representatives, civil and military, have toiled unceasingly, facing disease of a peculiarly sinister and fatal type, with patient and uncomplaining fortitude, to teach her how to use aright her new freedom. Never in history has any alien country been thus administered, with such high integrity of purpose, such wise judgment, and such single-minded devotion to the country's interests.[2]

During the four years following the evacuation of the island only two matters of consequence arose between the Cubans and the Americans. The first concerned the trade relations between the two countries.

The economic welfare of the Cubans depended upon their finding a market in which a reasonable profit could be realized for their principal products, sugar and tobacco.[3] Their natural market was the United States. Until the passage of the Wilson-Gorman Tariff Act (1894) sugar had

---

[1] *Ibid.*, pp. 14 f.; Military governor of Cuba, *Report* (1901), 8 vols.

[2] J. D. Richardson, *Messages and Papers of the Presidents*, X, 460; see also Roosevelt, *Autobiography*, p. 505. In his annual report (1902), Secretary Root said that he knew "of no chapter in American history more satisfactory than that which will record the conduct of the military government of Cuba" (*House Document No. 2* [Fifty-seventh Congress, second session], V, 9).

[3] *House Document No. 2* (Fifty-seventh Congress, first session), II, 50–52; *House Document No. 1* (Fifty-seventh Congress, second session), I, 348.

been admitted free for years. Even after the duty was placed on sugar, exchanges with the United States were extensive. In 1896 trade between Cuba and the United States exceeded a value of $47,000,000, and this in spite of the insurrection which had broken out the preceding year.

Although in 1901 the exports and imports of the island totaled over $69,000,000,[1] the welfare of the Cubans was seriously handicapped by the tariff policy of the United States, the high duties of the Dingley Tariff Act (1897) proving especially burdensome. According to Secretary Root, more than half of the population of the island depended directly or indirectly upon the success of the sugar industry. Concerning the industry he says in his official report in 1901:

> If it succeeds we may expect peace, plenty, domestic order, and the happiness of a free and contented people to reward the sacrifice of American lives and treasure through which Cuba was set free. If it fails we may expect that the fields will again become waste, the mills will again be dismantled, the great body of laborers will be thrown out of employment; and that poverty and starvation, disorder and anarchy will ensue; that the charities and the schools which we have been building up will find no money for their support and will be discontinued; that the sanitary precautions which have made Cuba no longer a dreaded source of pestilence, but one of the most healthy islands in the world, will of necessity be abandoned, and our Atlantic seaboard must again suffer from the injury to commerce and the maintenance of quarantines at an annual cost of many millions.[2]

[1] C. L. Jones, *Caribbean Interests of the United States*, pp. 87 f. For trade with the United States during the nineties see W. J. Clark, *Commercial Cuba* (New York, 1898), pp. 240–43. V. H. Olmsted and H. Gannett, *Cuba*, pp. 80–94, give detailed statistics covering imports and exports for 1899 to 1907. In 1899 native Americans in Cuba numbered 6,444, out of a total population of 1,572,797 (Olmsted and Gannett, *op. cit.*, pp. 150, 231). The British Foreign Office estimated the investment of capital in Cuba from Great Britain, France, and the United States at $50,000,000 in 1898 (Clark, *op. cit.*, p. 145).

[2] *House Document No. 2* (Fifty-seventh Congress, first session), II, 51.

Realizing the gravity of the situation to the Cubans, Roosevelt, in his first annual message to Congress (December 3, 1901), acted on the recommendation of Secretary Root,[1] and strongly urged a substantial reduction in the tariff rates on Cuban imports into the United States.[2] In accordance with Roosevelt's recommendation, a bill providing for reciprocal trade relations passed the House, but encountered vigorous opposition in the Senate, due largely to the activities and influence of the lobby maintained by the powerful beet-sugar and cane-sugar interests.[3]

When the debate was at its height Former President Cleveland wrote a public letter (January 21, 1902) warmly indorsing the position of Roosevelt.[4] But in spite of Cleveland's assistance, the support of most of the Democratic senators, and the sending of a special message to Congress (June 12, 1902),[5] the Senate refused the President's request.

During the controversy Roosevelt seems to have tried in a mild way the plan which he often adopted in later years, usually with success, when his policies were threatened by Congress: He took his case to the people.[6] On April 9, 1902, in an address at the Charleston (S.C.) Exposition, he said:

[1] *Ibid.*, pp. 51 f.

[2] *House Document No. 1* (Fifty-seventh Congress, first session), I, xxxi f.

[3] The opponents of Cuban reciprocity maintained that their opposition was based primarily upon their desire to protect the beet-sugar interests from the American Sugar Refining Co., which, they declared, would be the chief beneficiary of the Cuban treaty. See W. D. Orcutt, *Burrows of Michigan*, I, 299–306. Cf. with J. B. Bishop, *Theodore Roosevelt and His Time*, I, 188; A. W. Dunn, *From Harrison to Harding*, I, 364; J. H. Latané, *America as a World Power*, pp. 183–89; S. M. Cullom, *Fifty Years of Public Service*, pp. 375–78; Coolidge, *op. cit.*, pp. 373–76.

[4] Bishop, *op. cit.*, I, 188.

[5] Richardson, *op. cit.*, X, 458–60.   [6] Coolidge, *op. cit.*, p. 379.

CUBA AND INTERVENTION

Cuba is so near to us that we can never be indifferent to misgovernment and disaster within its limits. The mere fact that our administration in the island has minimized the danger from the dreadful scourge of yellow fever, alike to Cuba and to ourselves, is sufficient to emphasize the community of interest between us. Cuba's position makes it necessary that her political relations with us should differ from her political relations with other powers. This fact has been formulated by us and accepted by the Cubans in the Platt Amendments. It follows as a corollary that, where the Cubans have thus assumed a position of peculiar relationship to our political system, they must similarly stand in a peculiar relationship to our economic system.

We have rightfully insisted upon Cuba adopting toward us an attitude differing politically from that she adopts toward any other power; and in return, as a matter of right, we must give to Cuba a different—that is, a better—position economically in her relations with us than we give to other powers. This is the course dictated by sound policy, by a wise and farsighted view of our own interest, and by the position we have taken during the past four years. We are a wealthy and a powerful country, dealing with a much weaker one; and the contrast in wealth and strength makes it all the more our duty to deal with Cuba, as we have already dealt with her, in a spirit of large generosity.[1]

Undaunted by the opposition of the Senate, Roosevelt again urged the adoption of reciprocity at the next session of Congress,

not only because it is eminently for our own interests to control the Cuban market and by every means to foster our supremacy in the tropical lands and waters south of us, but also because we of the giant republic of the north should make all our sister nations of the American Continent feel that whenever they will permit it we desire to show ourselves disinterestedly and effectively their friend.[2]

But the President's message did not convert the recalcitrant group in the Senate, and only after an extra session

[1] Roosevelt, *Addresses and Presidential Messages*, pp. 7 f.

[2] *House Document No. 1* (Fifty-seventh Congress, second session), I, xx.

of that body were the necessary votes for the reciprocity treaty obtained (March 19, 1903).[1]

On the tenth of the following November, Roosevelt convened Congress in advance of its regular session to enact the legislation needed to put into operation the commercial treaty which had been concluded with Cuba.[2] On November 19, the bill passed the House by a vote of 335 to 21. In the Senate the opposition to the bill was so long continued that the extra session ended without action, but in the regular session which immediately followed the measure was made the special order each day until it finally passed, December 16, 1903. The arrangement thus consummated gave American shippers a cut of from 25 to 40 per cent in the normal Cuban tariff, while it gave to Cuban exporters an advantage of 20 per cent on sugar and other products of the soil and industry imported into the United States over the rates of the Dingley Act or in any other tariff measure which might be subsequently enacted.[3] A gateway to the economic welfare of the island was thus opened.

During the two-year struggle over reciprocity the Cubans watched their champion with appreciative eyes.[4] But their appreciation did not cause the Cuban officials to safeguard the sanitation of the island so as to prevent the

[1] Bishop, *op. cit.*, I, 189; Malloy, *op. cit.*, I, 353–57; Richardson, *op. cit.*, X, 588 f.

[2] Richardson, *op. cit.*, X, 559–61; Bishop, *op. cit.*, I, 257. In ratifying the commercial convention with Cuba (March 19, 1903), the Senate stipulated that the approval of Congress be given before the convention became effective.

[3] Malloy, *op. cit.*, I, 354; *United States Statutes at Large*, Vol. XXXIII, Part I, pp. 3 f. During the struggle a sensation was caused by the discovery that General Wood had expended $15,526.82 of Cuban funds to promote the cause of reciprocity.

[4] *House Document No. 1* (Fifty-eighth Congress, second session), I, 356, 365.

problem of health from becoming a source of serious irritation between the two countries.

Probably no single phase of the American military government in Cuba between 1898 and 1902 excited such keen interest in the world at large as the notable accomplishments of the army medical corps in stamping out tropical diseases in the island—in particular, yellow fever, a disease from which the United States, as well as all tropical America, had repeatedly suffered. In Havana, it is said, during more than a century not a year or a month had passed when the city was free from yellow fever. Within nine months after the campaign against mosquitoes was initiated, not a case of the disease could be found. Similar victories were won in other Cuban cities under army control.[1]

The success of the American military administration was due, not only to scientific research, but also to strict quarantine regulations and the construction of greatly needed sanitary works. Such undertakings were not complete when the United States evacuated the island and, as we have seen, the American authorities, in order to protect American cities along the Atlantic Coast as well as to promote the welfare of the Cubans, included in the Platt Amendment a provision obligating the Cuban government to continue and complete the work of sanitation initiated when the Americans were in control of the island.[2]

Although the need of appropriations for sanitation was mentioned by President Palma in his first message to the

---

[1] Secretary of War, *Annual Reports*, Vol. I (1901), Part I, pp. 39 f.; W. A. Kelly, *Walter Reed and Yellow Fever*; W. J. Showalter, "Redeeming the Tropics," *National Geographic Magazine*, XXV (1914), 344–58; H. J. Spinder, "Yellow Fever—First and Last," *World's Work*, XLIII (1921), 169–81.

[2] See pp. 70, 72 f., 78 above.

Cuban Congress (May 26, 1902), the American Minister to Cuba thought the subject had been "passed over very lightly" and had not received the attention which the necessity demanded; only three sentences—and these of a general character—were devoted to the subject.[1] Six months later, however, the budget submitted to the Congress (November 1, 1902) provided an expenditure of $1,158,728 for sanitation, and Palma's message, although still vague and general, treated the subject at greater length.[2] In his communication the next spring (April 6, 1903), the Cuban President called the attention of the Congress to the obligations in matters of public health incurred by the republic under the Platt Amendment.[3] A year later (April 4, 1904), after commenting on the work accomplished, he again urged the Congress to appropriate funds for the continuance of sanitation projects, particularly in Santiago.[4]

But disagreements, together with legal and financial difficulties, led to a disregard in large part of Palma's recommendations, and the outbreak of epidemics in the island caused Secretary Hay to direct the American Minister (November 25, 1904) to inform the Cuban government that, unless an efficient system of sanitation was carried out in Matanzas and Santiago before the beginning of the active quarantine season of the next year, the United States would find it necessary "to declare quarantine against Cuban ports."[5] Following the warning the Cuban

[1] *House Document No. 1* (Fifty-seventh Congress, second session), I, 333, 336.

[2] *Ibid.*, pp. 345, 347.

[3] *Ibid.* (Fifty-eighth Congress, second session), p. 363.

[4] *House Document No. 1* (Fifty-eighth Congress, third session), I, 242.

[5] *Ibid.*, pp. 250 f.

Congress voted funds for health purposes, but in amounts insufficient to meet the needs.[1] During 1905 the United States again made urgent and repeated representations to the Cuban government, calling for the establishment of effective sanitary regulations in Cuban cities.[2]

The replies of the Cuban government were for the most part vague and indefinite. On January 6, 1906, for example, the Cuban Secretary of State answered the American representative's reiterated request that a specific date in the near future be named for the carrying out of Cuba's obligations by saying that "he hoped the matter would be settled within the next four months or so."[3] This statement Secretary Root characterized in a message to the American representative at Havana as "very unsatisfactory, in that it gives little promise or assurance of an early compliance with the treaty engagements. This Government thinks the time has come when there should be action. You will so inform the Cuban Government."[4]

Root's vigorous communication produced results. Shortly after it was received, President Palma issued a decree (January 12, 1906) providing a sanitary organization for the whole island and regulating in detail all matters pertaining to sanitation. The Cuban government also agreed to help the municipal authorities of Havana meet the expense of sewering and paving the capital, this difficulty having been one of the chief causes of the delay.

On March 24, 1906, the regulations for house-cleaning introduced during the American occupation in 1899 but discontinued in 1900 were renewed. By the regulations all

[1] *Ibid.*, p. 253.

[2] *Ibid.* (Fifty-ninth Congress, second session), pp. 265–76.

[3] *Foreign Relations* (1906), p. 504.

[4] *Ibid.*, p. 506.

buildings in the city were to be inspected rigidly, and those found in an unsatisfactory condition were to be cleaned thoroughly by a sanitary squad. Old clothes, paper, and rubbish were to be carted away, loaded on scows, and dumped into the sea five miles beyond the mouth of the harbor. On June 11, 1906, funds were advanced to the sanitary authorities at Bolondron, Union de Reyes, and Alacranes where yellow fever had been reported.[1] Such energetic measures quickly improved health conditions in the island.

With the exception of the friction caused by the problem of sanitation the relations between Cuba and the United States during the four years following the American evacuation of 1902 were marked by great friendliness. The American government observed with satisfaction the progress of the island in economic matters, and as shown by its action in trade relations contributed to the prosperity of the Cubans. The success which the islanders seemed to be making in self-government was also a source of gratification. Commenting upon their advance in his annual message to Congress (December 6, 1904), President Roosevelt said:

If every country washed by the Caribbean Sea would show the progress in stable and just civilization which with the aid of the Platt Amendment Cuba has shown since our troops left the island, and which so many of the republics in both Americas are constantly and brilliantly showing, all question of interference by this Nation with their affairs would be at an end.[2]

But Cuban progress in self-government, as events were to demonstrate, was more apparent than real. When President Palma became the first president of the republic (May

[1] *Foreign Relations* (1906), pp. 506–10.
[2] *House Document No. 1* (Fifty-eighth Congress, third session), I, xli f.

20, 1902), he assumed an independent attitude toward the existing political parties and selected his cabinet irrespective of the political affiliations of the members.

The Cuban Congress acted in a much less commendable manner. Although required by the constitution to make the municipal offices elective,[1] the Congress refused to pass such legislation. As a result the municipal officers, who had been chosen by popular vote during the American régime, became subject under the revived Spanish law to removal by the national executive, who might displace them at will and appoint others to their positions. In like manner, owing to the failure of the Congress to carry out the provisions of the constitution, the judges also remained subject to appointment and removal by the executive. To aggravate the situation the Cuban legislature adopted an amendment to the electoral law, placing the control of elections largely in the hands of the heads of the municipalities. The provision of the constitution which required the passage of a law providing for minority representation in both Houses of Congress was also ignored by the legislature. The attitude of the Congress indicates clearly that the dominant political party intended to retain control of the government by ignoring constitutional stipulations; for the effect of its course was to place the control of the local governments and therefore of the elections in the hands of the national executive.

During the early period of Cuban independence two important political parties existed in the island: the Moderates and the Liberals. A third party called the

---

[1] Palma was not responsible for the attitude of the legislature. In his first message (May 26, 1902), he recommended that the Congress "formulate the municipal law, within the meaning of the constitution, as soon as possible" (*ibid.* [Fifty-seventh Congress, second session], p. 335).

[87]

Nationalists usually acted with the Moderates. Until early in 1905 President Palma remained independent of the political parties. Then, disappointed at the defeat of legislation which he had at heart, he decided to affiliate with the dominant party, the Moderates, hoping thereby to secure the desired legislation. Accordingly, he dismissed his composite cabinet, and organized another made up entirely of Moderates. Henceforth Palma conducted the government in accordance with party politics.

To understand what follows we must now examine the Cuban electoral law. This measure was most complicated. It provided in effect for two elections: first, a preliminary election in September for the selection of members of the House of Representatives, the governors of the provinces, and the senatorial and presidential electors; second, a final election in December for the choice of senators, president, and vice-president. In 1905 half of the members of the Senate were to be elected for terms of eight years; while half the House, all the governors, the president, and the vice-president were to be chosen for terms of four years. As a result of the reorganization of the cabinet, the election of 1905 was the first in which the president, the vice-president, the cabinet, and the secretary of government controlling the municipalities, the police, and rural guards, and the election machinery were all members of the same party.

Taking advantage of the situation, General Freyre Andrade, the secretary of government, changed the local officials in twenty or more municipalities just before the preliminary elections in September. His action aroused intense bitterness among the common people, who had chosen the municipal officials in the days of the American military government; in the popular estimation the local officers seemed of much greater consequence than were the officials of the central government.[1] That the purpose of Andrade's course was political seems beyond question; at any rate, his action was so interpreted by the large body of the people.

The result of the changes in the municipal offices appeared on election day. When the Liberals came to cast their ballots, they found the polling places surrounded by the police or the rural guards. In many instances the Liberals were denied the right to vote by the election officials. Convinced that a fair election was impossible, many Cubans made no effort to vote after noon of the preliminary election day.

But unfair methods had only begun. At the registration of voters, which followed in October and which was under the control of boards chosen at the preliminary election, a total of 432,000 names were enrolled. The registration included at least 150,000 fictitious names; for by no possibility could the number of voters in the island exceed 300,000, and from this total would need to be subtracted the large number of Liberals who did not register.[2]

According to the election law, native male Cuban citizens, of full age, were permitted to vote if they could read and write or owned property valued at $250, or had served in and been honorably discharged from the Cuban army. The first census of the island showed that two-thirds of the Cubans could neither read nor write. In the presidential election of 1908, when the Americans were in control of Cuba, the total vote was only 195,197. The total population of the island on September 30, 1907, was 2,048,980.[3]

[1] *House Document No. 2* (Fifty-ninth Congress, second session), II, 453.

[2] *Ibid.*, p. 454.

[3] V. H. Olmsted and H. Gannett, *Cuba: Population, History and Resources*, pp. 44, 131. According to a memorandum submitted in 1907 to President Roosevelt by Mr. Bennett of the New York *Herald*, the population of Cuba was at least 2,500,000 (Bennett to Roosevelt, February 11, 1907, *Roosevelt Papers*).

Realizing the futility of voting under the circumstances, the Liberals withdrew from the final election in December, 1905, preferring to adopt the Latin-American practice of revolution. The refusal of the Liberals to vote and the frauds of the registration officials resulted in the choice of Moderates to all offices filled at the election. Not a single Liberal candidate in the entire island was successful. Commenting on the situation at a later time, the American commissioners said:

We conferred with General Freyre Andrade and asked him . . . . whether there had not been registration so that at least 150,000 names must have been registered in addition to those who actually were entitled to register. He said that that was possibly true, but that it was impossible to hold an election in Cuba without fraud, and that the officers of registration who were elected, when they heard that the Liberals were not going to register or vote, merely out of spirit of mischief had increased the registration lists in this generous manner. We learned from a prominent official [a Moderate] who . . . . had had great experience in elections in the islands . . . . that the Liberals had been guilty of fraud in municipalities where they had control two years before; that there never had been, however, so much open coercion and fraud in the history of elections . . . . as was shown in the one in December, 1905; that he had remonstrated with General Andrade, and had pointed out that the election could be carried for the Moderates without going to such extremes, and that it would be very unwise to prevent the return of any liberals to Congress or the Senate in that election. The truth seems to be that General Andrade and those who sympathised with him in the plan which he pursued had become convinced that the universal-suffrage clause of the constitution and the holding of elections according to the constitution and the law, with the Cuban electorate in its present condition of ignorance, would produce such instability in the government as to prevent the growth and the development of the country on the prosperous lines which had been realized under President Palma, and that it was necessary in the best interests of Cuba to secure for him a solid support in both Houses of Congress in order that the proper policies might be followed.[1]

[1] *House Document No. 2* (Fifty-ninth Congress, second session), II, 454.

CUBA AND INTERVENTION

Immediately following the December election came rumors of plots against the government. An insurrection was begun, but it was quickly suppressed and the leader placed in jail. With the inauguration of President Palma in March, 1906, the Moderates believed apparently that danger was past. If so, their hope was vain; for in August a revolt of serious proportions began in the western and central parts of Cuba and quickly spread to other parts of the island. The explanation of the uprising, as subsequently given by the American commissioners, is as follows:

> The cause for the insurrection is to be found primarily in the election and the methods which were pursued in carrying it for the Moderate party. Of course, it could not have occurred in a country in which the common and ignorant people are not so easily aroused by personal appeals of local leaders as they are in Cuba. It could not have occurred in a country where such a thing as an insurrection and "going to the field," as it is called, does not offer relief from daily labor, the pleasures of a picnic, and the opportunity to live on the country and upon the earnings and prosperity of other people; but with all this and with the natural tendency to insurrection that has been cultivated by a long history of insurrection in Cuba, no such formidable force could have been organized, had there not been some real feeling of injustice and outrage on the part of the less educated and poorer classes, who seemed more or less dimly to understand that the victory of the Moderates at the polls was the beginning of the end of power which they might exercise in the government.[1]

It has occasionally been charged that the uprising was financed by American capitalists who desired to see the United States in control of the island. According to a confidential report from the Government Secret Service, however, the funds for the revolution came chiefly from wealthy Cubans who in most instances hoped by their contributions to insure the safety of their property. American residents of the Isle of Pines also gave considerable sums.

[1] *Ibid.*, p. 456.

It was rumored, but not proved, that the American minister to Cuba, Mr. Squiers, delivered large amounts to General Gomez. The Tobacco Trust was also said to have given freely to safeguard its properties from destruction. No evidence was found to support the charge that American politicians and merchants contributed money to help the revolt.[1]

It soon became evident that the Cuban officials were wholly incapable of reducing the insurrection. They had little popular support outside the cities, and their military forces consisted of only 600 artillery, some militia, and 5,500 rural guards indifferently armed.[2] The insurrectionists, on the other hand, soon numbered from 15,000 to 20,000 men, half of whom by the middle of September were ready to march into Havana.[3] Property valued at millions of dollars, most of it owned by foreign capitalists and the larger part by Americans, was threatened with destruction. Inquiries were at once made at Washington by several foreign governments concerning the steps that the United States contemplated in the crisis.

From the beginning of the difficulties the Department of State was kept informed concerning events by the American diplomatic agents in Cuba.[4] At the same time the American representatives repeatedly called the attention of the Cuban government to the necessity of protecting American lives and property. Early in September the inability of the Cuban officials to cope with the uprising

[1] Memorandum of agent of the Government Secret Service transmitted in a letter from Taft to Roosevelt, September 22, 1906, *Roosevelt Papers.*

[2] *House Document No. 2* (Fifty-ninth Congress, second session), II, 456, 468.

[3] *Ibid.,* p. 457.

[4] The unsettled and troubled condition of affairs is described, for example, in a long, confidential dispatch from Squiers to Hay as early as February 25, 1905, *Roosevelt Papers.*

became apparent. The danger of the destruction of millions of dollars' worth of property plus the loss of the sugar crop, the harvest of which was about to begin, loomed larger with each passing day.[1] Evidences multiplied that the Cuban government was not able to protect Americans and American interests in the island.[2]

By the eighth of September the Moderate leaders seem to have concluded that American intervention under the Platt Amendment was preferable to surrender or compromise with the insurgents.[3] On that day Steinhart, the American consul-general at Havana,[4] telegraphed the State Department at Washington:

Absolutely confidential. Secretary of state, Cuba, has requested me, in name of President Palma, to ask President Roosevelt send immediately two vessels; one to Havana, other to Cienfuegos; they must come at once. Government forces are unable to quell rebellion. The Government is unable to protect life and property. . . . . It must be kept secret and confidential that Palma asked for vessels. No one here except President, Secretary of State, and myself know about it. Very anxiously awaiting reply.[5]

On September 10 the State Department cabled Steinhart that two warships had been ordered to Cuba, but that President Roosevelt regarded it as "a very serious

[1] *House Document No. 2* (Fifty-ninth Congress, second session), II, 456, 531. On the extent of the sugar and allied industries at the time of the insurrection see Olmsted and Gannett, *op. cit.*, pp. 69–71.

[2] *House Document No. 1* (Fifty-ninth Congress, second session), I, 467, 471, 475.

[3] *House Document No. 2* (Fifty-ninth Congress, second session), II, 444, 462, 482.

[4] Owing to the fact that Steinhart had been in Cuba since 1899, he was on intimate terms with President Palma and his colleagues. For this reason Palma apparently preferred to send confidential communications through Steinhart rather than through Sleeper, the *chargé d'affaires* in the absence of the American minister, Mr. Morgan (*ibid.*, p. 444).

[5] *House Document No. 1* (Fifty-ninth Congress, second session), II, 444 f.

thing to undertake forcible intervention, and before going into it we should have to be absolutely certain of the equities of the case and the needs of the situation."[1]

The following day Bacon, the acting secretary of state during Root's absence in South America, cabled the American representative that the President "believes actual, immediate intervention to be out of the question."[2] Notwithstanding Roosevelt's attitude, President Palma on September 12 again asked for intervention, requesting that "President Roosevelt send to Havana with rapidity two or three thousand men."[3] The next day the request was repeated with the additional information that "President Palma has irrevocably resolved to resign and to deliver the government of Cuba to the representatives whom the President of the United States will designate as soon as sufficient American troops are landed in Cuba."[4]

The same day (September 13) witnessed the landing in Havana of a battalion of 125 men from the "Denver," at the request of President Palma and Jacob Sleeper, the American *chargé d'affaires*.[5] A few hours later Sleeper received instructions that no armed force was to be landed "under any circumstances . . . . except under orders from the Department of State." Upon receiving this dispatch Sleeper immediately directed the withdrawal of the troops, to the great regret of Palma.[6]

---

[1] *Ibid.*, I, 474.

[2] *Ibid.*, p. 475. [3] *Ibid.*, p. 476. [4] *Ibid.*, pp. 477 f.

[5] *House Document No. 2* (Fifty-ninth Congress, second session), II, 458. Sleeper states 100 men were landed; see *House Document No. 1* (Fifty-ninth Congress, second session), I, 478.

[6] *House Document No. 1* (Fifty-ninth Congress, second session), I, 378, 482 f. When the news reached Washington that the troops had been landed, a sharp telegram was sent to Sleeper to the effect that the soldiers should not have been landed and were not to be used without express authority (Bacon to Sleeper, September 13, 1906, *Roosevelt Papers*).

CUBA AND INTERVENTION

On September 14 Consul-General Steinhart cabled that Palma had resolved to resign, that the Vice-President had decided to refuse the office, that the cabinet ministers had declared their intention of resigning, that it would be impossible under the circumstances for the Cuban Congress to meet since no one would have the legal right to convoke it, and that anarchy would ensue "unless the United States Government will adopt the measures necessary to avoid this danger."[1]

In the crisis Roosevelt decided to send William H. Taft, secretary of war, and Robert Bacon, acting secretary of state, to Havana to do what was possible to end hostilities and re-establish order in the island. In explanation of his action Roosevelt addressed a public letter to the Cuban minister, Señor Quesada, in which he said:

You and I were intimately drawn together at the time when the United States intervened in the affairs of Cuba with the result of making her an independent nation. You know how sincere my affectionate admiration and regard for Cuba are. You know that I have never done, and never shall do, anything in reference to Cuba save with such sincere regard for her welfare. You also know the pride I felt because it came to me as President to withdraw the American troops from the island of Cuba and officially to proclaim her independence and to wish her godspeed in her career as a free republic. I desire now through you to say a word of solemn warning to your people, whose earnest wellwisher I am. For seven years Cuba has been in a condition of profound peace and of steadily growing prosperity. For four years this peace and prosperity have obtained under her own independent government. Her peace, prosperity, and independence are now menaced; for of all possible evils that can befall Cuba the worst is the evil of anarchy, into which civil war and revolutionary disturbances will assuredly throw her. . . . .

There is just one way in which Cuban independence can be jeoparded, and that is for the Cuban people to show their inability to con-

[1] *House Document No. 1* (Fifty-ninth Congress, second session), I, 479.

tinue in their path of peaceful and orderly progress. This nation asks nothing of Cuba, save that it shall continue to develop as it has developed during these past seven years, that it shall know and practice the orderly liberty which will assuredly bring an ever-increasing measure of peace and prosperity to the beautiful Queen of the Antilles. Our intervention in Cuban affairs will come only if Cuba herself shows that she has fallen into the insurrectionary habit, that she lacks the self-restraint necessary to secure peaceful self-government, and that her contending factions have plunged the country into anarchy.

I solemnly adjure all Cuban patriots to band together, to sink all differences and personal ambitions, and to remember that the only way that they can preserve the independence of their Republic is to prevent the necessity of outside interference, by rescuing it from the anarchy of civil war. . . . .

Under the treaty with your government, I, as President of the United States, have a duty in this matter which I cannot shirk. The third article of that treaty explicitly confers upon the United States the right to intervene for the maintenance in Cuba of a government adequate for the protection of life, property, and individual liberty. The treaty conferring this right is the supreme law of the land and furnishes me with the right and the means of fulfilling the obligation that I am under to protect American interests. . . . . It is in my judgment imperative for the sake of Cuba that there shall be an immediate cessation of hostilities and some arrangement which will secure the permanent pacification of the island.[1]

Roosevelt's letter and the news that American officials were coming to Havana immediately ended hostilities in Cuba.[2] The failure to adopt rules to govern the armed forces during the truce, however, made a clash between them probable at any moment. A renewal of the conflict under the circumstances would give to the strife all the added bitterness which would arise from the mutual charges of bad faith, certain to be made in such an event.

Meanwhile, Taft and Bacon left Oyster Bay, whither

[1] *Ibid.*, p. 480.

[2] *House Document No. 2* (Fifty-ninth Congress, second session), II, 449, 459.

they had been summoned by the President, stopped in Washington to consult military officers on the readiness of the Army to undertake forcible intervention if need arose and to confer with the Judge Advocate General concerning the right of the President to intervene in Cuba without action by Congress. But Roosevelt had no intention of confining himself to action approved by a counselor-at-law. In a long letter to Taft he stated emphatically that, if the need arose, as he hoped it would not, he intended to intervene; that he would not dream of asking the permission of Congress; that the Platt Amendment was the law of the land and he intended to execute it.[1]

On September 16 Taft and Bacon started for Cuba, reaching Havana on the morning of the nineteenth. During the next ten days the city was the center of a three-cornered contest between the insurgent leaders, the Cuban officials, and the American representatives. While attempting for political reasons to conceal the fact that they desired American intervention or even annexation, the Cuban officials endeavored during this period to turn the island over to the Americans.[2] Although not eager for intervention and in no way friendly to annexation, the insurgent leaders preferred the occupation of the island by the Americans to submission to rule by the Moderates. The American representatives, on the other hand, in accordance with Roosevelt's orders, tried in every way consistent with the re-establishment of peace and order to avoid intervention and to bring about an amicable solution of the controversy.[3]

Realizing the danger of a renewal of the conflict through

[1] Roosevelt to Taft, September 17, 1906, *Roosevelt Papers.*

[2] *House Document No. 2* (Fifty-ninth Congress, second session), II, 462, 482.

[3] *Ibid.*, pp. 459-62, 465, 515.

a violation of the truce, the American representatives first of all obtained the adoption by the commanders of the rival Cuban factions of definite rules to govern the conduct of the armed forces.[1] At the same time the commissioners held daily conferences with the leaders of both parties in an endeavor to find a basis of compromise.

But the efforts of the Americans were doomed to fail, primarily because of the obstinacy of the Moderates. Ten days before the arrival of Taft and Bacon a compromise which seemed to be acceptable to President Palma and his cabinet had been proposed. By this proposal, which as a whole impressed both Taft and Bacon as "a fair basis for settlement," the representatives, senators, and provincial governors chosen at the last election were to resign, the municipal officials who had been removed for partisan purposes were to be given redress, and the president and vice-president of the republic were to remain in office. Before the Americans landed, however, Palma rejected the proposal, having determined apparently to resign his office and force American intervention.

Believing Palma to be "the most disinterested patriot in the island,"[2] the American commissioners tried repeatedly to persuade him to retain office, proposing as a modification of the compromise explained above that a new election be held in three months under new laws to be prepared by a mixed commission containing at least one American, and that meantime the municipal officials remain as they were.[3] Although disappointed at the American proposal, the Liberal leaders indicated that they would probably accept it. But the Moderates continued obdurate, and Palma,

[1] *Ibid.*, pp. 459, 502–4.

[2] *Ibid.*, p. 460.   [3] *Ibid.*, pp. 460 f., 512 f.

having again declared his determination to withdraw from the presidency, called a session of Congress for September 28 to receive his resignation.[1]

The eagerness of the American commissioners to effect a compromise is evident at all times. For example, on September 28, Taft reported: "We said we would object to no agreement of any sort which would bring about peace; that we had no pride of opinion in the compromise suggested by us, but they might make any agreement they chose if it only brought about peace."[2]

While conferences and negotiations were in progress in Havana, Roosevelt sent dispatch after dispatch to the American commissioners urging them, if possible, to avoid intervention and effect some sort of compromise. In a personal note (dated September 17, 1906), written before Taft and Bacon reached Havana, Roosevelt said: "I most earnestly hope that there will be no necessity for intervention."[3] A few days later, when the situation seemed to demand the landing of troops, he cabled Taft a reluctant permission (September 21, 1906), but added: "I desire, if possible, that you communicate with me before taking such final steps as will irrevocably commit us to intervention."[4]

That Roosevelt was deeply influenced in his attitude by public opinion in the United States is evident from the dispatches. On September 22 he cabled the American commissioners: "It is important from the standpoint of public sentiment here that we shall make it plain that we are

[1] *Ibid.*, p. 460.

[2] *Ibid.*, p. 482.

[3] *Ibid.*, p. 448. See also Roosevelt's letter to Senator Foraker, September 28, 1906 (Foraker, *op. cit.*, II, 57–59).

[4] *House Document No. 1* (Fifty-ninth Congress, second session), II, 471.

exhausting every effort to come to an agreement before we intervene."[1]

In a telegram of September 26, he again urged the commissioners not to use the word "intervention," adding: "This I advise primarily with a view to complications here."[2]

About the same time he cautioned Secretary Taft:

Avoid the use of the word "intervention" in any proclamation or paper of yours and if possible place the landing of our sailors and marines on the grounds of conservation of American interests, emphasizing the temporary character of the landing and the hope that our keeping sailors, marines, or troops in the island will be but for a short time, until a permanent government has been formed.

In the same telegram he said: "I want to make it evident, beyond the possibility of a doubt, that we take no steps that we are not absolutely forced to by the situation."[3]

Later in the day he directed Taft

to do anything that is necessary, no matter how strong the course, but to try to do it in as gentle a way as possible, and to try to use terms which will be as little as possible of a challenge to opposition. But the main thing, after all, is to bring about a satisfactory result in Cuba, and with this in view I am willing, of course, to incur any criticism and run any risk.[4]

In reply to Taft's objection to the setting up of a Cuban provisional government on the ground that the office of provisional president was not authorized in the Cuban constitution, Roosevelt showed his impatience with constitutional limitations and at the same time revealed

[1] *Ibid.*, p. 472; see also pp. 475, 477, 480, 481, 484, 485.

[2] *Ibid.*, p. 480.

[3] *House Document No. 2* (Fifty-ninth Congress, second session), II, 477.

[4] *Ibid.*, p. 480.

again his repugnance to assuming control of the island. He said:

> I do not think that we should take such control except as a last resort and after every other expedient for securing pacification has been attempted, and I do not care in the least for the fact that such an agreement [the setting up of a Cuban provisional government] is not constitutional.[1]

The contrast between Roosevelt's denunciation of the Cuban revolutionists and his defense of the Panama seceders is striking. On September 26 he cabled Taft: "I sympathize most heartily with your abhorrence of the insurrectionary spirit, and appreciate keenly the evil necessarily done by the recognition of the insurrectionary party."[2] Later in the day he said: "It is undoubtedly a very evil thing that the revolutionists should be encouraged and the dreadful example afforded the island of success in remedying wrongs by violence and treason to the Government." In the same telegram he added: "If the Palma Government had shown any real capacity for self-defense and ability to sustain itself and a sincere purpose to remedy the wrongs of which your telegrams show that they have been guilty, I should have been inclined to stand by them, no matter to what extent, including armed intervention."[3] On September 28 he wrote Senator Foraker: "I share absolutely your indignation with the insurgents."[4]

Whether Roosevelt's views had undergone a sea change since 1903, or whether he regarded the situation in Cuba as entirely different from that which had obtained in Panama, or whether he did not believe that intervention in Cuba would promote the interests of the United States and

[1] *Ibid.*, p. 481. [3] *Ibid.*, p. 478.

[2] *Ibid.*, p. 477. [4] Foraker, *op. cit.*, II, 57.

his own desires, is not clear. At all events he intervened in Panama on the side of the revolutionists in record-breaking time, defending his action on the ground of treaty rights, international obligations, and justice to the oppressed Panamanians; while he intervened in Cuba with the utmost reluctance, not to assist Cubans who had been unjustly deprived of their political rights by a corrupt government, but to satisfy treaty obligations and to re-establish law and order.

As pointed out above, all efforts at compromise failed, and on September 28 Taft telegraphed the President:

> It looks today as if intervention would come tonight or tomorrow morning. I know how much you deplore this, but there is really no way out of it. The truth is that the two parties want it now, the Liberals because they can earn their victory in the holding of new elections, and the Moderates because if the elections have to be held they want them held under the auspices of the United States, and because the Moderates are in favor of annexation generally. But neither party is willing to take the responsibility of saying so out loud.[1]

During September, Roosevelt, while urging a compromise among the Cubans, neglected no step toward military and naval readiness in case armed intervention proved inevitable; he did not propose to have a repetition of the unpreparedness and mismanagement of 1898. On September 17 he expressed his satisfaction when informed that the

---

[1] *House Document No. 2* (Fifty-ninth Congress, second session), II, 482. Bacon seems to have disagreed with Taft, feeling apparently that nothing should be done until Root returned from South America. J. B. Scott (*op. cit.*, p. 118) quotes Bacon as saying: "I shall be ashamed to look Mr. Root in the face. This intervention is contrary to his policy and what he has been preaching in South America." On the other hand, Bacon telegraphed Adee that he greatly regretted not to be able to end the war by an agreement between the two parties, but that he was convinced that it was impossible (Bacon to Adee, September 29, 1906, *Roosevelt Papers*). Bacon was apparently indifferent to the injustice suffered by the Cuban Liberals, and he seems to have underrated the danger of a renewal of hostilities by a postponement of the settlement of the insurrection.

Army was ready.[1] Before Taft and Bacon left the United States, the President ordered a large detachment of the fleet to Havana. When intervention was proclaimed (September 29, 1906), therefore, Secretary Taft had at hand approximately 6,000 sailors and marines, while the Army was prepared to land 18,000 soldiers in the island within a few days.[2]

Fortunately, force was not needed. Shortly after the Americans took charge, the insurgents and the government militia surrendered their arms, disbanded, and returned to their homes. Political prisoners were at once set free. On October 13, 1906, Charles E. Magoon succeeded Secretary Taft as provisional governor of the island.[3] The second American occupation of Cuba had been peacefully inaugurated.

In his annual message to Congress (December 3, 1906) Roosevelt, after summarizing events in Cuba and describing his action in the crisis, stated that the provisional government would come to an end as soon as an election had been held and the new government had been established in a peaceful and orderly manner. He then announced the future policy of the United States toward the island as follows:

The United States wishes nothing of Cuba except that it shall prosper morally and materially, and wishes nothing of the Cubans save that they shall be able to preserve order among themselves and therefore to preserve their independence. If the elections become a farce, and if the insurrectionary habit becomes confirmed in the Island, it is absolutely out of the question that the Island should remain independent; and the United States, which has assumed the sponsorship

---

[1] Roosevelt to Taft, September 17, 1906, *Roosevelt Papers*.

[2] *House Document No. 2* (Fifty-ninth Congress, second session), II, 459.

[3] *Foreign Relations* (1906), p. 490; *House Document No. 2* (Fifty-ninth Congress, second session), II, 463–67, 487–89, 522–34.

before the civilized world for Cuba's career as a nation, would again have to intervene and to see that the government was managed in such orderly fashion as to secure the safety of life and property. The path to be trodden by those who exercise self-government is always hard, and we should have every charity and patience with the Cubans as they tread this difficult path. I have the utmost sympathy with them, and regard for them; but I most earnestly adjure them solemnly to weigh their responsibility and to see that when their new government is started it shall run smoothly, and with freedom from flagrant denial of right on the one hand, and from insurrectionary disturbances on the other.[1]

The second period of American occupation continued for a little over two years. In accordance with a law promulgated by Governor Magoon in April, 1908, elections were held in the fall of 1908, the Liberal candidates receiving a large majority of the popular vote over the Conservative candidates. With the inauguration of General Gomez as president (January 28, 1909), the American forces were withdrawn and the island was again placed in the hands of the Cubans.[2]

In an extemporaneous speech at a public dinner in Christiania, Norway, on May 5, 1910, Roosevelt stated that after the Spanish-American War he had been told repeatedly by European diplomats that in spite of its promises the United States would never leave Cuba. "You said you would, of course, but that is quite understood; nations don't expect promises like that to be kept." When the intervention of 1906 occurred, he said he was again told by the same gentlemen that the United States, having kept its promise by withdrawing in 1902, would now remain in

[1] *House Document No. 1* (Fifty-ninth Congress, second session), I, xlv. Roosevelt repeated his injunction in his annual message of December 3, 1907, and in his annual message of December 8, 1908. See *Foreign Relations* (1907), p. lxiv, and *ibid.* (1908), pp. lxvii f.

[2] Olmsted and Gannett, *op. cit.*, p. 44. The second occupation of Cuba cost the United States $6,000,000.

Cuba. "No, we shall not," he replied. "We will keep the promise not only in the letter but in the spirit. We will stay in Cuba to help it on its feet, and then we will leave the island in better shape to maintain its permanent independent existence."[1]

Roosevelt was right. The promise was strictly fulfilled. The second period of American occupation like the first was marked by order and prosperity, by growth in wealth and population, and by progress in sanitation and education.[2] Disorders have marred succeeding years and have occasionally caused the landing of American marines for the preservation of order; but with the passage of time the need for a third intervention becomes less likely. Whatever the future may hold for the Pearl of the Antilles, the record indicates that the second American occupation was a period of advance by the Cubans in the mastery of the difficult art of self-government.

[1] The speech is quoted, in large part, in Abbott, *Impressions of Theodore Roosevelt*, pp. 128–30.

[2] Roosevelt believed that advantage should be taken of the American occupation to put the island on a solid basis of sound legislation (Roosevelt to Taft, April 16, 1907, *Roosevelt Papers*).

Chapter V
THE VENEZUELAN CRISIS

DIFFICULTIES in Venezuela first brought Roosevelt into close contact with European diplomacy. Venezuela, it will be recalled, seceded from Colombia in 1829 and became an independent republic. For a decade and longer her history was relatively peaceful. Then she became involved in a series of wars and insurrections which continued with brief intervals of peace well into the twentieth century. In 1899, after one of the revolutions, there came to the head of the distressed state Cipriano Castro, who for the next ten years, with the exception of a short, self-imposed exile,[1] was the virtual dictator of Venezuela.

Like most Caribbean countries, Venezuela was heavily in debt when Castro became its ruler. During preceding decades both government and people had incurred heavy financial obligations for carrying on war, constructing railroads, building slaughter-houses, and developing natural resources.[2] Grants, concessions, and privileges of various sorts had been made to foreigners and to foreign corporations, sometimes in legitimate ways and for legitimate purposes, but more frequently in illegitimate ways and for

[1] *Foreign Relations* (1906), pp. 1440-42.

[2] *Senate Document No. 119* (Fifty-eighth Congress, third session), VII, 755-57, 771-73.

unproductive enterprises.[1] Loot, pillage, and exploitation in the worst sense of the term had characterized many of the self-seeking governments.

Throughout much of Venezuelan history both the people and their resources had been the prey of adventurers and unprincipled, self-seeking men. The ruling class, which ordinarily did not number more than one-tenth of the population, was usually divided into two rival factions, each endeavoring by fair means or foul to get control of the government. Once in power the successful faction usually acted on the principle that to the victors belong the spoils, the spoils being not merely the governmental offices, but also the revenues of the state, which too often were augmented by corrupt concessions, new loans, and forced contributions from foreign merchants and foreign corporations doing business in the country.

Under such conditions, which obtained during the greater part of the nineteenth century in most Latin-American countries, established and orderly government was often a farce. The political situation, as pictured by an American business man in 1903 in colors which perhaps are intentionally somewhat glaring, was as follows:

It does not take the observer long to ascertain that there is not in any of these countries such a thing as a legally constituted government. The constitutions prescribe that elections shall be held at stated periods and in a certain manner for the election of the president and other officials of the government, but no elections are ever held. Occasionally a newspaper correspondent, some disciple of Mark Twain, as a huge joke writes about an election in Venezuela or Colombia, the same as he might about a sea serpent, but not within the memory of any living man has there been a real election in those countries. . . . .

[1] For the commerce and resources of Venezuela see B. L. Miller and J. T. Singewald, *Mineral Deposits of South America*, pp. 531–45; W. S. Robertson, *Hispanic-American Relations with the United States*, pp. 187–93, 270, and Appendix.

The constitutions provide that the laws shall be passed by the legislatures of the several states or by the congress for the federal union, yet ninety-five laws out of every hundred are the edicts of the dictator, pure and simple, and no pretense is made that any legislative body ever read them, let alone passed them or engrossed them. . . . .[1]

Official correspondence supports in large measure the foregoing description. The American minister at Caracas, Francis B. Loomis, in a confidential communication to Secretary Hay (January 26, 1901), wrote:

The talk about the constitution is bosh. It is used as a convenience. When either it or the law can be quoted to advantage they are brought forward and referred to with a good imitation of solemn pride. When the constitution stands in the way of any course the Government desires to pursue, it is remorselessly and regularly ignored. This is not a constitutional government. General Castro is a dictator, and does pretty much as he pleases.[2]

On February 22, 1901, Loomis again wrote confidentially:

Since my residence here I have seen a majority of the members of the supreme court arrested, imprisoned, and finally removed from office for intimating that they would not decide a case in the manner desired by the Chief Executive.[3]

The political and financial conditions in Venezuela proved fertile soil for difficulties with other countries. Defaults repeatedly occurred on the external public debt, both in interest and principal. A British official paper said:

During the sixty-nine years that have elapsed since Venezuela became an independent State it may be reckoned that the external debt contracted in England has been in default for nearly forty years,—

[1] American Business Man, "Is the Monroe Doctrine a Bar to Civilization?" *North American Review*, CLXXVI (1903), 520.

[2] *Senate Document No. 413* (Sixtieth Congress, first session), XXIV, 324 f.

[3] *Ibid.*, p. 332; see also pp. 462, 480; cf. with Bowen's confidential report to Roosevelt, August 21, 1904, *Roosevelt Papers*.

and that during the same period the Republic has compelled the bond-holders to accept five arrangements, under each of which they have had to submit to large sacrifices of their rightful claims.[1]

The numerous insurrections and disorders which vexed the land usually resulted in injuries to the persons and property of aliens and to alien corporations, and led to extensive claims for indemnity—claims which, in most instances, were supported by the respective governments of the claimants. Such was the situation which led Great Britain, Germany, and Italy to take the action which brought about the Venezuelan crisis of 1902.

The controversy between Venezuela and the three European states named above arose primarily over pecuniary claims against the South American Republic. The claims were based for the most part on injuries and losses during the civil war in which Castro had risen to power and on the violation of contracts by the Venezuelan government. The most important German demands, for example, were, first, the recovery of interest seven years in arrears on 5 per cent Venezuelan bonds; second, the payment of dividends guaranteed by the Venezuelan government on a railroad built in Venezuela by a German corporation; and third, indemnity for losses, compulsory loans, and damages suffered by German subjects during the last Venezuelan revolution.[2] The claims of Great Britain and Italy, while differing in detail from those of Germany, were of the same general character.[3] Similar claims, it should be noted, were also made by the United States,

[1] "Memorandum of the British Government to the Hague Tribunal," *Senate Document No. 119*, VII, 772.

[2] *Foreign Relations* (1901), pp. 192–94; *ibid.* (1903), pp. 429–31; *Senate Document No. 316* (Fifty-eighth Congress, second session), XXXV, 641 f.

[3] *Senate Document No. 119*, VII, 757 f.; *Senate Document No. 316*, XXXV, 871–74.

Belgium, France, Mexico, the Netherlands, Spain, Sweden, and Norway.

Contrary to the view commonly held by historians, the leader in coercive measures against Venezuela in 1902, at least in the early phases of the controversy, was Great Britain, not Germany. In the first stages of the discussion the tone of the British dispatches to the Venezuelan government was usually one of sternness rather than conciliation. During the two years preceding the crisis of December, 1902, no hint or suggestion for submitting the British claims to arbitration or judicial decision can be found in the British communications.[1] In December, 1902, the Prime Minister stated on the floor of the House of Commons that the government had sent Venezuela three ultimatums during the preceding six months.[2]

The German government, on the other hand, on at least one occasion (July 16, 1901) urged upon Venezuela in friendly terms the examination of the German claims by joint arbitrators, with the suggestion that, in case the arbitrators could not come to an agreement, the claims on which they differed could be made the subject of special conferences between the imperial legation and the Venezuelan government; and the further suggestion that, in all instances in which the conferences failed, the disagreements should be submitted to the decision of the Hague Tribunal.[3] Less than a month before Great Britain and Germany delivered their ultimatums to Venezuela, the German government, while agreeing with the British suggestion that coercive measures be taken as soon as pos-

---

[1] *Senate Document No. 119*, VII, 161.

[2] *Parliamentary Debates* (4th series, 1902), CXVI, 1273 f., 1277; see also pp. 1107 f.

[3] *Senate Document No. 119*, VII, 261–63.

sible, pointed out the necessity of taking into consideration the fact that "the last notes between the German and Venezuelan Governments were exchanged more than six months ago, and were not couched in a tone which would justify an immediate resort to measures of coercion."[1] The British government suffered under no such handicap.

In spite of the moderation which marked the tone of its communications, Germany had for months contemplated a resort to stern measures, including possibly the "temporary occupation" of Venezuelan soil. As early as December 11, 1901, the German Ambassador at Washington had submitted to John Hay a prememoria which, after describing the German claims and reviewing the fruitless efforts that had been made to arrive at a settlement, concludes as follows:

Under these circumstances the Imperial Government believes that further negotiations with Venezuela are hopeless. The Imperial Government proposes therefore to submit the reclamations in question, which have been carefully studied and have been considered as well founded, directly to the Venezuelan Government and to ask for their settlement. If the Venezuelan Government continues to decline as before, it would have to be considered what measures of coercion should be used against it.

But we consider it of importance to let first of all the Government of the United States know about our purposes so that we can prove that we have nothing else in view than to help those of our citizens who have suffered damages, and we shall first take into consideration only the claims of those German citizens who have suffered in the civil war.

We declare especially that under no circumstances do we consider in our proceedings the acquisition or the permanent occupation of Venezuelan territory. . . . .

[1] *British and Foreign State Papers*, XCV (1901–2), 1083, 1095. The difference in the character of the German and British dispatches may be attributed in part to differences in the character of their claims against Venezuela (see *Senate Document No. 119*, VII, 637 f.). The significance of the contrast, however, lies in the light thrown upon the question as to whether Great Britain or Germany was the initial aggressor against the South American Republic.

After the posing of an ultimatum, first of all the blockade of the more important Venezuelan harbors—that is, principally the harbors of La Guaira and Porto Cabello—would have to be considered as an appropriate measure of coercion, as the levying of duties for import and export being nearly the only source of income of Venezuela would in this way be made impossible. Likewise it would be difficult in this way to provide the country, which depends on the import of cocoa, with food. If this measure does not seem efficient, we would have to consider the temporary occupation on our part of different Venezuelan harbor places and the levying of duties in those places.[1]

Hay replied to the German communication by a memorandum (December 16, 1901) in which he quoted from Roosevelt's annual message of December 3, 1901, as follows:

The Monroe doctrine is a declaration that there must be no territorial aggrandizement by any non-American power at the expense of any American power on American soil. It is in no wise intended as hostile to any nation in the Old World. . . . . This doctrine has nothing to do with the commercial relations of any American power, save that it in truth allows each of them to form such as it desires. . . . . We do not guarantee any State against punishment if it misconducts itself, provided that punishment does not take the form of the acquisition of territory by any non-American power.

Hay then goes on to state:

His excellency the German ambassador, on his recent return from Berlin, conveyed personally to the President the assurance of the German Emperor that His Majesty's Government had no purpose or intention to make even the smallest acquisition of territory on the South American Continent or the islands adjacent. This voluntary and friendly declaration was afterwards repeated to the Secretary of State, and was received by the President and the people of the United States in the frank and cordial spirit in which it was offered. In the memorandum of the 11th of December, his excellency the German ambassador repeats these assurances as follows: "We declare especially that under no circumstances do we consider in our proceedings the acquisition or the permanent occupation of Venezuelan territory." . . . .

[1] *House Document No. 1* (Fifty-seventh Congress, first session), I, 192–94.

THE VENEZUELAN CRISIS

The President of the United States, appreciating the courtesy of the German Government in making him acquainted with the state of affairs referred to, and not regarding himself as called upon to enter into the consideration of the claims in question, believes that no measure will be taken in this matter by the agents of the German Government which are not in accordance with the well-known purpose, above set forth, of His Majesty the German Emperor.[1]

Notwithstanding the German prememoria, almost a year elapsed before Germany resorted to coercion. The delay was not the outgrowth of a spirit of tolerance or benevolence toward the South American Republic. As early as January 20, 1902, Count von Bülow, the German chancellor, requested the Emperor's permission to enter into an agreement with the British government for joint action by the two countries for the collection of the claims, but William II preferred that no action be taken until after his brother, Prince Henry, visited America, lest the effect of the visit be destroyed by the suspicion which the coercive measures might arouse in the United States. Accordingly, the contemplated measures were postponed until the autumn.[2]

Why Germany acted in conjunction with Great Britain is a question on which the evidence is not conclusive. Perhaps the desire to establish closer relations with the British and thus hinder a *rapprochement* between the British and

[1] *Ibid.*, p. 195.

[2] *Die grosse Politik*, XVII, 242-44. As described in a note from Bülow to Prince Henry, the purpose of the latter's visit to America was not diplomatic, political, or commercial. "The purpose of the journey is solely that Your Royal Highness, as brother of His Majesty the Emperor, through the personality of Your Highness is to delight and win the Americans with manner and appearance, to convince them of the sympathy of His Majesty for the great and rapidly growing American people as well as of the usefulness of good relations between the German and American people who are not separated by any political differences but are bound instead by numerous and weighty interests, old traditions, and ties of blood."

the French played a part in her calculations. Perhaps the success of the enterprise and the payment of the claims seemed more certain, if Great Britain were an associate.[1] *Die Neueste Nachrichten* stated: "Had we Germans intervened alone with armed force in Venezuela, we should have run a risk which is not worth the prize we hope to obtain."[2]

The motives which caused Great Britain to act with Germany are equally obscure. Roosevelt and Hay believed that England was following Germany's lead in a half-hearted fashion. It may be that the co-operation of Great Britain with Germany was merely a part of the general British program of cultivating more friendly relations with continental neighbors.

But whatever the motives of the two governments may have been, they decided to act together. The first hint for combined action came apparently from England. On January 2, 1902, Villiers, the special correspondent for South America, told the German *chargé d'affaires*, Eckardstein, that there was a possibility after a later meeting of the German ministry that joint action against Venezuela would be proposed as soon as conditions there became clear. Owing to the vagueness of the suggestion[3] and to the approaching journey of Prince Henry to the United States, the German government, as pointed out above, did

[1] Concerning the motives that may have caused the two governments to act together against Venezuela see *Parliamentary Debates*, CXVI, 1251–58, 1269 f., 1275, 1280 f., 1286, 1490 f.

[2] *Ibid.*, p. 1252. So far as the action itself is concerned, the chief reasons for Germany's course seem to have been her desire to collect the claims, to enhance her reputation in Central and South America, and to protect the large German interests in those regions (see *Die grosse Politik*, XVII, 245, 248).

[3] On the margin of the letter in which the German Chancellor described to the Emperor the Venezuelan situation and related the British suggestion, the Emperor wrote "Too vague." See Bülow's letter of January 20, 1902 (*ibid.*, p. 243, n. 1).

not at the time give its assent to the suggestion. Six months later (July 23, 1902), however, Count Metternich, the German ambassador at London, in his turn cautiously sounded the British foreign minister, Lord Lansdowne, concerning joint action against Venezuela. Lansdowne indicated the willingness of the British government to confer with Germany with a view to such an enterprise and, at that time or later, seems to have proposed as an appropriate means of coercion a blockade of the Venezuelan ports.[1]

Less than a week after the German-English conferences concerning joint action were thus opened, Lord Lansdowne dispatched a stern note to Venezuela in which he declared that, unless certain British demands were granted, "His Majesty's Government will take such steps as may be necessary to obtain the reparation which they are entitled to demand."[2] About the same time, Lansdowne asked the British admiralty for information concerning the "most effectual and convenient manner of putting pressure on the Venezuelan Government," in case coercive measures were adopted.[3]

During the next four months, Great Britain took the lead in aggressiveness.[4] So vigorous was her course that on at least one occasion the German Ambassador in London expressed regret to Lansdowne that the British had

---

[1] *British and Foreign State Papers*, XCV (1901–2), 1069; *Die grosse Politik*, XVII, 245; see also *Senate Document No. 119*, VII, 618, 623.

[2] Note of July 29, 1902, *British and Foreign State Papers*, XCV (1901–2), 1078. The incident which precipitated the note was the seizure by Venezuelan authorities of certain British vessels (*ibid.*, XCV, 1064–68).

[3] *Senate Document No. 119*, VII, 617, 623, 629, 632.

[4] *Ibid.*, pp. 617, 623, 629, 632; see, in particular, pp. 630, 632, 635, 636; *Die grosse Politik*, XVII, 250 f.

acted alone when the German authorities stood in favor of the same action.[1]

During November the two governments completed their arrangements to proceed against Venezuela. On November 13, the British Ambassador at Washington informed Secretary Hay that, after one more effort to secure a settlement, the British government if unsuccessful would adopt whatever measures might be necessary to enforce their demands.[2] In reply to this communication Hay stated that ("the United States Government, although they regretted that European powers should use force against Central and South American Countries, could not object to their taking steps to obtain redress for injuries suffered by their subjects, provided that no acquisition of territory was contemplated."[3] On December 7 the British and German representatives delivered ultimatums to the Venezuelan government and on the following day, no satisfactory reply having been received, both legations withdrew from Caracas.

Meantime, the Italian government, which had also notified the United States that Italy might find it necessary to use coercion to secure satisfaction of the claims of its subjects, informed Great Britain and Germany of its desire to join in the action against Venezuela.[4] After some delay the request was granted, but the part Italy played in the enterprise was of minor consequence.

[1] See Metternich's telegram to the German Foreign Office, November 11, 1902, in *Die grosse Politik*, XVII, 250–52.

[2] *Senate Document No. 119*, VII, 635 f., 638 f.

[3] *Ibid.*, pp. 638 f. Cf. with Hay's reply to Germany (December 16, 1901); see pp. 145 f. above.

[4] *Senate Document No. 119*, VII, 657 f., 663 f., 665 f.; *House Document No. 1* (Fifty-eighth Congress, second session), I, 602 f.; M. A. de Wolfe Howe, *George von Lengerke Meyer*, pp. 65 f.

THE VENEZUELAN CRISIS

The plan of the allied powers was first to seize and retain the Venezuelan gunboats and then, if Venezuela did not submit to their demands, to blockade the Venezuelan ports.[1] Nothing further seems to have been contemplated, although at one time during the forming of the plans Lansdowne favored seizing the Venezuelan customs offices as a pawn in preference to establishing a pacific blockade.[2] There is no evidence, however, of an agreement to seize the ports or to take possession of Venezuelan soil. Indeed, on December 16, 1902, Lord Lansdowne declared in the House of Lords that it was "not intended to land a British force, and still less to occupy Venezuelan territory";[3] while the German government on December 14 declared that it had "no intention whatever . . . . to proceed beyond a warlike blockade."[4]

Following the severance of diplomatic relations with Venezuela events moved rapidly. On December 9, the day after the British and German legations left Caracas, the allied forces seized four Venezuelan gunboats.[5] Two days

[1] *Senate Document No. 119*, VII, 637, 641, 650, 669; *House Document No. 1* (Fifty-eighth Congress, second session), I, 453; *Parliamentary Debates*, CXVI, 1489, 1612; *Die grosse Politik*, XVII, 247, 263. The British *Blue Book* is not altogether trustworthy; when opposition to the Venezuelan blockade arose in England, Lord Lansdowne deleted the word "retain" from the correspondence as printed, fearing its publication would aggravate the excitement (*ibid.*, p. 263).

[2] See Bernstorff's note of November 17, 1902 (*ibid.*, pp. 254 f.).

[3] *Parliamentary Debates*, CXVI, 1290. On December 17 Balfour, the prime minister, declared in the House of Commons: "We have no intention, and have never had any intention, of landing troops in Venezuela or of occupying territory, even though that occupation might only be of a temporary character" (*ibid.*, p. 1489).

[4] *Foreign Relations* (1903), p. 421. See also Tower's telegram of December 17, 1902 (*ibid.*), and Lodge's speech in the Senate (*Congressional Record* [Fifty-ninth Congress, first session], Vol. XL, Part I, p. 1471).

[5] *Die grosse Politik*, XVII, 259, 261; *Senate Document No. 119*, VII, 666. Resentment was aroused in both England and America over the sinking of three of the gunboats by the Germans.

later Great Britain ordered a blockade of five Venezuelan ports and mouths of the Orinoco.[1] On December 13 the United States submitted the Venezuelan proposal for arbitration to the allied governments.[2] The same day the German cruiser "Vineta" and the British cruiser "Charybdis" bombarded two forts at Puerto Cabello, due to an alleged insult to the British flag and to the seizing of a British steamer.[3] On December 20 the British, German, and Italian governments declared a formal blockade of the Venezuelan ports.[4]

Meanwhile, a problem had arisen concerning the character of the blockade. When the use of force was first contemplated, the German government desired to establish a "peace blockade,"[5] primarily, it seems, in order to avoid the necessity of obtaining the assent of the Bundesrat to the proposed action, an assent essential under the German constitution for a declaration of war.[6] The United States objected to the plan, insisting that international law did not countenance a peaceful blockade and that the terms "blockade" and "peace" were contradictory in meaning.[7]

[1] *Senate Document No. 119*, VII, 670 f.

[2] *Ibid.*, p. 672.

[3] *Ibid.*, p. 676; *Die grosse Politik*, XVII, 259.

[4] *Senate Document No. 119*, VII, 683, 685.

[5] See the communication of the German government of December 20, 1901. *House Document No. 1* (Fifty-seventh Congress, second session), I, 196; also *ibid.* (Fifty-eighth Congress, second session), I, 421.

[6]*Die grosse Politik*, XVII, 242, 245, 257, 258; *House Document No. 1* (Fifty-eighth Congress, second session), I, 422.

[7] *Foreign Relations* (1903), pp. 452, 454 f. The initial impulse for the stand taken by the United States against a "pacific blockade" of Venezuela seems to have come from the former secretary of state, John W. Foster; see the account of his conference with Secretary Hay in J. W. Foster's *Diplomatic Memoirs*, II, 293. For the distinction made by the German government between a "peace" and a "war" blockade, see *Die grosse Politik*, XVII, 241 f.

The British government also finally denied the legality of the German position, the prime minister, Mr. Balfour, stating in the House of Commons (December 17) that "there can be no such thing as a pacific blockade" and that "evidently a blockade does involve a state of war."[1] Owing primarily to the attitude of the British government the German authorities consented (December 14, 1902) to a regular blockade,[2] which, as pointed out above, was duly established on December 20, 1902.

In the meantime, Roosevelt had informed both Germany and Great Britain of his hope that a peaceful solution of the controversy might be found. On December 5, 1902—two days before the delivery of the ultimatums to Venezuela—Hay cabled the American ambassadors at Berlin and London that J. and W. Seligman and Company, New York bankers, were trying to make arrangements to effect a settlement of the Venezuelan debt and that "the President would be glad if such an arrangement could be made as might obviate the necessity of any exhibition of force on the part of Germany and Great Britain." Hay adds that "the United States Government assumes no obligation whatever in the nature either of a material or moral guarantee of any liabilities created by the transaction." He also states that the communication is sent for the information of the American representatives "in case any one in interest make inquiry" of them.[3] No one in

---

[1] *Parliamentary Debates*, CXVI, 1490 f. According to Sir Edward Grey, Great Britain refused to recognize the "pacific blockade" which France established against Siam in 1893. For a time the controversy threatened to end in war (see E. Grey, *Twenty-Five Years* [New York, 1925], I, 12–15).

[2] *Die grosse Politik*, XVII, 255, 257 f.; *Foreign Relations* (1903), pp. 421 f., 454.

[3] The telegrams were sent at the request of J. and W. Seligman & Co. (*Foreign Relations* [1903], pp. 418 f., 452).

authority seems to have inquired about the matter, and the communication apparently was never brought to the attention of either Germany or Great Britain.

During the next few days the efforts of the American government were directed mainly toward the securing of arbitration between Venezuela and the allied powers. On December 13 the American ambassadors at London and Berlin transmitted "without comment" the proposal of the Venezuelan government "that the present difficulty respecting the manner of settling claims for injuries to British and German subjects during the insurrection be submitted to arbitration."[1]

Just what President Castro proposed to submit to arbitration is not clear. From the beginning of the controversy the Venezuelan government, basing its contention on the Calvo Doctrine, maintained that the settlement of the claims of aliens was an internal affair, subject to Venezuelan laws and the decisions of Venezuelan courts and in no sense an issue proper for diplomatic arrangement.[2] Castro's position was denied by the European states, chiefly on the ground that justice could not be obtained under Venezuelan legislation and jurisprudence.

Bowen, the American minister at Caracas, believed that the Venezuelan government meant to submit to arbitration all differences with the blockading powers.[3] A strict interpretation of the Venezuelan proposal, however, indicates that Castro intended to submit only the question of the claims for injuries sustained during the civil war, excluding others which the blockading powers considered as

[1] *Senate Document No. 119*, VII, 373, 672, 837; Foreign Relations (1903), pp. 791 f.

[2] *House Document No. 1* (Fifty-eighth Congress, second session), I, 419 f.

[3] *Foreign Relations* (1903), p. 790.

of equal or even greater importance. Indeed, it may even be argued that Castro's proposal included only the arbitration of the question whether the claims should be settled by diplomatic negotiations as the allies had insisted, or by judicial decision in accordance with Venezuelan law as the Venezuelan government had maintained.

Under the circumstances it is natural that Castro's proposal should have proved unacceptable to both Great Britain and Germany. The latter government, in addition, looked with unfriendly eyes upon the idea of arbitration. At a conference on December 15 the German Ambassador at London remarked to Lansdowne that, speaking for himself and without instructions, he thought there were "considerable objections to encouraging the idea of arbitration," an opinion indorsed by his government, for on the following day (December 16) he informed Lansdowne that the instructions he had received "agreed with the views he had expressed yesterday."[1]

Lansdowne replied that the British government, too, regarded the Venezuelan proposal in its present form as unacceptable for reasons that in the main corresponded to those advanced by the German government. He then went on to say that, while it was impossible to accept arbitration upon claims for compensation where injury had been done to British subjects through the misconduct of the Venezuelan government,

it was not necessary to exclude the idea of arbitration in reference to claims of a different kind. We had already provided for the reference of such claims to a mixed commission. It seemed to us, in these circum-

[1] "If President Castro should prematurely perceive that there exists on our part a leaning toward arbitration, he would interpret this as weakness and would certainly make no concessions," said Metternich to Lansdowne on December 16 (*Die grosse Politik*, XVII, 266; see also pp. 260 f., 262 f., 265, and *Senate Document No. 119*, VII, 674 f.).

stances, worthy of consideration whether we might not admit the principle of arbitration in regard to these claims, and perhaps invite the United States to arbitrate upon them.[1]

On December 17, the day after the conference between Lansdowne and Metternich, the American representatives at London and Berlin, at Hay's direction, repeated "with strong commendation" the Venezuelan proposal of arbitration.[2] The following day Lansdowne informed the American *chargé d'affaires* that

the cabinet had decided at its last meeting on the 16th to accept in principle the idea of settling the Venezuelan dispute by arbitration, and we had since ascertained that the view of the German Government was in accord with our own. We considered, however, that some of our claims were of such a kind that we could not include them in the reference.

Reserving such claims from adjudication,[3] Lansdowne then expressed the desire that the President of the United States would consent to act as arbiter on the claims submitted for arbitral action.

The decision of the German government to accept arbitration was reached on December 17 and before the receipt of the communication in which the United States had expressed the hope that the allied powers would accept arbitration.[4] For reasons pointed out below, Roosevelt declined to serve as arbitrator and, after some interchange of views, Germany, Great Britain, Italy, and Venezuela agreed to submit certain claims to the decision of the Hague Tribunal.[5]

[1] *Senate Document No. 119*, VII, 676; *Die grosse Politik*, XVII, 265.

[2] *Senate Document No. 119*, VII, 677; *Foreign Relations* (1903), pp. 421, 424, 453, 798.

[3] See pp. 138 and 146 f. below.

[4] *Foreign Relations* (1903), p. 424; *Senate Document No. 119*, VII, 679, 681.

[5] *Foreign Relations* (1903), pp. 799–803. For the claims to be submitted to arbitration, see pp. 146 f. below.

Such, in brief, is the story of the first phase of the Venezuelan crisis of 1902. The second phase will be discussed later. Let us now turn to the events that transpired behind the scenes, or are said to have transpired there, in order to discover, if possible, the rôle played in the affair by the American President.

Roosevelt's celebrated account of his action in the Venezuelan crisis is in a letter to William R. Thayer. In the *Life and Letters of John Hay*, published in October, 1915, Thayer had included a chapter entitled "The German Menace," in which there appeared for the first time an account of Roosevelt's course in the Venezuelan matter. The story was widely discussed during the pre-convention campaign of 1916 in which Roosevelt was a receptive candidate for the Republican nomination.[1] The accuracy of the narrative being questioned, Roosevelt wrote Thayer a detailed description of the episode. The letter, dated August 21, 1916, is in its essential details as follows:

There was no objection whatever to Castro's being punished, as long as the punishment did not take the form of seizure of territory and its more or less permanent occupation by some Old-World Power. At this particular point such seizure of territory would have been a direct menace to the United States, because it would have threatened or partially controlled the approach to the projected Isthmian Canal.

I speedily became convinced that Germany was the leader, and the really formidable party in the transaction; and that England was merely following Germany's lead in rather half-hearted fashion. . . . . I also became convinced that Germany intended to seize some Venezuelan harbor and turn it into a strongly fortified place of arms, on the model of Kiauchau, with a view to exercising some degree of control over the future Isthmian Canal, and over South American affairs generally.

For some time the usual methods of diplomatic intercourse were tried. Germany declined to agree to arbitrate the question at issue

[1] New York *Times*, LXV (May 27, 1916), 3; and *ibid.*, LXV (May 28, 1916), 1 and 7.

[123]

between her and Venezuela, and declined to say that she would not take possession of Venezuelan territory, merely saying that such possession would be "temporary"—which might mean anything. I finally decided that no useful purpose would be served by further delay, and I took action accordingly. I assembled our battle fleet, under Admiral Dewey, near Porto Rico, for "maneuvers," with instructions that the fleet should be kept in hand and in fighting trim, and should be ready to sail at an hour's notice. The fact that the fleet was in West Indian waters was of course generally known; but I believe that the Secretary of the Navy, and Admiral Dewey, and perhaps his Chief of Staff, and the Secretary of State, John Hay, were the only persons who knew about the order for the fleet to be ready to sail at an hour's notice. I told John Hay that I would now see the German Ambassador, Herr von Holleben, myself, and that I intended to bring matters to an early conclusion. . . . .

I saw the Ambassador, and explained that in view of the presence of the German squadron on the Venezuelan coast I could not permit longer delay in answering my request for an arbitration, and that I could not acquiesce in any seizure of Venezuelan territory. The Ambassador responded that his Government could not agree to arbitrate, and that there was no intention to take "permanent" possession of Venezuelan territory. I answered that Kiauchau was not a permanent possession of Germany's—that I understood that it was merely held by a ninety-nine years' lease; and that I did not intend to have another Kiauchau, held by similar tenure, on the approach to the Isthmian Canal. The Ambassador repeated that his Government would not agree to arbitrate. I then asked him to inform his Government that if no notification for arbitration came within a certain specified number of days I should be obliged to order Dewey to take his fleet to the Venezuelan coast and see that the German forces did not take possession of any territory. He expressed very great concern, and asked me if I realized the serious consequences that would follow such action; consequences so serious to both countries that he dreaded to give them a name. I answered that I had thoroughly counted the cost before I decided on the step, and asked him to look at the map, as a glance would show him that there was no spot in the world where Germany in the event of a conflict with the United States would be at a greater disadvantage than in the Caribbean Sea.

THE VENEZUELAN CRISIS

A few days later the Ambassador came to see me, talked pleasantly on several subjects, and rose to go. I asked him if he had any answer to make from his Government to my request, and when he said no, I informed him that in such event it was useless to wait as long as I had intended, and that Dewey would be ordered to sail twenty-four hours in advance of the time I had set. He expressed deep apprehension, and said that his Government would not arbitrate. However, less than twenty-four hours before the time I had appointed for cabling the order to Dewey, the Embassy notified me that His Imperial Majesty the German Emperor had directed him to request me to undertake the arbitration myself. I felt, and publicly expressed, great gratification at this outcome, and great appreciation of the course the German Government had finally agreed to take. Later I received the consent of the German Government to have the arbitration undertaken by the Hague Tribunal, and not by me.[1]

It is difficult to know how much credence should be given to Roosevelt's account. In support of the story, he cites the evidence of a Mr. A. W. Callisen, a friend and neighbor, and the testimony of Admiral Dewey who, in a letter to Mr. Henry A. Wise Wood, under date of May 23, 1916, says that, at the time of the Venezuelan difficulty, he was at Culebra, Porto Rico, in command of a fleet of over fifty warships, including every battleship and every torpedo boat in the Navy, "with orders from Washington to hold the fleet in hand and be ready to move at a moment's notice."[2] Callisen's testimony is in a letter to a friend. Commenting on Thayer's account of Roosevelt's action,[3] Callisen wrote:

. . . . The story is absolutely true, and here is the sequel.

The German and British Governments firmly counted on our well-established jellyfish squashiness and felt sure they had a free hand. The Kaiser and Junker party especially had everything cut and dried, and counted the affair as accomplished. The first time, Holleben in-

---

[1] J. B. Bishop, *Life and Times of Theodore Roosevelt*, I, 222–24; W. R. Thayer, *John Hay*, II, 412–15.

[2] Bishop, *op. cit.*, I, 226. [3] Thayer, *op. cit.*, II, 415 f.

formed his Government that probably Roosevelt's attitude was a bluff; but on second thought went to his friend Buenz[1] for advice, as B. knew the American people better than any German living, and was a close friend of Roosevelt's (I introduced him) and hence a good judge of the situation. Buenz at once assured him that Roosevelt was not bluffing, and that he could count on his doing as threatened; and that in a conversation Roosevelt had shown that he had an intimate knowledge of the strength and condition of the German fleet which was . . . . then no match for ours.

Holleben was obliged to eat his own words and telegraph in hot haste to Berlin, where his message fell like a bombshell.[2] You know the rest. This resulted in Holleben's being recalled and dismissed from the diplomatic service. . . . . When he sailed from Hoboken not a single member of the diplomatic corps or German official dared to see him off. Only Buenz (and I) dared to brave official disapproval, and went on board to bid him farewell. I went at Buenz's request.[3]

So far as the records are concerned, the evidence in support of Roosevelt's narrative seems to be limited to the testimony of Callisen and Dewey. The source of Callisen's information was apparently Dr. Buenz, who in turn presumably had the story from Holleben. Admiral Dewey seems to have known nothing about the crisis with Germany and states merely that he had orders to "be ready to move at a moment's notice."[4] Thayer, whose account was derived at first hand from Roosevelt,[5] cites no evidence to support the narrative; indeed, Thayer states that "neither Admiral Dewey . . . . nor any one else knew of the step that was to be taken."[6] On the other hand, Roosevelt

[1] Dr. Buenz was the German consul-general at New York City.

[2] According to Callisen, the *volte face* of Holleben seems to have been due to the information received from Buenz, not to the second interview with Roosevelt.

[3] Bishop, *op. cit.*, I, 225; but see n. 1 on p. 144 below.

[4] Bishop, *op. cit.*, I, 227; Thayer, *op. cit.*, II, 288.

[5] Thayer, "Bowen versus Roosevelt," *North American Review*, CCX (1919), 419.

[6] Thayer, *John Hay*, II, 288. See also Thayer's statements in the *North American Review*, pp. 52, 419 f.

implies that John Hay and possibly the secretary of the navy, William H. Moody, and the Chief of Staff knew about the contemplated action (see p. 124 above). Be this as it may, the fact remains that Thayer, Hay's biographer, with full access presumably to Hay's papers and letters, quotes nothing from Hay in support of the story, while Hay himself is silent upon the matter in his *Letters and Diary* as privately printed by his wife.[1] On the other hand, Hay, commenting upon the settlement of the Venezuelan problem in a letter to a private correspondent (February 16, 1903), says: "We have not interfered, except in using what good offices we could dispose of to induce all parties to come to a speedy and honorable settlement."[2] Two months earlier (December 18, 1902) Hay assured the German *chargé d'affaires*, Count von Quadt, that although the President and he both deeply regretted the Venezuelan affair they had come to the final determination to interfere in no way.[3] No indication that either Hay or Moody knew about the affair could be found in the *Roosevelt Papers*.

A critical study of Roosevelt's narrative necessarily centers on the five main points upon which he lays emphasis. These points are as follows: first, Germany was the leader in the enterprise; second, her purpose was to seize Venezuelan territory and convert it into a German dependency; third, Germany flatly refused to arbitrate her controversy with Venezuela; fourth, the President there-

[1] *Letters of John Hay and Extracts from Diary.*

[2] Thayer, *John Hay*, II, 289. Hay's comment quoted above seems to be confirmed by the following statement made by Roosevelt in Chicago (April 2, 1903): "By an offer of our good services in a spirit of frank friendliness to all the parties concerned, a spirit in which they quickly and cordially responded, we secured a resumption of peace" (*Addresses and Presidential Messages of Theodore Roosevelt, 1902–1904*, p. 120).

[3] *Die grosse Politik*, XVII, 269.

upon delivered an ultimatum to the German Ambassador to the effect that Germany must submit the issue with Venezuela to arbitration or Admiral Dewey would be ordered to the Venezuelan coast to prevent the German forces from taking possession of any territory; fifth, the German Ambassador, after a second interview, notified the President that the Emperor had agreed to arbitrate and requested Roosevelt to serve as the arbitrator. Each point deserves examination.

Historians who have discussed the Venezuelan affair have commonly accepted as true Roosevelt's assumption that Germany was the aggressor and that Great Britain was the dupe throughout the whole episode.[1] The assumption is not supported in the available official records. As has already been pointed out, the initial hint for joint action against Venezuela came from the British government.[2] At the moment the German authorities, in particular the Emperor,[3] proceeded very cautiously; while within governmental circles, as shown by the correspondence, there was a lack of confidence and even distrust of the British intentions. An indication of the lack of confidence may be seen in the arrangement proposed by Germany that in case coercion was undertaken the two countries should stand together throughout the action.[4]

Once the expedition had been launched, the German

---

[1] See, for example, J. H. Latané, *United States and Latin America*, pp. 249 f.; J. F. Rhodes, *McKinley and Roosevelt Administrations*, pp. 247–50; W. S. Robertson, *op. cit.*, pp. 114–18. John Bassett Moore seems to be the only writer who has attacked Thayer's narrative; see his "John Hay," *Political Science Quarterly*, XXXII (1917), 119–21.

[2] See pp. 110 and 114 f. above; see also *Die grosse Politik*, XVII, 288.

[3] See, for example, his notation on Bülow's letter to the Emperor, dated January 20, 1902, in *ibid.*, p. 243, n. 2.

[4] *Ibid.*, pp. 253, 256.

government showed the utmost solicitude to modify its course from time to time so as to accord with the desires of the British ministry, and with that end in view waived its own preferences repeatedly. For example, the German government consented shortly after the coercive measures were begun to substitute a war blockade for the peace blockade;[1] several days later it accepted the British suggestion to submit certain of the claims to arbitration;[2] some time afterward it adopted the British plan of returning captured Venezuelan vessels;[3] during the Washington negotiations to be described later it again yielded to the British suggestion, surrendering its claim for £66,000 cash and accepting instead £5,500.[4]

The acceptance of British leadership appears throughout the private correspondence of the German authorities as well as in their official dispatches. In a letter to the Emperor dated December 12, 1902, Bülow mentions the desire of the German government to go "hand in hand unreservedly with the English."[5] To this letter the Kaiser appends the remark: "We shall participate in the English program. We will allow our flag to follow the lead of the British."[6] Four days later Bülow makes the following marginal notation on a dispatch from Holleben: "His

---

[1] *Ibid.*, pp. 257, 258, 260.

[2] *Ibid.*, pp. 265, 267.

[3] *Ibid.*, pp. 275, 291.

[4] *Ibid.*, pp. 277–79. The change of front by the British government, according to the German dispatches, was due primarily to the popular hostility aroused in England by the joint blockade of Venezuela and the fear that a continuance of drastic measures would lead to the overthrow of the ministry. King Edward also seems to have changed his attitude completely (see *ibid.*, pp. 262 f., 265, 277 f., 281 f., 288–90).

[5] *Ibid.*, p. 258.

[6] *Ibid.*, p. 260 n.; see also p. 258 n.

Majesty will on no account go a single step farther toward
Venezuela than England and will take no step without
England."[1] While undoubtedly the policy of abnegation
adopted by Germany was dictated in large part by the
desire to avoid an appearance of aggression, the fact remains that in every point on which difference of opinion
arose between the two countries the action taken was that
proposed by Great Britain.[2] So much for the assertion
that Germany was the leader; leadership that *follows* is not
leadership.

Roosevelt's second assumption was that Germany intended to seize Venezuelan territory and convert it into
a permanent German colony. No evidence for the assumption appears in the *Roosevelt Papers* or in official records. From first to last the object of the expedition was
apparently the collection of the claims, although it is possible as in other instances that results not contemplated
originally might have eventuated.

To accomplish their purpose the allied powers agreed
first to seize the Venezuelan gunboats and then to blockade
the Venezuelan ports. Further than this no steps were
planned. As pointed out before, the German government
declared on December 14 that it had "no intention whatever ... to proceed beyond a warlike blockade."[3] Not a
word appears in the German correspondence to indicate
that the occupation of Venezuelan soil was ever contem-

---

[1] *Ibid.*, p. 264, n. 1.

[2] "I also reminded His Majesty the King [Edward VII] that the Imperial
Government during the whole course of the Venezuelan affair had met in the
most willing manner the wishes of the English Government and taken into account its difficult position" (dispatch of Count Metternich, January 29, 1903,
Die grosse Politik, XVII, 281 f.). See also *ibid.*, pp. 266 f., 271 f., 279.

[3] *Foreign Relations* (1903), p. 421.

plated.[1] Indeed, in an address in Chicago on April 2, 1903, Roosevelt himself said: "Both powers assured us in explicit terms that there was not the slightest intention on their part to violate the Monroe Doctrine, and this assurance was kept with an honorable good faith which merits full acknowledgment on our part."[2] This statement is confirmed in a long letter to Dr. Albert Shaw in which Roosevelt says that nothing that Germany and Great Britain had done or threatened to do so far had in any way or shape conflicted with his interpretation of the Monroe Doctrine.[3]

Nor does any evidence appear to support Roosevelt's statement that Germany refused to arbitrate her difference with Venezuela. On the contrary, the German government on July 16, 1901, proposed arbitration to President Castro, but the proposal was rejected.[4] After the blockade had been established, it is true, the German Ambassador at London did not view hospitably the idea of arbitration, on the ground that a premature acceptance would be inter-

[1] The only document that suggests the possibility of the occupation of Venezuelan soil by Germany is the German communication of December 11, 1901. To this suggestion the American government offered at the time no objection (see pp. 111 f. above). The Washington *Post* (December 21, 1902), prints an associated press dispatch from Berlin under date of December 20 announcing the acceptance of arbitration the day before by Germany and containing the following statement by Chancellor von Bülow: "Of course, we have not the slightest intention to make any territorial acquisitions in Venezuela. In that respect the United States government has months ago received from us explanations and of positive character." Bülow's last statement seems to be corroborated in Roosevelt's letter to Dr. Albert Shaw, December 26, 1902, *Roosevelt Papers*.

[2] *Addresses and Presidential Messages of Theodore Roosevelt, 1902–1904*, p. 120.

[3] Roosevelt to Shaw, December 26, 1902, *Roosevelt Papers*; see also Roosevelt to J. G. Shaffer, December 22, 1902, and Roosevelt to Taft, December 26, 1902 (*ibid.*).

[4] See pp. 110 f. above.

preted by Castro as a sign of weakness.[1] Nevertheless, the following day (December 17) the German government waived its views and gave its consent to the principle of arbitration.

In so far as Roosevelt's ultimatum is concerned supporting evidence is limited, as shown above, to the testimony of Dewey and Callisen.[2] The vagueness of Roosevelt's narrative, especially in the time order of events, makes it difficult to check the account. Throughout the story, as given in his letter to Thayer, he employs repeatedly such expressions as "for some time," "within a certain specified number of days," and "a few days later." From the account, therefore, it is impossible to determine the exact time which is said to have intervened between the beginning of the crisis and the last interview with the German Ambassador. But the narrative indicates beyond question that a considerable period elapsed.[3]

[1] *Die grosse Politik*, XVII, 266; see also p. 121, n., above.

[2] See pp. 125 f. above. James Ford Rhodes, in his *McKinley and Roosevelt Administrations*, pp. 251 f., quotes a letter from President Roosevelt to Henry White, dated August 14, 1906. In the letter Roosevelt refers to a private interview which he had with the German Ambassador at the time of the Venezuelan trouble, stating that he told Holleben, after mentioning the presence of Dewey's fleet in the West Indian waters, "that the popular feeling was such that he should be obliged to interfere, by force if necessary, if the Germans took any action which looked like the acquisition of territory there or elsewhere along the Caribbean." Rhodes cites no source for the letter; it differs markedly from one of the same date addressed to White in Bishop, *op. cit.*, II, 270, in which Roosevelt in comment upon the Emperor says: "I have had to speak with express emphasis to him on more than one occasion; and on one occasion (that of Venezuela) have had to make a display of force and to convince him definitely that I would use force if necessary." This letter to White contains the earliest reference by Roosevelt to the possible need for force in connection with the Venezuelan incident.

[3] In a speech in Chicago on September 27, 1917, Roosevelt gave an account of the Venezuelan affair that differs in some details from that given to Thayer. In the Chicago address, as reported in the Chicago *Daily News* of September 27, 1917, Roosevelt says that he gave the German Ambassador the following

THE VENEZUELAN CRISIS

From Roosevelt's letter to Thayer it will be observed, in the first place, that "the usual methods of diplomatic intercourse were tried" by the United States for some time before Roosevelt's first interview with the German Ambassador and that during this period "Germany declined to arbitrate." It will be noted, in the next place, that several days intervened between the first and the second inter-

---

ultimatum: " 'Tell your government that in ten days it must arbitrate the matter or I will send Dewey down there.' Thirty days before I had ordered Dewey to take our fleet into West Indian waters. . . . .

"About a week later the ambassador called on me and talked about the weather and tennis, and when I asked about the Venezuelan answer, he admitted that he had not dared send the message to his country. He told me he knew I could not be serious in the matter.

"I then told him that instead of allowing the three days that remained for an answer I would order Dewey to sail in forty-eight hours. . . . .

"Inside of thirty-six hours he came back smiling and said he had received instructions from the German Government to notify me that they would arbitrate. . . . ."

A third account of the episode, with variations, appears in Roosevelt's speech before the Union League Club of New York, March 20, 1917. Here he said in part:

"The story came out in connection with his [Hay's] papers after his death. England was endeavoring to placate Germany. She was not successful. . . . . England was trying to placate Germany by tagging after her. . . . . I soon became convinced that Germany . . . . intended to take possession of some point of territory in Venezuela, fortify it, and hold it so as to control the approach of the Isthmian Canal. . . . . After a while I sounded out England and found that England was uncomfortable in the alliance and would certainly not fight us—that she would be neutral, which was all I wanted. Then, before seeing the German Ambassador, I took our fleet, every battleship and every destroyer, and put it in the West Indies under Dewey—to maneuver—just friendly maneuvers.

"Then I saw the German Ambassador and said that I must have a promise from Germany to arbitrate the matter. He said he was very sorry, that they could not give it, but that he would assure me they would only take 'temporary possession' of any port. . . . ." Roosevelt then gave the ten-day ultimatum. "The Ambassador said he was very sorry, but he knew that his Government would not arbitrate."

One week later Holleben called and, upon inquiry, answered that he had had

views—"a week," according to Thayer.[1] Finally, Roosevelt states that some additional time passed before the German Emperor at last consented to arbitrate.[2] Thus, the acceptance of arbitration seems to have been in doubt for nine or ten days.

But, according to the official record, the request of the Venezuelan government for arbitration was not transmitted to the allied powers until December 13, and then "without comment."[3] Moreover, neither Great Britain nor Germany seems at the time to have interpreted the action of the American government as indicating that the United States supported the request.[4] Three days after the Venezuelan proposal was received, the German Ambassador at London informed Lansdowne that the German government regarded the idea of arbitration as open to considerable objections. In reply Lansdowne stated that, while he agreed with the objections of Germany to the submission of certain claims to arbitration, he thought it was worthy of consideration whether a different kind of claims might not be settled by that method. On the same day Holleben sent a dispatch from New York in which, without mention

---

no word from Berlin. Roosevelt then said that Dewey would be ordered to sail in forty-eight hours. "Some eighteen hours before the time for Dewey to sail, the Ambassador turned up," with the word that Germany would arbitrate. Cf. also Oscar K. Davis, *Released for Publication*, pp. 84–90.

[1] *Op. cit.*, II, 287; "about a week later," said Roosevelt in his Chicago speech (see note above).

[2] "Within thirty-six hours," says Thayer, *op. cit.*, II, 288. Roosevelt says: "Less than twenty-four hours before the time I had appointed for cabling the order to Dewey"; Bishop (*Theodore Roosevelt*, I, 224). "Some eighteen hours before the time for Dewey to sail" are Roosevelt's words in the speech before the Union League Club, March 20, 1917.

[3] *Foreign Relations* (1903), p. 792; *Die grosse Politik*, XVII, 260 n.

[4] *Senate Document No. 119*, VII, 673 f.; *Die grosse Politik*, XVII, 261.

of Roosevelt or allusion to the American government, he reviews public opinion as expressed in the press and in commercial circles and concludes with the opinion that "it would be wise and would create a good impression in all America if our government would accept the principle of arbitration."[1] The following day, December 17, the German government signified its acceptance of arbitration in accordance with the British suggestion, a decision reached before the receipt of the dispatch from the United States in which the hope was expressed that the blockading powers would accept arbitration. In other words, the Venezuelan request for arbitration which was submitted without comment by the United States on December 13 was accepted by Germany on December 17, prior to the receipt of the American dispatch expressing the hope that arbitration would be accepted by the blockading powers.[2]

Thus, according to the official record, the German government, while at first disinclined to arbitrate, accepted the principle four days after the Venezuelan proposal reached Berlin. It appears, therefore, that instead of the issue

[1] *Die grosse Politik*, XVII, 264. (The dispatch from which the quotation in the text is taken is the only communication relating to the Venezuelan affair from Holleben that appears in *Die grosse Politik*.) A much stronger recommendation for the acceptance of arbitration than that made by Holleben was sent to Berlin the same day (December 16) by Count Metternich after a conference with Lord Lansdowne in which the latter stated that he had been empowered by the cabinet to submit for the consideration of the German government the question of partial arbitration with the possibility of a request that the United States accept the office of arbiter. After explaining Lansdowne's proposal (*ibid.*, p. 266) Metternich concludes: "With reluctance I therefore feel it my duty to express the view that the sooner we, together with England, can honorably withdraw from the affair, so much the better. I see how the opposition and repugnance toward the action in Venezuela grows here daily, and it will possibly be easier to endeavor to bring the matter to a conclusion on the basis of Lord Lansdowne's suggestion now than later."

[2] *Foreign Relations* (1903), p. 424; *Die grosse Politik*, XVII, 267.

of arbitration consuming the nine or ten days indicated by Roosevelt's account, the entire discussion from the submission of the Venezuelan request to the acceptance of the principle by Germany occupied barely more than half a week. Nothing in the dispatches shows that the German government was aware of any pressure, threats, or ultimatum from Roosevelt. At a later date Bülow wrote: "During the critical period through which our country passed at the beginning of the new century America never once opposed our policy."[1] Throughout the entire episode German policy seems to have been dominated by a desire to collect the claims and at the same time to remain on good terms with England and the United States.

What, then, shall we conclude concerning Roosevelt's part in the Venezuelan affair? In the light of the available evidence his narrative at best can be accepted only with reservations. That his account is inaccurate in matters of detail is evident; that he urged arbitration upon the German government in interviews with the German ambassador can scarcely be doubted, although no record of such interviews can be found[2] and although the initial move for arbitration came from Venezuela. That Roosevelt's words had the decisive influence which he ascribed to them more than a decade after the event is opened to serious question;[3] that he would have offered naval and military resistance to

[1] *Imperial Germany*, p. 52.

[2] During the entire month of December, 1902, Roosevelt's "Memorandum of Engagements," which seems to be particularly full and complete for the period and is in part in the President's handwriting, records only one conference with the German Ambassador (December 6) and this for the purpose of presenting the German Commissioners to the St. Louis Exposition (*Roosevelt Papers*).

[3] See H. R. Bowen, "Roosevelt and Venezuela," *North American Review*, CCX (1919), 415 f. On February 11, 1903, the Bureau of Navigation informed the President that there were only four German ships in American waters (*Roosevelt Papers*).

a seizure of Venezuelan soil if attempted by either Germany or Great Britain seems beyond argument.[1]

At no point in Roosevelt's account does he refer to the influence of Great Britain upon Germany. His attitude is doubtless explained by the fact that public opinion in England generally condemned the course of the British ministry and by the fact that Roosevelt wrote his account during the world-war when his hostility to the German government was intense. He had long been suspicious of Germany.[2] Thayer's narrative of the episode which, as pointed out above, owed its origin to Roosevelt, reveals even more animosity.[3]

So far as the official record is concerned, the German reluctance to accept arbitration seems to have been due

[1] See Roosevelt's letter to Lodge, June 19, 1901, in the Chicago *Daily News* (February 26, 1925), p. 4.

[2] See Roosevelt's letter to Lodge, March 27, 1901, *Roosevelt-Lodge Correspondence*, I, 484 f. Criticism of England's course may be implied in Roosevelt's letter to Lodge, June 20, 1903, Chicago *Daily News* (March 4, 1925), p. 4.

[3] Thayer's account is untrustworthy in many particulars. There is no evidence that Germany made any offers to the Tory government to enlist their co-operation; Thayer says (*op. cit.*, II, 285): "By offers which cannot yet be made public, Germany persuaded the Tory Government to draw closer to her." The allied governments did not establish a "pacific blockade" on December 8, 1901 (cf. with Thayer, *loc. cit.*). Hay did not urge arbitration upon Great Britain and Germany during 1901 (cf. *op. cit.*, II, 286); Germany, however, on July 16, 1901, offered to submit her claims to arbitration (*Senate Document No. 119*, VII, 261 f.), to which proposal neither Roosevelt nor Thayer refers. Nothing in the German, British, or American records supports Thayer's statement (*op. cit.*, II, 286) that after "England and Italy were willing to come to an understanding, Germany refused." The Venezuela claims did not go to The Hague for arbitration (*ibid.*, II, 289). See Thayer's "The President and the Kaiser, "*North American Review*, CCX (1919), 50–54; Bowen's "Roosevelt and Venezuela," *ibid.*, pp. 414–17; Thayer, "Bowen versus Roosevelt," *ibid.*, pp. 418–20; Bowen's letter in the New York *Times* (March 28, 1917), p. 12. See also the criticism of Thayer's narrative by J. B. Moore, in "John Hay," *Political Science Quarterly*, XXXII (1917), 119–21.

chiefly to an unwillingness to submit all the claims to an arbitral tribunal; the British ministry agreed fully with the German government on this point, and on the issue neither Germany nor Great Britain receded from their original position. In so far as the German government may have had other reasons for objecting to arbitration, they do not appear in the record; such objections, if they existed, were overcome primarily by the attitude and influence of Great Britain. Thus, as in other significant aspects of the episode, the British ministry, rather than Roosevelt, seems to have been the main factor in effecting a change in the initial attitude of the German government.[1]

The consent of the allied powers to the principle of arbitration, viewed from the practical standpoint, was a barren victory for Venezuela. Claims of the "first rank," including German claims originating in the Venezuelan civil war from 1898 to 1900 and British claims based upon the seizure of British shipping and the imprisonment of British subjects, were strictly excluded from arbitration; in all such instances the allied powers demanded and secured cash payments or adequate guaranties. All other claims set forth in the ultimatums of December, 1902, were to be submitted to arbitration only on condition that the Venezuelan government first admit in principle its responsibility. In short, a comparison of the demands in the ultimatums with the conditions set forth by the allied power as prerequisite to the agreement to arbitrate reveals that the only important difference between the two was the substitution of arbitration for the mixed commissions.[2]

By the arrangement the blockading powers attained their original objectives; while Venezuela, which had from

[1] *Foreign Relations* (1903), pp. 421, 454.

[2] *Senate Document No. 119*, VII, 272–75, 687–89, 693 f., 844 f.

the beginning insisted that the claims be adjudicated in the Venezuelan courts in accordance with Venezuelan law, was compelled to submit the controversy to diplomatic settlement. The principle asserted by Venezuela, thus overthrown by the allied powers with the consent and approval of President Roosevelt, was warmly indorsed, in so far as the payment of the public debt was concerned, by Señor Drago; minister of foreign affairs of the Argentine Republic, in an able memorandum submitted to the American government. In the communication, which bears the date of December 29, 1902, Drago says:

The capitalist who supplies any money to a foreign State always takes into consideration the resources of the country and the more or less probabilities that the obligations contracted shall be fulfilled without difficulty.

Because of this every Government obtains different credit in view of its grade of civilization and culture and its conduct of affairs, and these circumstances are measured and weighed before the contracting of any loan, and serve to make its conditions more or less onerous. . . . . Besides, the creditor knows that he contracts with a sovereign entity and that it is an inherent condition of all sovereignty that executive proceedings against it can not be entered into or carried out, as that form of payment would compromise its very existence, making its independence to disappear. . . . .

The recovery of loans by military methods supposes a territorial occupation to render it effective, and a territorial occupation signifies the suppression or subordination of local government in the countries wherein it is extended.

Such a condition to all appearances contradicts visibly the principles oftentimes proclaimed by the nations of America, and especially so the Monroe Doctrine upheld and defended at all times with so much zeal by the United States. . . . .

We do not pretend in any way that the South American nations should remain on any account exempt from the responsibilities of every order that the infractions of international law involve upon civilized communities. . . . . The only thing that the Argentine Republic maintains, and which she would see with great satisfaction consecrated, in view of the events that have occurred in Venezuela, by a nation such as the United States, which possesses so great authority and power, is the principle that there can not be European territorial expansion in America, or oppression of the peoples of this continent, because their unfortunate financial condition might oblige one or more of them to put off the fulfilment of its obligations; that is to say, the principle which I should like to see acknowledged is that a public debt can not give rise to the right of intervention, and much less to the occupation of the soil, of any American nation by any European power. . . . .[1]

Secretary Hay replied to the communication by a memorandum in which, "without expressing assent to or dissent from" the views of the Argentine government, he quoted the following passages from the two annual messages of President Roosevelt as indicating the general position of the American government:

We do not guarantee any State against punishment if it misconducts itself, provided that punishment does not take the form of the acquisition of territory by any non-American power [December 3, 1901].

No independent nation in America need have the slightest fear of aggression from the United States. It behooves each one to maintain order within its own borders and to discharge its just obligations to foreigners. When this is done, they can rest assured that, be they strong or weak, they have nothing to dread from outside interference [December 2, 1902].

Hay then concludes:

Advocating and adhering in practice in questions concerning itself to the resort of international arbitration in the settlement of controversies, not adjustable by the orderly treatment of diplomatic negotiations, the Government of the United States would always be glad to see the questions of the justice of claims by one state against another growing out of individual or national obligations, as well as guarantees for the execution of whatever award may be made, left to the decision of an impartial arbitral tribunal, before which litigating nations, weak and strong alike, may stand as equals in the eye of international law and mutual duty.[2]

[1] *Senate Document No. 119*, VII, 401–5.   [2] *Ibid.*, p. 406.

The conclusion of the Venezuelan imbroglio was attended with difficulty. On December 9, the day after the serving of diplomatic relations between Venezuela and the allied powers, the Venezuelan government had requested Herbert W. Bowen, the American minister at Caracas, to act as arbitrator for Venezuela in the settlement of the differences with Great Britain and Germany. To this request Hay gave his approval the following day, on condition that Venezuela propose arbitration and that Great Britain and Germany accept the proposal.[1] On December 20 the allied powers requested President Roosevelt to act as arbitrator, a proposal in which Venezuela joined the next day.[2] According to Thayer, Roosevelt was at first inclined to serve, but was dissuaded by Hay, who agreed with Bowen that it would be improper for the United States, which also had claims against Venezuela, to sit in judgment on the case.[3] Instead, Hay suggested that the controversy be submitted to the Hague Court, maintaining that the decision by that body of a case in which so many powerful nations were involved would strengthen the tribunal and would promote the cause of international arbitration. With some hesitation Roosevelt adopted Hay's suggestion, and the allies and Venezuela, although manifesting disappointment at Roosevelt's refusal to serve, acquiesced in his decision.[4]

The negotiations that comprise the second phase of the

[1] *Foreign Relations* (1903), pp. 790 f.

[2] *Senate Document No. 119*, VII, 676; but see *Die grosse Politik*, XVII, 267.

[3] Thayer, *John Hay*, II, 288. The one reason which tempted Roosevelt to act as arbitrator was to occupy a position which would remove all possibility of a decision in conflict with the Monroe Doctrine (Roosevelt to Shaw, December 26, 1902, *Roosevelt Papers*).

[4] *Senate Document No. 119*, VII, 690; *Foreign Relations* (1903), pp. 459, 461; Thayer, *op. cit.*, II, 288 f.

Venezuelan crisis were carried on in Washington, Bowen serving as the representative of Venezuela. Not until he had consented to every demand of the allies and had pledged 30 per cent of the total income of La Guaira and Puerto Cabello, the two most important Venezuelan ports, to the payment of claims, did the allied powers consent to issue orders for the raising of the blockade (February 14, 1903).[1]

The six weeks' delay in settling the controversy was caused in large part by a sharp disagreement between Bowen and the representatives of the allied powers over the securities to be given by Venezuela to guarantee the payment of the claims and over the question of priority of payment. Primarily on the ground that the blockade forced Venezuela to consent to the claims against her, Great Britain, Germany, and Italy maintained that their subjects should be paid in full before payment should be made to the citizens of the other creditor states. The view of the allies was vigorously combatted by Bowen who on January 29 declared:

I object to paying first the claims of the allies and the claims of the other nations afterwards, because:

1. I think it is unjust, unfair, and illegal to tie the hands of the said other nations for the period of five or six years that it would take to pay the claims of the allied powers;

2. If I recognize that brute force alone can be respected in the collection of claims, I should encourage the said other nations to use force also;

3. If the allied powers wanted preferential treatment, they should have asked for it in the beginning, and should not now propose it after I understood that all the conditions of the allied powers had been stated.

[1] *Senate Document No. 119*, VII, 748. In case Venezuela failed to pay the 30 per cent of the income, the creditor nations were authorized to put Belgian officials in charge of the two custom-houses to collect the duties until the entire foreign debt was paid.

If, however, this demand for preferential treatment is raised simply as a point of honor, I am willing to agree that the entire thirty per cent be paid to the allied powers for the first month.[1]

Bowen's attitude caused a temporary deadlock. As a way out of the difficulty Great Britain finally proposed that the question of preferential payment be left to the decision of President Roosevelt.[2] In spite of the objections of Count Metternich[3] and the refusal of Bowen to accept the suggestion,[4] the British Ambassador submitted the proposal to Hay on February 6.[5] Yielding doubtless to the advice of the Secretary of State, Roosevelt again declined to serve as arbitrator and suggested that the question of preferential payment be referred to the Hague. All the powers consenting, a protocol was concluded for the arbitration of the dispute by a special court to be convened in accordance with the Hague Convention.[6]

An incident that occurred during the preceding negotiations offers a possible explanation of the incongruities between the official records and Roosevelt's narrative of his action during the Venezuelan crisis. In the latter part of January, 1903, hostility against Germany was aroused in the United States as a result of the bombardment of Fort San Carlos by the German gunboat "Panther," one of the warships engaged in the Venezuelan blockade. "I hear indirectly," cabled Count Quadt, "that Secretary Hay expressed himself very bitterly concerning our action. . . . . At no time since the Venezuelan entanglement has feeling against us been so heated as now."[7]

---

[1] Ibid., p. 738.

[2] Ibid., pp. 740, 742.

[3] Die grosse Politik, XVII, 283.

[4] Senate Document No. 119, VII, 398.

[5] Ibid., p. 747.

[6] Ibid., pp. 31–38.

[7] Die grosse Politik, XVII, 274; cf. with A. D. White, Autobiography (New York, 1905), II, 246–48.

A few days later Count Speck von Sternburg, who had been sent to Washington on special mission,[1] reports (January 31, 1903) a conference with President Roosevelt in which the latter emphasized the desirability of bringing the Venezuelan negotiations to a satisfactory conclusion as soon as possible "since they begin to highly irritate public opinion both here and in Europe."[2] Three days later Sternburg reports that "the little sympathy which Germany still had in the United States she had sacrificed." He then adds that "Dewey's fleet had received secret orders to hold itself in readiness," and recommends that Bowen's offer concerning payment of the claims be accepted.[3] It was at this time (February 5, 1903) that Roosevelt made inquiry concerning German naval strength in the West Indies and the Atlantic.[4]

Most significant of all, perhaps, is Sternburg's account of a conversation with Roosevelt a few days after the completion of the negotiations. Under date of February 19, 1903, he sent the Foreign Office the dispatch given below;[5] the footnotes are the comments written on the margins of the communication by the German Emperor.

[1] *Ibid.*, p. 273. The rumor that Holleben had been recalled because of dissatisfaction with his work (see Callisen's letter on pp. 125 f. above) brought forth the following statement from the German Foreign Office: "He [Holleben] has not been recalled and his leave is granted upon his own initiative. The government would never recall an ambassador in the midst of important negotiations without grave reasons, and these certainly do not exist in this case . . . . (*Washington Post*, January 10, 1903).

[2] *Die grosse Politik*, XVII, 285.

[3] *Ibid.*, p. 286.

[4] H. C. Taylor to G. B. Cortelyou, February 9, 1903, and Bureau of Navigation to the President, February 11, 1903, *Roosevelt Papers*.

[5] *Die grosse Politik*, XVII, 291 f.; Roosevelt's "Memorandum of Engagements" includes the engagement with Sternburg for February 18, but it is silent concerning the conference of January 31 (*Roosevelt Papers*).

THE VENEZUELAN CRISIS

During a long ride which I had with the President yesterday[1] he discussed several pending questions. First he declared himself pleased to a high degree over the result of the Venezuelan negotiations which had made the best impression imaginable here with reference to Germany. He had emphasized at my arrival here the urgent necessity of the most rapid settlement of the Venezuelan question since public opinion was highly irritated because of the continued blockade. The sinking of the Venezuelan ships and the bombardment of the forts during the negotiations had immediately created sympathy here for Venezuela and had produced a critical situation. The German warships on the blockade had seen their future enemy in the fleet of Admiral Dewey.[2] Dewey's sailors on the other hand[3] had regarded the German ships as their next object of attack. It was high time to make an end to these conditions. Then it had been the German ships, but in six weeks it might probably be the English.

After the President had turned the conversation to the South American republics, he remarked that the best guarantee he saw for improving conditions there lay in the expansion of German influence[4] which had already gained so firm a foothold in southern Brazil. In the creation of an independent state of Germans in Brazil he saw the best solution of the South American question.[5] I felt a certain cooling of sympathy of the President for England.[6]

Touching upon the Alaskan question the President said: "In case the approaching negotiations should come to nothing we would without further ado proceed to mark out the boundary line claimed by us and insist on its recognition."[7]

Speaking of the causes underlying the anti-German movement in the United States, the President explained candidly that it had been provoked through the action of Admiral Diederich in Manila. The American people had seen therein an insult to their national hero, Admiral Dewey.[8]

[1] "How good it is if the German representative of His Majesty can ride out with the President.—W. *Approved.*"
[2] "They never dreamed of it."
[3] "Very foolish of them."
[4] "Right."   [5] "Right."   [6] "Good."
[7] "So. Let them try that on John Bull and see what happens."
[8] "! !"

I felt that the President does not place absolute confidence in Germany's assurances toward respecting the Monroe Doctrine. I took the occasion to assure him emphatically that Germany did not think of acquiring territory in South and Central America.[1]

In view of the foregoing evidence a number of interesting queries arise. Considering the fact that Roosevelt did not write[2] an account of the Venezuelan crisis until almost fourteen years after the event, is it possible that he may have confused the incidents of January and February with those of the preceding December? Is it possible that he may have mixed the question of arbitration decided in December with the problem aroused six weeks later by the German bombardment of Fort San Carlos? Did he perchance in retrospect confuse conversations with Holleben with those he had with Sternburg? Was Roosevelt's narrative, possibly, colored by an active imagination, enlarging upon the substratum of facts revealed by the official records and recalled more or less dimly after a lapse of many years? Was the coloring of the account due in part to the intense hostility Roosevelt felt toward Germany during the world-war when he first wrote the story? If the foregoing questions should be answered in the affirmative, most of the inaccuracies in Roosevelt's narrative are explained.

The question of preferential treatment, together with the related problem of the manner in which the revenues for the payment of the claims should be divided among the various powers, were the only matters submitted to the Hague Tribunal. At the suggestion of the Venezuelan government it had previously been agreed that all claims, excepting those designated as "first claims," be decided by

[1] "Good."

[2] In a volume published in 1925 (*Released for Publication*, pp. 84 ff.) O. K. Davis, for many years Washington correspondent of the New York *Times*, says that Roosevelt told him about the Venezuelan episode on August 7, 1908; see also Roosevelt's letter to White quoted on p. 132, n. 2, above.

mixed commissions. The final arrangement was incorporated in a series of protocols, each of which provided that, with the exceptions noted above, all claims should be settled at Caracas by mixed commissions composed of two members: one appointed by the Venezuelan government, and the other appointed by the government representing the claimants. All disagreements between the commissioners were to be settled by an umpire, to be selected by the chief magistrate of a third nation named in the protocol.[1] The equity of the demands of the allied powers may be judged from the fact that out of claims totaling 190,-676,670 bolivars,[2] the commissions awarded only 38,429,-376 bolivars, or barely one-fifth of the sum demanded.[3]

In the arbitration proceedings at The Hague in the fall and winter of 1903-4, the counsel for both sides[4] agreed that international law afforded no clear rule for the decision of the controversy as to preferential payment. Nor could any similar case be cited by either party. The Chinese indemnity claims, arising from the Boxer Insurrection in 1900, furnished the nearest parallel; in this instance all creditor nations received equal treatment regardless of their participation or non-participation in the relief of the besieged legations in Pekin. Counsel for the United States strongly urged the similarity of the Chinese indemnity collection, but in vain; for on February 22, 1904, the tribunal gave a unanimous decision in favor of the blockading powers.[5] The verdict completed the series of defeats met by Venezuela.

[1] *Senate Document No. 119*, VII, 23-31, 38-40.

[2] A bolivar is worth about twenty cents in gold.

[3] *Senate Document No. 316*, XXXV, 260, 291, 480, 510, 641, 871, 888, 916, 942, 954.

[4] Great Britain, Germany, and Italy *vs.* Venezuela, Mexico, Spain, France, Belgium, the Netherlands, the United States, and Sweden and Norway.

[5] *Senate Document No. 119*, VII, 93-99.

Chapter VI

THE COLLECTION OF DEBTS

WATCHFUL vigilance," as President Roosevelt styled his attitude in the Venezuelan crisis,[1] was succeeded by a policy that might be called "preventive action." In the Venezuelan affair he had confined himself to negative and mediatory measures. Informed by Great Britain and Germany of their contemplated coercion of Venezuela, he had expressed his regret that "European powers should use force against Central and South American countries," but had added that the United States "could not object to their taking steps to obtain redress for injuries suffered by their subjects, provided that no acquisition of territory was contemplated."[2] Once the blockade was established he had at first transmitted the Venezuelan request for arbitration "without comment,"[3] and subsequently had used his influence to secure a peaceful solution of the controversy.

Convinced of the dangers inherent in the policy of negation and mediation which he had pursued in the Venezuelan difficulty, Roosevelt embarked shortly after that crisis upon a course of positive action, a course more in harmony with his own character and better designed, so he believed, to prevent the recurrence of crises such as the one

[1] Address at Chicago, Ill., April 2, 1903 (Theodore Roosevelt, *Presidential Addresses and State Papers*, I, 260).

[2] See pp. 116 f. above. [3] See p. 120 above.

just surmounted. The same year which witnessed the decision of the Hague Tribunal in the Venezuelan case saw the announcement of the new policy in Roosevelt's annual message to Congress, December 6, 1904:

All that this country desires is to see the neighboring countries stable, orderly, and prosperous. Any country whose people conduct themselves well can count upon our hearty friendship. If a nation shows that it knows how to act with reasonable efficiency and decency in social and political matters, if it keeps order and pays its obligations, it need fear no interference from the United States. Chronic wrong-doing, or an impotence which results in a general loosening of the ties of civilized society, may in America, as elsewhere, ultimately require intervention by some civilized nation, and in the Western Hemisphere the adherence of the United States to the Monroe Doctrine may force the United States, however reluctantly, in flagrant cases of such wrong-doing or impotence, to the exercise of an international police power.[1]

The immediate cause for Roosevelt's pronouncement was the condition of affairs in Santo Domingo. Like Venezuela, the republic that occupies the eastern portion of the island of Santo Domingo had long been a prey to ambitious, self-seeking adventurers and a victim of disorders and insurrections usually originating in the efforts of rival leaders to obtain possession of the resources of the republic and, more especially, of the custom-houses, the chief source of governmental revenue.[2] So numerous were the revolutions during the forty years that followed the establishment of Santo Domingo as an independent state (1844) that no Dominican president completed his term of office and hardly a year passed without civil war.[3]

With the rise to power of Ulysses Heureaux in 1886,

---

[1] *House Document No. 1* (Fifty-eighth Congress, third session), I, xli; cf. *ibid.* (Fifty-ninth Congress, first session), I, xxxiv.

[2] *Foreign Relations*, Part I (1907), pp. 324, 333, 335, 357, 360.

[3] T. C. Dawson, "Chronology of Political Events in Santo Domingo," *Foreign Relations* (1906), pp. 572–84; *ibid.* (1905), p. 382.

however, there began a period relatively free from disorder. Heureaux was a full-blooded negro. He trusted no one. Notorious for his orgies and crimes, he was said to be a Nero and Caligula combined. He was accused of some two thousand murders. A list of his alleged victims, when printed, covered several columns in the newspaper. Unconcerned about the future, he boasted that "he cared not what history might record of him and of his conduct since he would not have to be here to read it."[1]

Establishing his position in the presidency over the armed resistance of his opponents, Heureaux maintained himself in power during the next thirteen years by bribery, intrigue, hard work, courage, and ruthlessness. To insure order and obtain support he secured a following in all parts of the country by employing an army of officials and by paying pensions to those whose position or influence made their allegiance valuable. In a single province, according to the American Minister, Heureaux had one-tenth of all the able-bodied men on his pay-roll, the majority with no pretense of service to the state, except that of rendering armed resistance in case of insurrection. When bribery failed, he employed intimidation, exile, assassination, and execution.

But extravagance and inefficiency combined to overwhelm Heureaux in financial ruin. Distrustful of everyone, he attempted to manage the finances himself without competent assistance or adequate bookkeeping. Swamped by the demands made upon him, he borrowed large funds from foreign bankers at exorbitant rates of interest and upon ruinous terms. When interest became due, he went deeper into the financial mire by borrowing additional

[1] J. H. Hollander, "Readjustment of San Domingo's Finances," *Quarterly Journal of Economics*, XXI (1907), 411.

funds to meet the accruing obligations. Outwitted by shrewd and unscrupulous moneylenders and the victim of an appreciating money market, he found himself in 1898 burdened with a debt of more than twenty millions, with barely a dollar in the treasury, and faced by a sullen and unhappy citizenry thousands of whom had been debauched by the pension system he had established.

Notwithstanding the agricultural and commercial prosperity which had resulted from the thirteen years of peace and order that Heureaux had given to the country, discontent and unrest were widespread among the educated and military classes. The issuance of a large sum of paper money in 1898 lost him the support of the peasantry. The following year, in the midst of signs of revolt which appeared in all parts of the republic, Heureaux was assassinated by Ramon Caceres, whose father had been killed by Heureaux and who believed that Heureaux was on the point of arresting him and his relatives and putting them out of the way.[1]

The death of Heureaux was followed by the speedy collapse of his government. Under the leadership of Jimenes and Horacio Vasquez a revolution ensued within a month, as the result of which the former assumed the presidency and the latter the vice-presidency. Abolishing the pension lists and repudiating obligations to foreign creditors, Jimenes found himself in possession of a large income; for the country was prosperous and the imports and exports large.

[1] For the character and rule of Heureaux, see *Foreign Relations* (1905), pp. 382 f.; *ibid.* (1906), 585–91; *Congressional Record* (Fifty-ninth Congress, first session), Vol. XL, Part I, p. 1177; J. H. Hollander, "The Convention of 1907 between the United States and the Dominican Republic," *American Journal of International Law*, Vol. I, Part I, p. 288.

But instead of setting aside a sum sufficient to meet the legitimate obligations and debts of the government, Jimenes unfortunately squandered the revenues of the country on new pensions and generous allowances to his followers. To add to the calamities of the republic, disagreement soon arose between Jimenes and Vasquez culminating in 1902 in civil war. In the struggle that ensued victory came to the Horacistas, as the followers of Vasquez were called, and for a brief period Vasquez occupied the presidency. The new president seems to have made an earnest effort to govern with honesty and efficiency, but disaffection soon appeared, an insurrection took place, and the republic fell for a short time into the hands of Alejandro Wos y Gil who promptly repudiated the attempts of his predecessor at financial reform.

The next year was a time of confusion, anarchy, and disaster. Fighting was almost constantly in process in some part of the country. Those in charge of the short-lived governments—Jimenista, Horacista, or coalition—lived a hand-to-mouth existence on funds secured by confiscations, by short-time loans at high rates of interest, and by deals permitting the importation of goods at less than the legal rates. The local authorities ordinarily conducted their affairs as they pleased, for the central government was usually powerless to interfere. Every town and city in the republic suffered from capture and recapture by the contending forces, while every province was a scene of bloodshed and destruction of property. Finances were demoralized, interest on the public debt unpaid, revenues mortgaged and uncertain.

The strife and chaos were brought to an end by a compromise. At a conference held on board the cruiser "Detroit," then in Dominican waters to protect American lives and interests, the Jimenista leaders recognized as president Carlos F. Morales, one of the younger Jimenista chiefs who had joined forces with the Horacistas; Morales and his followers in turn acknowledged certain Jimenista leaders as the legal governors in the provinces of Monte Christi and Azua.

For a time peace reigned. The government troops for the most part laid down their arms, the roving bands of marauders disintegrated, agriculture was resumed, business revived, and irreconcilable revolutionists left the country.

But the republic still faced serious dangers. The country continued to suffer from the ravages of the late civil conflict. The exiled Jimenistas, like the *émigrés* during the French Revolution, waited only for a favorable moment to return and renew the struggle. Intrigues were constantly in progress within the Horacista party. Deep anxiety existed concerning the foreign debt and the action which might be taken to collect it by the various creditor states.[1]

As in other backward regions the debts of Santo Domingo had been incurred for the exploitation of the natural resources of the country, the building of railroads, the conduct of government, the waging of war, and the gratification of the greed of those who were temporarily in control of affairs, Loans had been secured on exorbitant terms, at excessive interest rates, and at the price of valuable concessions and grants.

In 1869, for example, the Dominican government contracted a 6 per cent loan of £757,700 for the construction of roads and railways. As provision for a sinking fund and the payment of interest Santo Domingo agreed to pay for

[1] For the civil wars between 1899 and 1905, see *Foreign Relations* (1905), pp. 383–86; *ibid.* (1906), pp. 591–96.

twenty-five years an annuity of £58,900. The bonds, issued at rates ranging from 50 to 70 per cent of their par value, were secured upon a first charge on the customs duties of the ports of Santo Domingo and Puerto Plata, the guano royalties, and the revenues for the mines and forests of the province of Samana. Of the total income from the sale of the bonds the Dominican government acknowledged the receipt of only £38,000—little more than half the amount it obligated itself to pay in return every year during the next quarter of a century.[1] The episode is typical of the equity of many of the financial transactions between Latin-American countries and their creditors.[2]

In 1904 the face value of the Dominican public debt, not including all claims, was estimated at $32,280,000. Of this total about $22,000,000 was owed to European creditors, over $18,000,000 of the sum being formally recognized by the Dominican government.[3] For a number of years the creditor states had energetically pushed the claims of their subjects, securing as a result a more or less definite acknowledgment of the obligation together with arrangements which seemed to point to the ultimate extinction of the debt. In 1901, for example, the French and Belgian bondholders were given a mortgage on the revenues of the ports of Santo Domingo and Macoris. By the arrangement

[1] See *Thirty-first Annual Report of the Council of the Corporation of Foreign Bondholders*, extract from which appears in *Congressional Record*, Vol. XL, Part I, p. 797.

[2] See the total of the arbitral awards against Venezuela as compared with the amount of the claims (p. 147 above). Claims presented by the United States, Mexico, Great Britain, Spain, France, and Chile against one another during the last third of the nineteenth century totaled more than $719,000,000, while the entire allowances of arbitral commissions amounted to less than $8,500,000 (*Senate Document No. 119* [Fifty-eighth Congress, third session], VII, 182 f., 418 f.).

[3] *House Document No. 1* (Fifty-ninth Congress, first session), I, 336 f.

the French and Belgian governments might at any moment demand the control of the custom-houses at the two ports in case the payments specified in the contract were not met by the Dominican government. Since the revenues collected at Santo Domingo and Macoris constituted the chief income of the republic, such a demand, if enforced, would overthrow the government; for no government can exist without the funds necessary for its running expenses. Naturally the civil wars which had vexed the country since the overthrow of Heureaux made the fulfilment of the contract impossible.

To increase the gravity of the situation, the Italian, German, and Spanish governments in July, 1903, required the Dominican authorities to sign protocols agreeing to pay specific monthly sums on the debts owed to their citizens. A year later (May, 1904) the declaration of the Italian government that a definite settlement must be made with its nationals led to the drafting of new protocols assigning certain revenues to the Italian creditors. The climax was reached on July 14, 1904, when the arbitrators who had been appointed to determine the manner of payment of the $4,500,000 which had previously been agreed upon as the sum due the Santo Domingo Improvement Company, a New York corporation, rendered a decision requiring the payment of almost $40,000 a month to the company, in default of which the custom-house of Puerto Plata was to be delivered to an American representative of the company together with a lien upon the duties collected at Monte Christi, Sanchez, and Samana. As a result of the decision, the Morales government, unable to pay the prescribed monthly instalment, turned over (October 17, 1904) the custom-house at Puerto Plata to the American agent.

Since the administrative expenses of the city as well as

two important interior provinces were paid from the revenues collected at Puerto Plata, the surrender of the custom-house placed additional financial burdens upon the southern ports and threatened immediate disaster to the government. Moreover, the award at once brought strong protests from the Italian, French, and Belgian representatives who insisted that the effect of the decision was to end the opportunity for realizing on the claims provided for in protocols Santo Domingo had entered into with their respective governments.

Discouraged at the outlook, President Morales was at first disposed to let matters take their course. But the danger of European intervention and of internal insurrection finally brought him to the conclusion that with the help of the United States he might find a way out of the morass. Not the least of the reasons that led him to this conviction was his belief that a guaranty against insurrection would be afforded by placing the custom-houses in charge of financial agents responsible to and protected by the American government.[1] The opposition to American intervention was so strong in the cabinet and among the Dominican people, however, that it was not until the American Minister, by the direction of Secretary Hay (December 30, 1904), suggested that the Dominican government ask the United States to take charge of the collection of the revenues that Morales consented to make the request.[2] Even then weeks passed before internal opposition could be sufficiently overcome so that a definite arrangement could be formulated.[3]

During the preceding year, it is true, the Dominican

[1] *Foreign Relations* (1904), p. 280.

[2] *Ibid.* (1905), pp. 298–300.   [3] *Ibid.*, p. 305.

authorities had made repeated efforts to obtain American assistance. In January, 1904, the Minister of Foreign Affairs visited Washington and sought the help of the United States to enable Santo Domingo to meet its financial problems, but his request was denied.[1] In a letter to J. B. Bishop, February 23, 1904, Roosevelt expressed his own attitude as follows:

I have been hoping and praying for three months that the Santo Domingans would behave so that I would not have to act in any way. I want to do nothing but what a policeman has to do in Santo Domingo. As for annexing the island, I have about the same desire to annex it as a gorged boa constrictor might have to swallow a porcupine wrong-end-to. Is that strong enough? I have asked some of our people to go there because, after having refused for three months to do anything, the attitude of the Santo Domingans has become one of half chaotic war towards us. If I possibly can, I want to do nothing to them. If it is absolutely necessary to do something, then I want to do as little as possible. Their government has been bedeviling us to establish some kind of protectorate over the islands, and take charge of their finances. We have been answering them that we could not possibly go into the subject now at all.[2]

Roosevelt's reluctance to act in the Dominican imbroglio was overcome by the attitude of the European creditor states and by the likelihood that non-intervention by the United States would bring a repetition of the Venezuelan crisis with all the dangers latent in such a situation.[3] In 1903 he had rejected the suggestion of the representative

[1] J. B. Bishop, *Theodore Roosevelt and His Time*, I, 430; *House Document No. 1* (Fifty-ninth Congress, first session), I, 340. In a letter to Senator Cullom (March 13, 1905), Hay gives the date of the visit to the Dominican Minister as the spring of 1904 (S. M. Cullom, *Fifty Years of Public Service*, p. 388).

[2] Bishop, *op. cit.*, I, 431. In a message to the Senate on March 6, 1905, Roosevelt stated that "under no circumstances do we intend to acquire territory in or possession of either Haiti or Santo Domingo" (J. D. Richardson, *Messages and Papers of Presidents*, X, 859).

[3] *House Document No. 1* (Fifty-ninth Congress, first session), I, 340.

of a foreign country that a joint fiscal control of the Dominican Republic be established to collect the revenues of Santo Domingo and, after giving a certain percentage to the republic, to divide the balance ratably among the creditor nations.[1] In the spring of 1904 the offer of the Dominican President to turn over all the custom-houses to the United States government was again declined.[2] But when the financial problems of the island republic became critical in the latter half of 1904, Roosevelt finally became convinced that he must act. In his annual message to Congress in December, 1905, he describes the situation which brought him to the foregoing decision as follows:

There was imminent danger of foreign intervention. The previous rulers of Santo Domingo had recklessly incurred debts, and owing to her internal disorders she had ceased to be able to provide means of paying the debts. The patience of her foreign creditors had become exhausted, and at least two foreign nations were on the point of intervention, and were only prevented from intervening by the unofficial assurance of this Government that it would itself strive to help Santo Domingo in her hour of need. In the case of one of these nations, only the actual opening of negotiations to this end by our Government prevented the seizure of territory in Santo Domingo by a European power.[3]

The initial move in negotiations, as pointed out above, was made by John Hay, a few months after the award in favor of American creditors.[4] In a confidential telegram dated December 30, 1904, he directed the American minister, T. C. Dawson, to

sound the President of Santo Domingo, discreetly but earnestly and in a perfectly friendly spirit, touching the disquieting situation which

[1] Bishop, *op. cit.*, I, 430; *House Document No. 1* (Fifty-ninth Congress, first session), I, 340.

[2] *Ibid.*, I, 300; Cullom, *op. cit.*, p. 388.

[3] Richardson, *op. cit.*, XI, 1155; see also Roosevelt, *Autobiography*, p. 507; *House Document No. 1* (Fifty-ninth Congress, first session), I, 298, 323.

[4] See p. 155 above.

is developing owing to the pressure of other governments having arbitral awards in their favor and who regard our award as conflicting with their rights. . . . . You will ascertain whether the Government of Santo Domingo would be disposed to request the United States to take charge of the collection of duties and effect an equitable distribution of the assigned quotas among the Dominican Government and the several claimants.[1]

To assist Dawson in arranging a plan with the Dominican authorities for the management of Dominican revenues by American representatives, Roosevelt sent (January 5, 1905) as special commissioner to the Dominican government Commander Dillingham, a naval officer possessing wide knowledge of conditions in the island.[2] After Dillingham's arrival (January 14) negotiations proceeded rapidly, and on January 20 an agreement known as the Dillingham-Sanchez protocol was signed providing for a guaranty by the United States of the territorial integrity of the Dominican Republic and for the control by the United States of all Dominican custom-houses, 45 per cent of the revenue to be turned over to the Dominican government and the balance used by the United States to pay the

[1] *House Document No. 1* (Fifty-ninth Congress, first session), I, 298. Roosevelt's action was clearly foreshadowed over a quarter of a century earlier. In 1872 and again in 1881 the United States entered into negotiations with Venezuela looking toward the administration of the customs revenues of Venezuela by the United States. When Blaine became secretary of state (1881), France was endeavoring to collect claims from Venezuela. Upon Venezuela's refusal to pay, France proposed to seize the Venezuela custom-houses, collect the duties, and reimburse the creditors. Blaine objected, but urged Venezuela to pay, with the suggestion that the money be forwarded through the American agent at Caracas. Should Venezuela not pay within three months, Blaine proposed that the United States take possession of the custom-houses, collect the duties, and pay the revenues to the creditor nations. Blaine's short term of office prevented the fulfilment of this plan (*Foreign Relations* [1881], pp. 1207, 1213, 1216–18; see also J. B. Moore, *Digest of International Law*, VI, 711 f.).

[2] *House Document No. 1* (Fifty-ninth Congress, first session), I, 300 f.

creditors of Santo Domingo.[1] The stipulation concerning the territorial guaranty, as well as other details in the protocol, proved unacceptable to the American government, and the exchange of views and arrangement of compromises that followed delayed the completion of negotiations and the signing of a new protocol until February 7, 1905.[2] Popular hostility to Americans, the fear that Santo Domingo was to be annexed, and official suspicion of the designs of the United States, especially among members of the Dominican ministry, proved difficult obstacles to overcome. According to the dispatches, American warships, as well as American tact, were needed to prevent disorder and insurrection.[3]

Roosevelt submitted the new protocol to the Senate on February 15, 1905. Opposition at once developed, and the session came to an end without action. A similar fate attended the arrangement at the special session of the Senate which immediately followed Roosevelt's inauguration. The failure to confirm the protocol, according to the President, was due to the opposition of the Democrats and the absence of certain Republican senators.[4]

When the news that the treaty had been rejected reached Santo Domingo, rumors of revolution immediately spread through the capital. The next day brought word, however, that the Senate had merely adjourned and that the treaty was still pending. Hereupon calm was temporarily restored, but the arrival of an Italian cruiser on March 14 aroused instant alarm in government circles,

---

[1] *Ibid.*, p. 306. The United States government had not authorized the signing of the protocol (see Hay's letter to Senator Cullom, in Cullom, *op. cit.*, p. 388).

[2] *House Document No. 1* (Fifty-ninth Congress, first session), I, 313–24.

[3] *Ibid.*, pp. 305–7, 316 f., 322, 324, 327–33, 351–54.

[4] Bishop, *op. cit.*, I, 433; but see also Cullom, *op. cit.*, pp. 391 f., and Roosevelt to Taft, August 21, 1907, *Roosevelt Papers*.

being interpreted as an intention by the Italian government to force the immediate settlement of the Italian claims. About the same time representatives of other creditor states began to press the Dominican authorities for the resumption of payments under their protocols.

In the crisis the Dominican Minister of Finance informed Dawson that "he could stand the strain no longer and that he contemplated resigning." Dawson urged him to retain his office in order to avoid plunging the country into deeper difficulties. The Dominican Minister then intimated that he would continue in his position providing a practical *modus vivendi* was adopted pending the ratification of the treaty. Finding that an arrangement by which an American citizen should act as receiver of the customs would be satisfactory to the creditor states and would prevent intervention by them, Dawson cabled the Dominican proposal to Washington.

After a conference with leading senators Roosevelt accepted the proposal. He describes his action in a confidential letter to Hay, then in Germany endeavoring to regain his health:

There has been a rather comic development in the Santo Domingo case. Morales asked us to take over the custom-houses pending action by the Senate. I decided to do so, but first of all consulted Spooner, Foraker, Lodge, and Knox. All heartily agreed that it was necessary for me to take this action. Rather to my horror Taft genially chaffed them about going back on their principles as to the "usurpation of the executive." But they evidently took the view that it was not a time to be overparticular about trifles. I also consulted Gorman, who told me that he had taken it for granted that I would have to take some such action as that proposed, and believed it necessary. I understand, however, that this was merely his unofficial opinion, and that officially he is going to condemn our action as realizing his worst forebodings.[1]

[1] Bishop, *op. cit.*, I, 433; *Congressional Record* (Fifty-ninth Congress, first session), Vol. XL, Part II, pp. 1426, 1473.

By the *modus vivendi* the President of the United States was to suggest for nomination by the Dominican President American citizens who were to act as receivers of customs at the various ports. Of the money collected, 45 per cent was to go to the Dominican government and the remainder was to be deposited in a New York bank designated by the President of the United States, there to be kept until the Senate acted upon the treaty. If the action of the Senate was adverse, the money was to be turned over to the Dominican government; if the Senate ratified the treaty, the fund was to be distributed among the creditors in proportion to their just claims.[1] The arrangement was to take effect April 1. As general receiver and collector Roosevelt nominated Colonel George R. Colton, for a number of years a customs collector in the Philippine Islands.[2] Colton was at once appointed by President Morales.

Roosevelt's action immediately became the target of fierce criticism in the Senate. Following the lead of Senator Morgan, of Alabama, who had served on the Committee on Foreign Relations for a longer period than any other senator,[3] the President's opponents denounced his course as unconstitutional, declaring that he had put into execution a treaty which the Senate had refused to approve and that he had established a protectorate over Santo Domingo. Only the pressure of American warships, it was maintained, enabled Colton and his assistants to act as collectors of customs—a declaration openly accepted in the Senate by Roosevelt's supporters.[4]

[1] *House Document No. 1* (Fifty-ninth Congress, first session), I, 360–62, 365 f.

[2] *Ibid.*, p. 367.

[3] Senator Morgan had been a member of the Senate Committee on Foreign Relations since his appointment in 1879 (Cullom, *op. cit.*, p. 348).

[4] See speech by Senator Spooner (Wis.) on January 23, 1906 (*Congressional Record*, Vol. XL, Part II, p. 1428).

THE COLLECTION OF DEBTS

Although the Americans who acted under the *modus vivendi* were technically officers of the Dominican government, in reality they were under the control of the United States.[1] Roosevelt frankly reorganized the situation in an address at Chautauqua, New York, on August 11, 1905.[2] After describing conditions in Santo Domingo he said:

Accordingly the executive department of our Government negotiated a treaty under which we are to try to help the Dominican people to straighten out their finances. The treaty is pending before the Senate, whose consent to it is necessary. In the meantime we have made a temporary arrangement which will last until the Senate has had time to take action upon the treaty. Under this arrangement we see to the honest administration of the custom-houses, collecting the revenues, turning over forty-five per cent to the Government for running expenses and putting the other fifty-five per cent into a safe deposit for equitable division among the various creditors, whether European or American, accordingly as, after investigation, their claims seem just.

The custom-houses offer well-nigh the only sources of revenues in Santo Domingo, and the different revolutions usually have as their real aim the obtaining possession of these custom-houses. The mere fact that we are protecting the custom-houses and collecting the revenue with efficiency and honesty has completely discouraged all revolutionary movement. . . . .

[1] Concerning the legal nature of the receivership the following statement from the final report of the general receiver is of interest: "The receivership to which this final report relates was never in actual control of the Dominican customs service proper. The receivership has been a separate and distinct branch, the work of which was confined largely to the receipting for, safekeeping, and honest disbursement of those funds collected by the Dominican officials designated as deputy receivers in charge at the several custom-houses. . . . . The receivership attempted to act in an advisory capacity in order to accomplish certain reforms, establish uniformity in matters of classification, and stamp out, if possible, questionable practices, which naturally prevented an honest enforcement of the customs laws. But in some respects it was not entirely successful, owing to the lack of cooperation" (*Foreign Relations*, Part I [1907], p. 330).

[2] New York *Times*, August 12, 1905. See also Roosevelt's letter to Sidney Brooks, December 28, 1908, Bishop, *op. cit.*, II, 130, and Roosevelt, *Autobiography*, p. 510.

Without question the presence of American warships in Dominican waters discouraged insurrections. A week after the arrangement went into effect Roosevelt wrote Taft that American citizens were in the custom-houses to stay until the United States took them out and that no revolutionists would be allowed to interfere with them.[1] Later, when signs of insurrection appeared during the fall, Roosevelt went so far as to send the following note to the Secretary of the Navy (September 5, 1905):

> As to the Santo Domingo matter, tell Admiral Bradford to stop any revolution. I intend to keep the island in *statu quo* until the Senate has had time to act on the treaty, and I shall treat any revolutionary movement as an effort to upset the *modus vivendi*. That this is ethically right, I am dead sure, even though there may be some technical or red tape difficulty.[2]

The foregoing order throws light on one of the chief causes of opposition to the *modus vivendi*. Senators opposed the arrangement not only because they regarded Roosevelt's action as an exercise of unconstitutional authority, but also because they interpreted the phrase relating to the maintenance of the *status quo* as meaning that the United States would support the existing Dominican government against any insurrectionary movement, thereby establishing in fact the very protectorate to which they vigorously objected. Their interpretation seems warranted by a sentence in a statement given to the press on March 28, 1905, by Acting Secretary of State Adee to the effect that the object of the arrangement with Santo Domingo was "to maintain the *status quo*."[3] Certainly the order to the Secretary of the Navy, quoted above, indicates that

[1] Roosevelt to Taft, April 8, 1905, *Roosevelt Papers*.

[2] Bishop, *op. cit.*, I, 433.

[3] New York *Times*, March 28, 1905.

the fears of those opposed to a suzerainty over Santo Domingo were not without grounds.

Toward the end of 1905, Roosevelt seems to have changed his mind about the prevention of revolutionary movements. The change may have been due to the influence of Secretary Root who became secretary of state after the death of John Hay (July 1, 1905). Root manifested much less arrogance in dealing with Latin-American peoples than did his predecessor. The dispatches of Root repeatedly lay emphasis upon the use of American marines and warships only after an explicit request had come from the Dominican authorities and only for the "temporary protection of life of American citizens which Dominican Government [declared] itself for a time being unable to protect."[1] When disagreements developed between President Morales and his cabinet in December, 1905, Root telegraphed the American Minister urging an amicable settlement of differences within the government. He then continued:

We can not take any part in differences between factions or officers of Dominican Government. No troops are to be landed except when absolutely necessary to protect life and property of American citizens, and if landed they must confine themselves strictly to such protection, which will extend to the peaceful performance of duty by the Americans who are collecting revenue in the custom-houses so long as the Dominican Government desires them to continue that service. If Dominican Government determines to end the *modus vivendi* and the collection of duties by Americans nominated by President of the United States, protection will extend to their safe withdrawal with their property. Notice of such termination should be given formally. We are about to withdraw several of our ships, which will return to United States with Admiral Bradford.[2]

[1] *Foreign Relations* (1905), pp. 405, 408.

[2] *Ibid.*, p. 408. On November 18, 1905, Dawson had cabled that "all the ports except Azua and Barahona are guarded" by American vessels (*ibid.*, p. 406).

[165]

Root's appeal for peace proved fruitless. The discord within the Dominican government culminated on December 24, 1905, in an armed conflict between the followers of Morales and those of Vice-President Caceres. In the struggle the forces of Caceres were completely victorious, and Morales, injured and destitute, offered to resign the presidency and withdraw from the country if his life were spared. His offer was accepted, and on January 12, 1906, Morales left Santo Domingo for San Juan, Porto Rico, on board the cruiser "Dubuque." With his departure the serious phases of the revolution came to an end. Throughout the disturbance the United States safeguarded the custom-houses, but seems to have given neither assistance nor favor to either of the contending factions,[1] in this respect pursuing a policy in striking contrast to that followed in 1903 in Panama.

Meanwhile, the struggle in the American Senate over Dominican affairs continued. The original Dillingham-Sanchez protocol drafted January 20, 1905, was so objectionable that Roosevelt never submitted it to the Senate.[2] The arrangement of February 7, 1905, which in all essential respects was put into operation by the *modus vivendi*, was so severely attacked that Roosevelt became convinced finally that changes would have to be incorporated to secure its ratification. Accordingly, negotiations were renewed, alterations were made, and in the amended form

[1] M. H. Urena, *Los Estados Unidos y La Republica Dominicana*, pp. 32–34; *Foreign Relations* (1905), pp. 404–13; *ibid.*, Part I (1906), pp. 536–49, 551; Roosevelt, *Autobiography*, p. 510.

[2] See pp. 159 f. above. Senator Spooner declared (January 23, 1906) that he regarded the Dillingham-Sanchez protocol "as an attempt to do a thing which the Executive Department or its agents had no power to do" (*Congressional Record*, Vol. XL, Part II, p. 1426).

the protocol was approved by the Senate on February 25, 1907.[1]

Roosevelt insisted that the changes in the protocol were "utterly unimportant."[2] A comparison of the arrangement as ratified with the protocol as originally submitted to the Senate reveals, however, three significant differences, as well as a number of important variations in the financial details of the two conventions. In the first place, the agreement of the United States "to respect the complete territorial integrity of the Dominican Republic" was omitted from the treaty as ratified in order to meet the objections of senators who maintained that there was no difference between "respecting" and "guaranteeing" the territorial integrity of Santo Domingo. In the second place, the clause by which the United States pledged its assistance in the internal affairs of Santo Domingo whenever it considered such assistance wise was deleted in deference to senators who believed that the provision would involve the United States in the internal affairs of the republic. In the third place, the clause by which the United States agreed to attempt to determine the validity and the amount of all claims pending against Santo Domingo was amended in the treaty as ratified so that the obligation of evaluating the claims remained with the Dominican government.[3] Thus three

[1] W. M. Malloy, *Treaties and Conventions*, I, 418–20. Roosevelt believed that the chief difficulty in securing ratification was due to the lack of popular interest in the situation (Roosevelt to Taft, August 21, 1907, *Roosevelt Papers*).

[2] Roosevelt, *Autobiography*, p. 511.

[3] Cf. *Foreign Relations* (1905), pp. 342 f., and *ibid.* (1907), pp. 307–9. See also H. Howland, *Theodore Roosevelt and His Times*, pp. 167–70; Cullom, *op. cit.*, pp. 391 f.; Hollander, "The Convention of 1907 between the United States and the Dominican Republic," *American Journal of International Law*, Vol. I, Part I, pp. 289 f., 293–95; Hollander, "Readjustment of San Domingo's Finances," *Quarterly Journal of Economics*, XXI (1907), 425 f.; and Fabula, *Los Estados Unidos contra la Libertad*, pp. 226–29.

important political features in the earlier protocol were omitted in the treaty as ratified.

During the twenty-eight months in which the *modus vivendi* was in operation, the arrangement proved satisfactory to the creditor European governments and beneficial to the Dominicans. When the plan went into effect April 1, 1905, the Dominican treasury was empty and the government was behind in its current expenses approximately $100,000. Not a wagon road in the entire republic was as long as ten miles. Public buildings were in worse condition than they had been for forty years. The Dominican government did not own or control as much as a rowboat in its entire customs service. Smuggling both by land and by sea was commonplace.

Twelve months after the *modus vivendi* became effective the cash on hand amounted to $1,228,536.44, and at the termination of the arrangement (July 31, 1907) the total had risen to $3,223,986.02. In addition, the Dominican government had been able to meet its current expenses out of the 45 per cent of the receipts allotted to it, receiving in its share of the revenue a larger cash income than when it had controlled the entire receipts. It had also acquired a revenue service consisting of four new steel cutters, had established an effective patrol system on the frontier, and had provided for the opening of schools, the improvement of roads, and the repair of public edifices.[1]

Naturally the professional revolutionists in Santo Domingo were bitterly hostile to the *modus vivendi* as well as to the conventions of 1905 and 1907. Substantial citizens, however, seem for the most part to have approved

[1] *Foreign Relations* (1905), pp. 378–82; *ibid.* (1907), Part I, pp. 322–60; Hollander, "The Convention of 1907 between the United States and the Dominican Republic," *American Journal of International Law*, Vol. I, Part II, pp. 287–97.

the action of the United States. During the twenty-eight months in which the *modus vivendi* was in operation, according to the American receiver-general, Colonel Colton, not one single complaint nor line of criticism has been received from the Dominican Government, nor from any consul or special representative, residents of the city of Santo Domingo, particularly charged with safeguarding the interests of and reporting upon matters of moment to those of their countrymen, holders of Dominican bonds long since due, and for which settlement repeatedly has been urged.[1]

In short, to quote the words of Colonel Colton, Santo Domingo in a little more than two years was transformed "from a bankrupt State—without credit at home or abroad, consumed by revolutions within, and threatened by creditors without—into a solvent and peaceful country of some dignity and promise."[2] In the light of the evidence Roosevelt had grounds for feeling that he had "put the affairs of the island on a better basis than they had been for a century."[3]

The influence of Roosevelt's policy in the collection of debts proved far reaching.[4] With modifications his plan has remained in operation in Santo Domingo to the present time.[4] It has also been followed with variations in other Latin-American countries by all of his successors. During

[1] *Foreign Relations* (1907), Part I, pp. 323 f.   [2] *Ibid.*, p. 333.

[3] Letter to Sidney Brooks, December 28, 1908, in Bishop, *op. cit.*, II, 130; see also Roosevelt, *Autobiography*, p. 511.

[3] Hollander, "The Dominican Convention and Its Lessons," *Journal of Race Development*, IV, 398–408.

[4] The story of the military administration of the republic by the United States and the benefits and abuses to which it led does not fall within the scope of this volume. On such matters see *Hearings before a Select Committee on Haiti and Santo Domingo* (U.S. Senate), Part I, esp. pp. 51–60, 90–94, 96–104, and Part IV, pp. 1238–1341; *Report of the Secretary of the Navy* (1920), pp. 321–42; *Current History*, XIV, 397; Carl Kelsey, "The American Intervention in Haiti and the Dominican Republic," *Annals of the American Academy*, C, No. 189, 166–200; Urena, *op. cit.*, pp. 51 ff.

President Taft's administration Secretary Knox negotiated treaties with Honduras (January 10, 1911) and with Nicaragua (June 6, 1911) by which the two countries were to be placed under the financial supervision of the United States.[1] In each instance provision was made for the appointment of collectors of customs who had previously been approved by the President of the United States. In Nicaragua the collector was immediately appointed without waiting for the Senate to approve the arrangement, and loans were made to Nicaragua by New York bankers. Some time later the Senate rejected the treaties, financial and political disorder followed, and in 1912 United States marines and a warship were stationed at Corinto.

A more recent instance of action modeled on Roosevelt's Dominican policy occurred during the Wilson administration. On February 16, 1916, the Senate ratified a treaty with Haiti by which a receivership of customs closely resembling that introduced in the Dominican Republic was established in the negro republic. Clauses in the treaty also extended the chief provisions of the Platt Amendment over Haiti and, in addition, gave the United States control over the native constabulary and the internal financial administration of the government. The manner in which Americans managed Haitian affairs has been subject to much criticism.[2]

[1] On March 16, 1909, according to the secretary of the navy, George Meyer, Knox read in the cabinet meeting a paper defining the policy of the Taft administration in Central America: "It ensures the neutrality of Honduras and contemplates establishing its credit by their suggesting that we put in a financial agent such as we furnished to San Domingo" (M. A. de Wolfe Howe, *George von Lengerke Meyer*, pp. 427 f.).

[2] On relations with Haiti, see *Senate Committee Hearings*, Part I, pp. 5–33, 336, 344, 348; *ibid.*, Part II, pp. 394 f.; *United States Statutes at Large*, Vol. XXXIX, Part II, pp. 1654–60; *Senate Report No. 794* (Sixty-seventh Congress, second session); C. Kelsey, *op. cit.*, pp. 118–65.

Roosevelt did not approve of the use of force by the United States for the collection of the contractual claims of American citizens in other lands. Nor did he indorse intervention for such purposes by other governments. In his annual message to Congress in 1905, he said: "Our own Government has always refused to enforce such contractual obligations on behalf of its citizens by an appeal to arms. It is much to be wished that all foreign governments would take the same view."[1]

Elsewhere in the same message, it is true, Roosevelt stated that there were "limits to the wrongs which any self-respecting nation can endure." An instance of what he regarded as such a wrong, or tort, occurred in Venezuela after the settlement of the crises described in the preceding chapter.[2] In spite of repeated representations, remonstrances, and threats by the United States, President Castro, in accordance with his attitude toward claims,[3] refused to recognize as subject to diplomatic consideration the forcible expulsion of an American citizen from Venezuela and certain claims of American citizens and corporations, running in some instances over a considerable period of years. After long-continued and fruitless efforts to secure redress, Roosevelt withdrew the American legation from Caracas (June 13, 1908). The overthrow of Castro a short time before the expiration of Roosevelt's admin-

[1] *House Document No. 1* (Fifty-ninth Congress, first session), I, xxxiv. See also Roosevelt's special message to the Senate (February 15, 1905), *ibid.*, p. 335. For an earlier statement of American policy see Secretary Bayard's note of June 24, 1885, in which the declaration is made that in the case of mere contractual claims all that the United States would undertake to do would be to interpose its good offices by calling the attention of the foreign sovereign to the claims (J. B. Moore, *Digest of International Law*, VI, 716).

[2] See Roosevelt's letter to Taft, August 21, 1907, *Roosevelt Papers.*

[3] See pp. 120 f. and 138 f. above. For the character of Castro's rule, see Bowen's confidential report to Roosevelt, August 21, 1904, *Roosevelt Papers.*

istration opened the door for a renewal of diplomatic relations and a settlement of the dispute between the two countries on terms satisfactory to the United States.[1]

While the controversy with Venezuela was at its height, Roosevelt reasserted his position on the collection of international debts by giving the American delegates who attended the Third International Conference of American Republics at Rio de Janeiro during July and August, 1906, the following instructions:

> It has long been the established policy of the United States not to use its armed forces for the collection of ordinary contract debts due to its citizens by other governments. We have not considered the use of force for such a purpose consistent with that respect for the independent sovereignty of other members of the family of nations, which is the most important principle of international law and the chief protection of weak nations against the oppression of the strong. . . . . We regret that other powers, whose opinions and sense of justice we esteem highly, have at times taken a different view and have permitted themselves, though we believe with reluctance, to collect such debts by force. It is doubtless true that the non-payment of public debts may be accompanied by such circumstances of fraud and wrongdoing or violation of treaties as to justify the use of force. This Government would be glad to see an international consideration of the subject which shall discriminate between such cases and the simple non-performance of a contract with a private person, and a resolution in favor of reliance upon peaceful means in cases of the latter class.[2]

In accordance with the suggestion of the American delegation, the Rio de Janeiro Conference decided to recommend to the governments therein represented the consideration of an invitation to the Second Peace Conference at The Hague to canvass "the question of the com-

[1] *Senate Document No. 413* (Sixtieth Congress, first session), pp. 13–58, 91–269, 278, 284, 510 f., 528, 592; *Foreign Relations* (1908), pp. 774–80, 786–96, 820; *ibid.* (1909), p. 609; Roosevelt, *Autobiography*, pp. 506 f.

[2] *Foreign Relations*, Part I (1906), p. xlix; see also Secretary Root's speech, August 17, 1906, *ibid.*, pp. 29–31.

pulsory collection of public debts." In harmony with this recommendation General Horace Porter, by the direction of President Roosevelt, presented to the Hague Conference that assembled the following year a resolution which, as finally adopted by that body,[1] stipulated that none of the contracting powers would resort to armed force for the recovery of contract debts claimed from the government of one country by the government of another country as being due to its citizens unless the debtor state should disregard an offer of arbitration or, after accepting the offer, should fail to submit to the award.[2] The action, while falling short of American hopes and while failing to realize the Drago Doctrine,[3] marked a distinct step forward in the elimination of causes which have too often resulted in international conflict. All in all, the Roosevelt policy and action in regard to the collection of debts involving nations was promotive of international amity and peace.

[1] Thirty-nine of the forty-four states represented in the Conference voted for the resolution in its final form.

[2] *American Journal of International Law*, II (suppl.), 82; Urena, *Los Estados Unidos y La Republica Dominicana*, pp. 43-49.

[3] See pp. 139 f. above.

Chapter VII
MEDIATION IN CENTRAL AMERICA

THE history of the countries of Central America during the nineteenth century is a dreary tale of successive disorders, revolutions, and wars. Temporarily and partially united on various occasions, the five republics quickly fell apart only to engage in conflicts recurring so frequently that the number is well-nigh uncountable. The daring attempts to exploit Central America that were made from time to time by such Americans as the famous adventurer, William Walker, added to the confusion. Such expeditions were uniformly denounced by the United States; for the official attitude of the Republic of the North throughout the period was in general that of a disinterested, friendly neighbor, concerned only in the welfare of the Central American countries and eager only to co-operate in efforts to establish a union among them.[1]

The Spanish-American War brought no immediate

---

[1] In 1851 Daniel Webster wrote: "How little the probability is that Central America . . . . can ever attain her proper dignity and proper destiny while divided into so many small states." *Senate Document No. 25* (Thirty-fourth Congress, first session), X, 20. In 1881 Secretary Blaine declared: "The United States is ready to avow that no subject appeals more strongly to its sympathy, nor more decidedly to its judgment than Central American Union. Nor is this a new policy. For many years this government has urged upon Central American states the importance of such a union" (*Foreign Relations* [1881], p. 816). The various attempts at union prior to 1906 are summarized in J. B. Scott, "Central American Peace Conference of 1907," *American Journal of International Law* (1908), pp. 121–25.

change in American policy in Central America, although the enlargement of American interests that followed the conflict naturally increased the desire of Americans for peace and progress in the Caribbean. With the construction of the Panama Canal the United States had utilitarian as well as altruistic reasons for wanting political stability in the region. Such facts furnish the historical background and the fundamental explanation of Roosevelt's policy in the mid-American republics.

Central America consists of five states with an aggregate area approximating one hundred and seventy thousand square miles, thrice the size of Illinois. The five countries have a combined population of about four million. In form, the government of each state is republican with powers divided among the legislative, executive, and judicial departments; in fact, the president is the center of political authority. Representative government as known in the United States does not exist.

With the exception of the Costa Ricans, among whom the Spanish element is dominant, the people of Central America are largely of Indian or mixed blood. The governing class as a rule come from the latter group. Although separated politically, the people of the five republics are essentially one in language, religion, customs, ideals, and traditions.

The attitude of Central Americans toward the United States has usually been one of fear, hatred, and distrust. In the capital of Costa Rica, by far the most advanced of the five states,[1] stands a heroic statue depicting a despised Yankee being driven from the soil of Central

---

[1] W. B. Hale, "Our Danger in Central America," *World's Work*, XXIV (1912), 445; S. MacClintock, "Revolutions and Interventions in Central America," *World Today*, XXI (1911), 956.

America.[1] In common with most Latin-Americans the aversion of the Central Americans to the United States is caused in part by a different attitude toward life. The American Minister to Honduras explains the difference in these words:

. . . . We must be prepared to recognize that there exists,—if not a live antagonism,—certainly, a wide gulf, between the Spanish American and the Anglo-Saxon. Their ways are not our ways and our ways are not theirs. Our direct methods of thought and action to them are often intolerably inconsiderate and rude. Possessed of great charm of manner and brilliant powers of mind, their indirect processes of reasoning and elaborate formalism, however, make extreme demands on our patience. Their political habits, their attitude toward law and the courts, are almost the reverse of our own. Their literary and social enjoyment are very distinct and their general sympathies are much more closely related to Europe than to the United States.[2]

When we consider the differences in viewpoint between a man like Roosevelt and a people such as are described above, the success of the American President's policy in dealing with them seems little short of phenomenal. From beginning to end his policy in the region was that of the peacemaker. Viewed as a whole he was highly successful.

Roosevelt's first attempt at mediation occurred in the summer of 1906 as the result of a war between Guatemala and Salvador in which Honduras subsequently joined as the ally of Salvador. Throughout June and the early part of July the American representatives in the region exerted themselves to avert an armed clash between the countries named, but their efforts resulted in failure.

[1] P. M. Brown, "American Diplomacy in Central America," *American Political Science Review*, VI (suppl.), 159.

[2] Brown, *op. cit.*, pp. 154 f.; on Central American resources and political and social conditions see *Senate Document No. 119* (Fifty-eighth Congress, third session), pp. 165 f.

MEDIATION IN CENTRAL AMERICA

Shortly after the opening of hostilities (July 10, 1906) Acting Secretary of State Bacon telegraphed Mr. Thompson, the American ambassador at Mexico, that the United States was "most anxious to do everything possible to preserve peace," but that such an outcome was "evidently impossible without active co-operation of Mexican Government." Accordingly, Bacon directed Thompson "to say to President Diaz that the President, earnestly wishing to help in avoiding war in Central America, desires to rely largely upon the advice of President Diaz."[1]

The Mexican President replied at once that he would join in anything that Roosevelt might desire to do in the matter and that he (Diaz) would send a telegram to the President of Salvador urging in strong terms the maintenance of neutrality. In conclusion Diaz suggested that Roosevelt send a dispatch of the same tenor, adding that he (Diaz) would hold his telegram until the next day in order that the two messages might reach their destination about the same time. In accordance with Diaz' suggestion Roosevelt on July 13, 1906, sent the following dispatch, *mutatis mutandis*, to the presidents of Salvador and Guatemala:

> I earnestly appeal to Salvador to take immediate steps toward settling questions pending with Guatemala, either by agreement to arbitrate or by direct negotiation for a definitive agreement between the two countries. Disturbance of the peace of Central America inflicts grievous injury upon the affected States and causes the gravest concern to the United States, whose sole desire is to see its neighbors at peace. The recent deplorable renewal of hostilities should not be allowed to be the precursor of a protracted and disastrous struggle, perhaps involving other States and leading to results of which the scope can not be fore-

[1] *Foreign Relations* (1906), p. 836. The American policy culminating in the peace of the "Marblehead" seems to have been guided by Bacon; see J. B. Scott, *Robert Bacon*, pp. 110–12; also editorial, *American Journal of International Law*, I (1907), 141.

seen. In the interest of humanity and the indispensable peace of Central America it becomes my duty to urge a settlement before it may be too late. I offer the deck of the *Marblehead*, now on the way to the coast of Salvador, as a neutral place where representatives of Guatemala and Salvador may meet to consider terms of agreement, an armistice between the contestants being meanwhile effected. . . . . My action has the full concurrence of the President of Mexico.[1]

Roosevelt's proposal was immediately accepted by both Guatemala and Salvador.[2] In his acceptance the President of Salvador expressed the belief that the prospect of peace would be enhanced if the American ministers to Guatemala and Salvador and the Mexican Minister to Central America would participate in the conference. His suggestion was adopted by the State Department, but with the express stipulation that the American representatives, as well as the Mexican Minister, were to be present "purely in an advisory and friendly capacity"[3] and that the negotiations were to be conducted directly between the representatives of the belligerents. The rôle of the American representatives, it may be noted, is an early instance of a practice commonly followed by the United States in European conferences after the rejection of the Versailles Treaty in 1919.

On the same day that Guatemala and Salvador accepted Roosevelt's proposal, Costa Rica informed the State Department of its desire to extend its good offices in behalf of peace "conjointly with the Government of the United States," but its offer does not seem to have been accepted.[4] Shortly afterward Honduras expressed the wish to join with Salvador in the peace negotiations.[5] As one of

---

[1] *Foreign Relations* (1906), p. 837.

[2] *Ibid.*, pp. 839 f.

[3] The expression occurs in three different dispatches (*ibid.*, pp. 844–46).

[4] *Ibid.*, p. 840.   [5] *Ibid.*, p. 841.

the parties to the controversy, its participation was welcomed.

Peace negotiations began on the "Marblehead" on July 18, 1906. In addition to representatives from the three belligerent states the conference included the Mexican Minister to Central America, a special delegate from Nicaragua, and the two American ministers accredited to Guatemala and to Salvador and Honduras respectively. The American Minister to Salvador and Honduras also served *pro forma* as the special delegate from Costa Rica. Negotiations were conducted and controlled throughout by the representatives of the belligerents. The delegates from Nicaragua and Costa Rica were "entirely complimentary without notes or influence," the former country being invited by Salvador without consultation with the American Minister. The representatives from Mexico and the United States confined their activities apparently to friendly suggestions.[1]

The conference was a complete success, an amicable agreement being reached by the belligerents within two days after the negotiations began. The fact that the convention was signed on the high seas in rough weather was declared by some of Roosevelt's critics to be proof that the delegates had been deliberately carried to sea in order to force them to sign an agreement that they would not have signed on land.[2] By the convention Guatemala, Salvador, and Honduras agreed as follows: first, to end hostilities; second, to exchange prisoners and recommend a general amnesty; third, to prevent the abuse of asylum; fourth, to negotiate within two months a general treaty

[1] *Ibid.*, pp. 848–51.

[2] Brown, *op. cit.*, p. 152, n. 2; see J. B. Scott, *Robert Bacon*, pp. 111 f., and *American Journal of International Law*, I, 141 f.

of peace and friendship, the capital of Costa Rica being designated as the place of meeting for the conference; fifth, to submit their recent difficulties and all new disagreements that might arise to the joint arbitration of the President of the United States and the President of Mexico.[1]

Roosevelt was greatly pleased over the outcome of his mediatory efforts. His course in securing the co-operation of Mexico, the first instance in which the United States had solicited the assistance of another American state in the settlement of international difficulties, was apparently justified by the results. At the same time his policy had promoted friendly relations with Mexico. He expressed his appreciation of the aid of President Diaz in the warmest terms.[2] The third Pan-American Conference, then in session at Rio de Janeiro, adopted by acclamation a resolution in which it expressed its gratification over the successful mediation of the two presidents in bringing about a peace agreement between the warring republics in Central America.[3]

The conference provided for in the "Marblehead" convention met upon invitation of the Costa Rican government at San José, the capital of Costa Rica, on September 15, 1906. The date had been selected as an auspicious one since it marked the anniversary of the independence of Central America. An invitation to participate was extended to Nicaragua as well as to the countries represented at the "Marblehead" conference, but the Nicaraguan presi-

[1] *Foreign Relations* (1906), pp. 851 f.; dispatches between Mexico and the Central American states are in Mexico, *Boletin oficial*, XXII, 235–41.

[2] *Foreign Relations* (1906), p. 849; note also Roosevelt's statement in his annual message to Congress (*ibid.*, p. 1).

[3] *Ibid.*, p. 852; see also Root to Roosevelt, August 2, 1906, *Roosevelt Papers*.

dent, Zelaya, after sending his acceptance withdrew it upon the ground that, not being a belligerent in the late conflict, Nicaragua had no connection with the proposed treaty.

A second invitation calling attention to the fact that neither Nicaragua nor Costa Rica need become parties to the treaty, but that mutual acquaintanceship and friendly feeling would result from the participation by all in the celebration of the anniversary of Central American independence, brought no reply.[1] President Zelaya's refusal to co-operate is said to have been due to his unwillingness to recognize the right of the United States to have a hand in Central American affairs.[2]

The San José Conference lasted ten days. It resulted in the following agreements: first, a general treaty of peace between the four republics; second, a convention for the establishment of an international Central American bureau in the city of Guatemala; third, a convention for the establishment of a Central American pedagogical institute in San José, Costa Rica.[3] The most notable provisions in the general treaty were the following: first, that differences among Salvador, Guatemala, and Honduras should be submitted to arbitration by the presidents of the United States and of Mexico; and second, that difficulties among Costa Rica, Salvador, and Honduras should be arbitrated by Central American tribunals established in accordance with the Corinto Convention of 1902 to which Guatemala had not been a party. Although the agreements of the San José Conference were short lived, they are

---

[1] *Foreign Relations* (1906), pp. 854–56.

[2] Nicaragua, *Memoria de Relaciones Exteriores* (1907), pp. xxvii, 5, cited in D. G. Munro, *Five Republics of Central America*, p. 207; see also Brown, *op. cit.*, p. 160. Cf. with Scott, "Central American Peace Conference of 1907," *op. cit.*, p. 126.

[3] *Foreign Relations* (1906), pp. 857–66.

significant as providing a basis for the work of the Washington Conference the following year and as indorsing the principle of arbitration by outsiders rather than by members of the Central American family, the mode that had been established previous to the "Marblehead" convention.

An understanding of the notable events of the next year makes it necessary at this point to turn back to earlier arrangements among the Central American republics. By the Corinto agreement of 1902, mentioned above, Costa Rica, Honduras, Nicaragua, and Salvador bound themselves to accept arbitration in order to settle "every difficulty or question" that might arise between them, agreeing to submit all controversies to a tribunal of Central American arbitrators.[1] In accordance with the arrangement a Central American Court of Arbitration was established in the autumn of 1902. The next year Guatemala, Honduras, Nicaragua, and Salvador entered into a treaty in which they agreed "to adjust the disputes that may arise" between them by arbitration.[2] Costa Rica does not seem to have accepted an invitation to ratify the treaty.[3] On August 21, 1904, the governments of the contracting republics issued a manifesto in which they declared that they would "aid each other by military force, if necessary, in maintaining the *status quo*."[4]

As a result of the foregoing agreements two methods of arbitration were in existence in Central America at the opening of the year 1907. By the Corinto Treaty of 1902 Costa Rica, Honduras, Nicaragua, and Salvador had agreed to submit their differences to arbitration by Central American tribunals. By the San José Treaty of 1906 Sal-

[1] *Ibid.* (1902), p. 882.
[2] *Ibid.* (1904), pp. 351 f.
[3] *New Pan-Americanism*, III, 115.
[4] *Foreign Relations* (1904), p. 541.

vador, Guatemala, and Honduras had agreed to submit
their difficulties to the arbitrament of the presidents of the
United States and Mexico. The first method was arbitration by members of the family; the second was arbitration
by outsiders. Which, if either, was to prevail?[1]

The question came to a crisis in 1907. Late in the preceding year a revolution had broken out in Honduras
against the government of President Bonilla. The rebels
seem to have received aid from the president of Nicaragua,
José Zelaya, who cherished ambitions to make himself head
of a united Central American state.[2] The insurrectionists
operated close to the Nicaraguan border, and in an effort
to crush their forces the Honduran troops crossed the
frontier early in January, 1907.

The Nicaraguan government immediately demanded
an explanation of the invasion and, shortly afterward,
claimed indemnity for the violation of Nicaraguan soil.
Later in the month the two governments, in accordance
with the Corinto Treaty, agreed to submit their grievances
to an arbitral tribunal composed of one member from each
of the republics of Honduras, Nicaragua, Salvador, and
Costa Rica. The refusal of Nicaragua or Honduras, or both
countries,[3] to disband their armies pending arbitration, as
directed by the arbitrators, resulted in the dissolution of
the tribunal (February 8). Thus the Corinto plan, when
put to the test, proved a failure.

[1] Munro, *op. cit.*, pp. 119 f. Munro errs in his statement that Costa Rica
was a party to the agreement to submit her differences with Honduras, Salvador,
and Guatemala, to American-Mexican arbitration. See Arts. 3 and 4 of the San
José Treaty (*Foreign Relations* [1906], pp. 857 f.).

[2] Munro, *op. cit.*, pp. 172 f., 209 f.; *New Pan-Americanism*, III, 123.

[3] The President of Honduras declared that his government "yielded from
the beginning and without restriction to every disposition the tribunal saw fit
to make" (*Foreign Relations* [1907], p. 618; see also pp. 616, 619, 621, 626, and
New Pan-Americanism, Vol. III, p. 120, n. 2).

In the emergency President Roosevelt, having previously secured the indorsement of Mexico, Guatemala, Salvador, and Costa Rica, telegraphed the presidents of Nicaragua and Honduras (February 11) urging the preservation of peace through the reconvening of the arbitral tribunal or the establishment of a new one.[1] President Bonilla of Honduras accepted Roosevelt's mediation and suggested that arbitration be intrusted to either Salvador or Costa Rica. Zelaya gave a partial assent, agreeing that the arbitrators might determine only "the reparations for violation of territory, without discussing the existence of offensive acts."[2] In a later dispatch to the President of Guatemala who, in common with the presidents of Costa Rica and Salvador, exerted his influence in behalf of arbitration, Zelaya declared that Nicaragua would accept "nothing but reparation."[3]

Efforts for arbitration failing, an armed conflict ensued in which the Nicaraguan forces and the revolutionists were victorious. Within a few weeks they captured the Honduran capital Tegucigalpa, the port of Amapala, and overthrew the government of Bonilla in spite of the military support he received from Salvador which had entered the conflict as the ally of Honduras. In the crisis Guatemala, fearing the designs of Zelaya, seems also to have given secret aid to Honduras. During the chaos that followed the capture of Tegucigalpa, the American *chargé d'affaires*, Philip Brown, assumed control with the aid of consuls and preserved order.[4]

The negotiations that resulted in the treaty of peace

[1] *Foreign Relations* (1907), p. 616.

[2] *Ibid.*, p. 619.

[3] *Ibid.*, p. 623.

[4] *Ibid.*, p. 627; cf. with Brown's explanation, *op. cit.*, p. 157.

between Nicaragua and Salvador were aided by Brown, although he reports that he "refrained from taking any part whatever, except when directly solicited to do so, when any particular point at issue was submitted" to him.[1] By the treaty of Amapala the two countries agreed to invite the other governments of Central America to join in a Central American Congress to be held at Corinto "to conclude a general treaty of peace and friendship having for a base obligatory arbitration" to replace the Corinto agreement of 1902 and the San José Treaty of 1906. Pending the conclusion of the general treaty, Nicaragua and Salvador agreed to submit any differences that might arise between them to "the obligatory arbitration of the Presidents of the United States and Mexico, conjointly." Upon the insistence of the Salvadorean and Nicaraguan ministers, Brown signed the treaty as a representative of the "moral force" of the United States.[2]

Four months of comparative quiet followed the treaty of Amapala. During the period Roosevelt gave no official recognition to President Dávila, the leader of the Honduran revolutionists who had become the head of the republic upon the overthrow of Bonilla.[3] In August the danger of a renewal of hostilities between Salvador and Nicaragua, caused apparently by Zelaya's intrigues and ambitions, brought an urgent request from the Honduran government for American support in an effort to maintain the neutrality of Honduras in the approaching conflict.

The predicament of Honduras will become apparent by a glance at the map (frontispiece). Owing to the geographical situation of Honduras, military operations between Salvador and Nicaragua are practically impossible except

[1] *Foreign Relations* (1907), p. 632.

[2] *Ibid.*, pp. 633 f.   [3] *Ibid.*, pp. 601–6.

through a violation of Honduran soil. Most Central American conflicts have in fact been fought in Honduras.

The imminence of war, in which it seemed probable that all of the Central American republics would become involved, led to an immediate recognition by Roosevelt of Dávila's government. It also led to a new attempt at mediation by the American and Mexican presidents, the initiative on this occasion coming from President Diaz.[1]

The effort was most successful, favorable responses being received almost immediately from the Central American governments. On September 17, 1907, the ministers of the five republics in Washington agreed upon a protocol which had been drawn up by Adee and Godoy, the Mexican *chargé d'affaires*, and had been approved by Root.[2] The protocol, subsequently approved by the Central American governments, provided for a Conference in Washington by representatives of the Central American countries in order to settle mutual differences and establish durable bases for peace. The protocol also stipulated that the presidents of Mexico and of the United States should be invited to appoint representatives "to lend their good and impartial offices in a purely friendly way toward the realization of the objects of the Conference." Pending the conclusion of the Conference the five republics bound themselves "to maintain peace and good relations among one another."[3]

A few days before the Conference was to assemble the way to peace was further advanced at a meeting at

---

[1] *Ibid.*, p. 637.

[2] Adee to Roosevelt, September 11, 1907; see also Adee to Roosevelt, September 12, 1907, *Roosevelt Papers*.

[3] *Foreign Relations* (1907), p. 645. The protocol is in *Foreign Relations* (1907), pp. 644 f., and in Mexico, *Boletin oficial*, XXIV, 343-45.

Amapala between the presidents of Salvador, Honduras, and Nicaragua. Here the common difficulties were discussed, and a unanimous agreement was reached that "all past differences, no matter what their nature may have been, shall be forgotten."[1]

On November 14, 1907, the Central American Peace Conference formally convened in the Bureau of American Republics in Washington. On the two preceding days the delegates held preliminary meetings to elect officers and adopt rules. Only the delegates from the five republics attended the preliminary sessions.

With the exception of the opening and the closing sessions the meetings of the Conference were not open to the general public.[2] The opening session was called to order by the American Secretary of State, Elihu Root, who delivered an address in which he urged the delegates to establish a durable peace among their several countries and to make such provision for the future as would render impossible a return of the unfortunate conditions that had existed in the past. One fancies that he can detect the voice of Roosevelt in the following passage from Root's address:

We can not fail, gentlemen, to be admonished by the many failures which have been made by the people of Central America to establish agreement among themselves which would be lasting, that the task you have before you is no easy one. The trial has often been made and the agreements which have been elaborated, signed, ratified, seem to have been written in water. . . . .

The all-important thing for you to accomplish is that while you enter into agreements which will, I am sure, be framed in consonance

[1] *Foreign Relations* (1907), p. 663.

[2] On November 15 Andrew Carnegie was cordially received by the Conference and upon request addressed the delegates urging upon them the adoption of arbitration for settling their difficulties (see *Monthly Bulletin of the International Bureau of the American Republics*, XXV [1907], 1371–73).

with the most peaceful aspirations and the most rigid sense of justice, you shall devise also some practical methods under which it will be possible to secure the performance of these agreements. The mere declaration of general principles, the mere agreement upon lines of policy and of conduct are of little value, unless there be practical and definite methods provided by which the responsibility for failing to keep the agreement may be fixed upon some definite person, and the public sentiment of Central America brought to bear to prevent the violation. The declaration that a man is entitled to his liberty would be of little value with us in this country were it not for the writ of habeas corpus that makes it the duty of a specific judge, when applied to, to inquire into the cause of his detention and set him at liberty if he is unjustly detained. . . . .

To find practical definite methods by which you shall make it somebody's duty to see that the great principles you declare are not violated, by which if an attempt be made to violate them the responsibility may be fixed upon the guilty individual—those, in my judgment, are the problems to which you should specifically and most earnestly address yourselves.[1]

After an address by the Mexican Ambassador the foreign minister from Costa Rica, Senor Anderson, replied in the name of the delegates. In his address Anderson explained the true cause of the conflicts that had disturbed Central America for almost a century. In a statement requiring courage he declared:

Our peoples are not warlike, and the only part they have played in the several wars which from independence to our day have stained the Central American soil with blood is that of dying with heroism and self-denial for a cause which they have not understood. The Central American wars have never been wars between nations, but wars between governments.[2]

The second meeting of the Conference began with the reading of the first article of the protocol of September 17, in which the object of the gathering was declared to be the

[1] *Foreign Relations* (1907), p. 688.

[2] *Ibid.*, p. 692; see also S. MacClintock, *op. cit.*, XXI, 959 f.

discussion of "the steps to be taken and the measures to be adopted in order to adjust any differences which exist, among said Republics, or any of them, and for the purpose of concluding a treaty which shall determine their general relations."

The reading of the foregoing article brought the question of claims or controversies growing out of the late conflict in Central America before the Conference as the first matter for discussion and settlement. The strained relations that had existed for months among several of the republics made the problem a delicate one, and for a moment each delegation waited for another to take the lead. The silence was broken by the chairman of the delegation from Salvador. He rose and said: "Salvador has no claim of any kind to present against any of the other republics." His statement was immediately followed amid applause by similar declarations by the chairmen of the other delegations. The mutual surrender of claims was a happy augury for the success of the Conference; come what might, the gathering was to be free apparently from disaster due to events in the past.[1]

The question of the claims having been satisfactorily settled, the Conference next attacked the problem of the future relations of the Central American republics. A wide divergence in views at once appeared. On the one hand, the delegation from Honduras, supported by representatives from Nicaragua, proposed a union of the five countries. On the other hand, the delegates from Costa Rica objected strongly even to the discussion of union, insisting that under the protocol the Conference had no authority to consider such a matter; they urged, instead, that the

[1] The action of the delegates was, of course, the logical result of the Amapala Conference described on pp. 186 f.

Conference proceed to draw up a general treaty of peace along the lines of the San José Treaty of 1906.

To solve the difficulty a committee composed of one representative from each delegation was appointed, but the committee proved unable to arrive at an agreement. Two reports were submitted to the Conference, one supporting the proposal of Honduras and the other the course advocated by Guatemala. A way out of the *impasse* was suggested by the American representative, William I. Buchanan, who proposed that the Conference postpone the consideration of both reports and proceed, instead, to prepare projects for conventions covering matters outside the scope of either report and, in particular, to provide for an international court. Buchanan's suggestion was supported by the Mexican representative and was adopted by the Conference. As the work of the gathering proceeded, the question of union became less vital, and was eventually disposed of to the general satisfaction of the delegates at one of the closing sessions by an agreement to include in the minutes a statement of the views of the advocates of consolidation.

The work of the Conference as embodied in treaties and conventions was as follows: first, a general treaty of peace and friendship; second, an additional convention relating to revolutions, civil wars, and presidential elections; third, a convention for the establishment of a Central American court of justice; fourth, a convention for the extradition of criminals; fifth, a convention on railway communications; sixth, a convention concerning future Central American conferences; and seventh, conventions for the establishment of an international Central American bureau and for a Central American pedagogical institute.[1]

[1] The treaties and conventions are printed in Malloy, *op. cit.*, II, 2391-2420.

The last session of the Conference was held on December 20. In the forenoon the delegates called in a body on President Roosevelt and Secretary Root to inform them that the Conference had completed its work and to express gratitude for the assistance given by the American government. In the afternoon the Conference was formally closed at a session over which Secretary Root presided and in which addresses were given by the President of the Conference, the Mexican Ambassador, and the American Secretary of State.[1]

The most important results of the Conference were the general treaty of peace, the convention for the creation of a Central American court of justice, and the convention for the establishment of an international Central American bureau. The general treaty of peace and the convention providing for the court of justice were to remain in force for ten years; the convention establishing the Central American bureau was to run for fifteen years.

The most significant articles in the general treaty of peace and the additional convention relating thereto were those in which the Central American republics bound themselves first to "decide every difference or difficulty that may arise amongst them, of whatsoever nature it may be, by means of the Central American Court of Justice" (Art. 1); second, to observe the "absolute neutrality" of Honduran territory in the event of any conflict between the other republics (Art. 3); third, to recognize mutually all Central Americans as citizens upon their compliance

[1] The account of the Conference given above is based largely on the official report of William I. Buchanan, the American representative, and on the appended documents. Buchanan's report is published in *Foreign Relations* (1907), pp. 655–727. See also Mexico, *Boletin oficial*, XXV, 138–80, 245–52; and *Monthly Bulletin of the International Bureau of American Republics*, XXV (1907), 1334–73.

with the respective constitutional laws (Art. 6); fourth, to refuse recognition in another Central American republic to a government resulting from a coup d'état (Art. 1, additional convention); and fifth, to abstain from intervention in case of civil war in another country (Art. 2, additional convention).[1]

The establishment of the Central American court of justice aroused more general interest than any other act of the Conference. According to Buchanan, the court was "an outgrowth of the efforts made by Secretary of State Root in his instructions to the delegates of the United States to the Second Peace Conference at The Hague toward endeavoring to secure a 'world's international court of justice.' "[2]

In the convention creating the court the five republics bound themselves, as in the general treaty explained above, to submit all controversies to the tribunal in case diplomatic efforts to reach an understanding should fail, and to accept in all instances the judgment of the court as final. The convention included various provisions designed to make the court independent: the five judges were to be appointed, one by the legislature of each republic, and were to serve for a term of five years; they were to enjoy the privileges of diplomatic representatives, but were not to practice their profession or hold public office during their terms of service; as representatives of "the national conscience of Central America," they were allowed to act in cases involving the republics to which they owed their appointment.

[1] The treaty and additional convention are printed in *Foreign Relations* (1907), pp. 692–96.

[2] *Ibid.*, p. 676; see also Luis Anderson, "Peace Conference of Central America," *American Journal of International Law*, II (1908), 146, 151.

The court was to be competent to determine its own jurisdiction. In deciding points of fact it was to be governed only by its free judgment. In passing upon points of law it was to be controlled by the principles of international law. It was to have power to fix the *status quo* in any controversy pending before it, and to have authority to appoint special commissioners to carry out its measures in Central America, although its orders were to be sent through the governments of the countries concerned. The decisions of the court were to receive the concurrence of at least three of the judges. The five republics bound themselves to obey and enforce all orders of the court. They also joined in a solemn declaration that "on no ground nor in any case [would] they consider the present convention as void."[1]

The conventions providing for the establishment of an international Central American bureau and for the creation of a Central American pedagogical institute[2] were both based on the San José treaties of 1906. The Bureau proved to be especially useful. By its service as a clearing house of information, its publication of the periodical *Centro America*, its assistance to commerce and industry, and its activity in preparing plans for joint action in matters of common concern, it has done much to promote national feeling throughout Central America.[3] According to D. G. Munro, the Bureau "has perhaps been the only institution provided for at the meeting in 1907 which has thus far fully justified its creation."[4]

[1] *Foreign Relations* (1907), pp. 697–700.

[2] *Ibid.*, pp. 705–8.

[3] W. F. Slade, "Federation of Central America," *Journal of Race Development*, VIII (1917), 234–41.

[4] *Op. cit.*, p. 225.

The general treaty of peace and the Central American court of justice have not fully realized the hopes of their originators and sponsors. It is hardly to be expected, perhaps, that five governments that had eyed one another with open or veiled hostility for decades should suddenly become harmonious neighbors.

Peaceful relations at all events did not immediately develop in Central America. Six weeks had not elapsed since the inauguration of the court of justice (May 25, 1908)[1] before need arose for the services of the tribunal. Early in July the Nicaraguan President telegraphed the President of Costa Rica that a revolutionary movement had broken out in Honduras; that Guatemala and Salvador had instigated the insurrection and were participating in it; and that to prevent the situation from becoming serious the matter should be taken up immediately by the court of justice.[2]

The truth seems to be that the Nicaraguan president, Zelaya, for years a disturbing element in Central America, had by his intrigues in Honduras aroused the fears of Salvador and Guatemala and that the two countries, aided by Honduran rebels, had decided to strike without imperiling their safety by further delay.

Upon the receipt of Zelaya's telegram the President of Costa Rica immediately informed the presidents of the other republics that he had brought the controversy before the court of justice. At the request of the court, Costa Rica subsequently proposed mediation or the submission of the

---

[1] An account of the elaborate ceremonies accompanying the establishment of the court is given in *Foreign Relations* (1908), pp. 217–47.

[2] The court was located at Cartago, Costa Rica. Andrew Carnegie gave $100,000 for the creation of a temple of peace for the exclusive use of the court. The destruction of Cartago by an earthquake resulted in the removal of the court in 1910 to San José.

dispute to the decision of the tribunal. Honduras and Nicaragua at once filed formal complaints before the court while the court promptly responded by requesting proof of the charges. At the same time the court ordered Guatemala, Salvador, and Nicaragua to reduce their military forces to a peace basis and to refrain from any movements that might suggest interference in the internal affairs of Honduras.[1] The orders of the court were obeyed, the immediate danger of war was ended, the revolution died away, and in December the court rendered a decision in which by a vote of three judges it absolved Salvador from all responsibility for the insurrection in Honduras, and by the vote of four judges it exonerated Guatemala. Neither side was required to pay the costs.[2]

Although the decision was criticized adversely owing to the fact that most of the judges had voted in accordance with the interests of the governments that had appointed them, the case is significant because it prevented a general war, because it constituted the first action of the court, and "because it was probably the first instance of States not parties to a difficulty haling the actual parties before a court for a trial of their case."[3] Since the Washington Conference of 1907, it should be added, no international war has taken place in Central America.

The later history of the Central American court of justice has been unfortunate. On two different occasions during President Taft's administration the tribunal made notable efforts to intervene in Central American revolutions, but without success. Its efforts, however, increased

---

[1] Editorial, "First Case before the Central American Court of Justice," *American Journal of International Law*, II (1908), 835–41.

[2] *New Pan-Americanism*, III, 136 f.; Munro, *op. cit.*, pp. 217–19.

[3] *New Pan-Americanism*, III, 137.

its prestige. Then came its deathblow. In the Bryan-Chamorro Treaty of August 5, 1914, Nicaragua, in return for $3,000,000 in gold, granted the United States the right to build and operate an interoceanic canal across Nicaragua as well as to establish on Nicaraguan territory a naval base bordering upon Fonseca Bay.[1] Costa Rica, Salvador, and Honduras looked upon the grant as an impairment of their rights and, after making vigorous protests, they attempted to prevent Nicaragua from carrying out the provisions of the treaty by an appeal to the court. The decision of the court was in favor of the three republics, but both the United States and Nicaragua refused to accept the verdict.

Their attitude proved fatal to the court; it was of course unable to enforce its decision. When the question of continuing its existence came up the following year, nothing could be done owing to the withdrawal of Nicaragua. As a result a tribunal, described at one time as "the most remarkable judicial organ in the world,"[2] came to an end.

In the death of the court Roosevelt, of course, had no part. The exact extent of his responsibility for its birth and for the major features of American policy in Central America during his administration is to a degree a matter of conjecture. In his public addresses he gives little attention to Central American affairs. In comparison with the other problems that engaged his attention conditions in Central America may have seemed of small consequence.

But it must be remembered that the Panama Canal and all that affected the passageway loomed large in Roosevelt's mind. He was never indifferent to developments in its neighborhood. Moreover, his versatility, his energy, his

[1] Malloy, *op. cit.*, III, 2740–42.
[2] *New Pan-Americanism*, III, 129.

intimate contact with the Department of State, his dominant interest in all that affected American foreign relations, make it certain that he was concerned in the affairs of mid-America. His messages to Congress, his dispatches to President Diaz and to the executive heads of the five Central American republics, as well as the comments in his correspondence,[1] furnish concrete evidence of his interest in the "Marblehead" convention, the San José treaties, and the Washington Conference.

Roosevelt's passion for law and order, as well as his desire to promote the social and economic stability and progress of the countries of the Caribbean, seen in particular in his policy in Cuba and Santo Domingo, furnish corroboratory evidence of his controlling influence in determining the policy of the American government toward the five republics. In view of such facts it is not open to question that back of the work of the Department of State in promoting mediation in Central America there was, as usual, the guiding hand of Theodore Roosevelt.

[1] See, for example, Roosevelt to Hay, January 14, 1905, and Root to Roosevelt, August 2, 1906, *Roosevelt Papers*.

Chapter VIII

ROOSEVELTIAN IMPERIALISM

ROOSEVELTIAN imperialism as manifested in the Caribbean was opportunist in character, not planned or predetermined. Like the conscript fathers of ancient Rome, Roosevelt was led from one action to another by the swift current of events which during his administration seemed to change with kaleidoscopic rapidity. Inheriting the results of the Spanish-American War, he came to the presidency when the government was engaged in measures initiated by his predecessor. With negligible exceptions he was heartily in sympathy with the undertakings which had been begun. Launched upon the project of an isthmian canal, which he had advocated for years, he soon found himself engaged in problems arising from the relationship which that enterprise bore to the wider circle of the Caribbean. Thus he became involved first in Colombia, next in Venezuela, then in Santo Domingo, and finally in Central America. With each problem he dealt in the manner of the practical man of affairs rather than in the fashion of the doctrinaire or the man of predetermined policies.

Although Roosevelt seems to have realized the dangers inherent in the employment of force by European governments in the Venezuelan episode of 1902, he confined his action in the crisis to a tender of good offices and mediation and to declarations that the United States under the

Monroe Doctrine did "not guarantee any State against punishment if it misconducts itself, provided that punishment does not take the form of the acquisition of territory by any non-American power."[1] Convinced of the dangers in a policy of inaction, he adopted a different plan of procedure when a similar situation developed two years later in Santo Domingo. To meet the new problem he enlarged the scope of the Monroe Doctrine, justifying his interpretation on the ground that "if we had refused to apply the Doctrine to changing conditions it would now be completely outworn, it would not meet any of the needs of the present day, and indeed would probably by this time have sunk into complete oblivion."[2]

Accordingly he assumed the rôle of receiver in order to prevent European governments from intervening in Santo Domingo for the collection of claims against the island republic. Balked in his purpose temporarily by the failure of the Senate to ratify the convention authorizing the arrangement, he proceeded to meet the situation by a *modus vivendi* under which the Dominican revenues were administered for more than two years by an American army officer.

In adopting such measures Roosevelt usually paid little attention to the far-reaching issues involved or the influence his action might have on his successors.[3] On most occasions "he was pure act."[4] An exception was his course in Cuba. Here he said he intended to establish a precedent, if intervention became necessary, by refusing to ask per-

[1] *House Document No. 1* (Fifty-seventh Congress, first session), I, 195; see also *Senate Document No. 119* (Fifty-eighth Congress, third session), VII, 406.

[2] *House Document No. 1* (Fifty-ninth Congress, first session), I, xxxiii.

[3] See, for example, *ibid.*, p. xxxv, and Roosevelt to Taft, August 21, 1907, *Roosevelt Papers*.

[4] Henry Adams, *Education of Henry Adams*, p. 417.

mission of Congress because he believed that it was for the enormous interest of the government for the executive to have greater independence in dealing with foreign powers.[1] Years after the Santo Domingo episode he expressed the opinion that the action taken in the island "should serve as a precedent in all similar cases,"[2] but at the time his main thought seems to have been to solve the immediate problem confronting him.

Roosevelt's opportunism was not due to lack of vision or purpose. His policy was rather the outgrowth of his conception of the nature and limitations of democracy. In a letter devoted largely to the Russo-Japanese situation, he sets forth his view as follows:[3]

I appreciate to the full the difficulty of committing oneself to a course of action in reliance upon the proposed action of a free people which is not accustomed at present to carrying out with an iron will a long-continued course of foreign policy. It would be well-nigh impossible, even if it were not highly undesirable, for this country to carry out any policy save one which had become part of the inherited tradition of the country, like the Monroe Doctrine. Not merely could I, for instance, only make such an engagement for four years, but I would have to reckon with a possible overthrow in Congress, with the temper of the people, with many different conditions. In consequence, my policy must of necessity be somewhat opportunist.[4]

In most instances Roosevelt's opportunism was guided or dominated by his devotion to the cause of national

[1] Roosevelt to Taft, September 17, 1906, *Roosevelt Papers.*

[2] *Autobiography*, p. 507.

[3] Roosevelt to Cecil Spring-Rice, December 27, 1904, quoted in T. Dennett, *Roosevelt and the Russo-Japanese War*, pp. 44 f.

[4] At a later time (1913) Roosevelt wrote: "Nine-tenths of wisdom is to be wise in time, and at the right time; and my whole foreign policy was based on the exercise of intelligent forethought and of decisive action sufficiently far in advance of any likely crisis to make it improbable that we would run into serious trouble" (*Autobiography*, p. 508).

defense. With him national defense was a passion; it was, indeed, almost a religion. No language was too forceful to express his scorn of national weakness nor his admiration of national strength.

At one time he says, "No friendliness with other nations, no good will for them or by them, can take the place of national self-reliance. . . . . We must work out our destiny by our own strength."[1] At another time he declares, "The nation that cannot fight, the people that have lost the fighting edge, that have lost the virile virtues, occupy a position as dangerous as it is ignoble."[2] On another occasion he maintains, "Diplomacy is utterly useless where there is no force behind it; the diplomat is the servant, not the master, of the soldier."[3]

"To play a great part in the world," David Starr Jordan quotes him as saying, "a nation must perform those deeds of blood which above all else bring national renown."[4] "In public as in private life a bold front tends to insure peace and not strife," he insists; "if we possess a formidable navy, small is the chance indeed that we shall ever be dragged into a war to uphold the Monroe Doctrine. If we do not possess such a navy, war may be forced upon us at any time."[5] In his *Autobiography* he writes, "I advocate preparation for war in order to avert war; and I should never advocate war unless it were the only alternative to dishonor."[6] "Merely for the protection of our

[1] *American Ideals* (Homeward Bound ed.), p. 377.

[2] *Autobiography*, p. 253.

[3] J. B. Bishop, *Theodore Roosevelt*, I, 76.

[4] *Days of a Man*, p. 305.

[5] Bishop, *op. cit.*, I, 76; see also Roosevelt's letter to Schurz, September 8, 1905, *Speeches, Correspondence, and Political Papers of Carl Schurz* (New York, 1913), VI, 434–36.

[6] *Op. cit.*, p. 207.

own shores we need a great navy," he declares; "and what is more, we need it to protect our interests in the islands from which it is possible to command our shores and to protect our commerce on the high seas."[1]

Roosevelt's zeal for strength and power dates from his boyhood. Weak and puny from long-continued attacks of asthma, he fell a victim on one occasion to two stronger lads who proceeded to make life miserable for him. Describing the incident in later years he wrote:

> The worst feature was that when I finally tried to fight them I discovered that either one singly could not only handle me with easy contempt, but handle me so as not to hurt me much and yet to prevent my doing any damage whatever in return.[2]

Impressed by the bitter and humiliating experience, he began to make his body,

> faithfully going through various exercises, at different times of the day, to broaden the chest narrowed by this terrible shortness of breath, to make the limbs and back strong, and able to bear the weight of what was coming to him later in life.[3]

The next chapter in the development of Roosevelt's passion for strength came probably from his study of the War of 1812. In that conflict, it seemed to him, the dishonor and failure that characterized American military efforts were the inevitable fruits of the lack of preparation for which he held Jefferson primarily responsible.

Third in the series of causes which brought about his devotion to vigor was probably his life in the open— camping trips in Maine, hunting expeditions in the

---

[1] *American Ideals*, p. 279; see also *Addresses and Presidential Messages*, p. 323, and *Roosevelt-Lodge Correspondence*, I, 214, 218 f.

[2] *Autobiography*, p. 32.

[3] Comment of Roosevelt's sister, quoted in H. Howland, *Theodore Roosevelt and His Times*, p. 2; see also C. R. Robinson, *My Brother Theodore Roosevelt*, pp. 50, 92.

Rockies, ranch life in the Dakota Bad Lands. Here, as on the frontier, the things that counted were courage, endurance, action, physical prowess. Impressed by such experiences Roosevelt became the country's outstanding exponent and advocate of personal and national self-defense and security.

The first manifestation of President Roosevelt's ardor for national defense appears in his course in the isthmian canal project. From the beginning his interest in the enterprise was primarily in the relation of the canal to naval strength and strategy. On February 14, 1900, he gave the following explanation of his opposition to the first Hay-Pauncefote Treaty in a letter to Captain A. T. Mahan: "I do not see why we should dig a canal if we are not to fortify it so as to insure its being used for ourselves and against our foes in time of war."[1]

In like manner, Roosevelt justified his Panama policy. The military motive which occupied so important a place in the inception of the canal was, indeed, one of the reasons for the rejection of the Hay-Herran Treaty by the Colombians, who believed that the canal should be constructed and dedicated primarily to serve the needs of peace, not war.

Roosevelt's anxiety concerning the European blockade of the Venezuelan ports in 1902 was also caused largely by his concern lest an approach to the Panama Canal should fall into the possession of a potential enemy. His intervention in Santo Domingo was in like manner partly an outgrowth of his intention to prevent another of the outposts of the canal from coming under the control of a European

---

[1] Bishop, *op. cit.*, I, 143. See also Roosevelt's address at Chicago, April 2, 1903, in *Addresses and Presidential Messages*, p. 115, and his letter to his brother-in-law, in *Letters to Anna Roosevelt Cowles*, pp. 236 f.

country. His desire for coaling stations in Cuba and his attempt to purchase the islands of St. Thomas and St. John from Denmark were also due to the strategic value of such possessions for the defense of Panama.

Rooseveltian imperialism rested on the belief that civilized peoples have definite obligations toward the backward tribes or races of the earth. He mentions[1] with approval Kipling's verses on "The White Man's Burden":

> Take up the White Man's burden—
> Send forth the best ye breed—
> To bind your sons to exile
> To serve your captives' need;
> To wait in heavy harness,
> On fluttered folk and wild—
> Your new caught, sullen peoples,
> Half-devil and half-child.

Roosevelt was outspoken in his praise of British imperialism. When governor of New York, he said :

England's rule in India and Egypt has been of great benefit to England, for it has trained up generations of men accustomed to look at the larger and loftier side of public life. It has been of even greater benefit to India and Egypt, and finally, and most of all, it has advanced the cause of civilization.[2]

Some time later he paid an even higher tribute to England:

It is the great expanding peoples who bequeath to the future ages the great memories and material results of their achievements, and the nations which shall have sprung from their loins, England standing as the archetype and best exemplar of all such mighty nations.[3]

[1] "The White Man's Burden" is evidently the poem to which Roosevelt refers in his letter to Lodge (January 12, 1899) and of which he writes: "Rather poor poetry, but good sense from the expansion standpoint" (*Roosevelt-Lodge Correspondence*, I, 384).

[2] Address to Hamilton Club, Chicago, April 10, 1899, in *Strenuous Life* (Homeward Bound ed.), pp. 19 f.

[3] *Ibid.*, p. 34.

ROOSEVELTIAN IMPERIALISM

Five years afterward he wrote his friend Spring-Rice: "It was a good thing for Egypt and the Soudan, and for the world, when England took Egypt and the Soudan. It is a good thing for India that England should control it."[1]

Nor was his praise of imperialism limited to that of Great Britain. He writes:

Every expansion of civilization makes for peace. In other words, every expansion of a great civilized power means a victory for law, order, and righteousness. This has been the case in every instance of expansion during the present century, whether the expanding power were France or England, Russia or America. In every instance the expansion has been of benefit, not so much to the power nominally benefitted, as to the whole world.[2]

In view of such opinions it is natural that rulership over primitive peoples should have appealed strongly to Roosevelt. In a letter to Senator Lodge (January 22, 1900), he says: "The thing I should really like to do would be to be the first civil Governor General of the Philippines. I believe I could do that job, and it is a job emphatically worth doing."[3]

In Roosevelt's comments concerning the treatment of the backward races—and his letters and speeches contain numberless references to the subject—he always insists upon the necessity of government in the interests of the governed, not of the governing. For example, in speaking of American duties in the West and East Indies (February 13, 1899), he says: "We must not fail to perform them in a

[1] Bishop, *op. cit.*, I, 297. See also Roosevelt, *American Ideals*, pp. 290, 293, 300, 305 f.; and the address "On British Imperial Administration," at the Guildhall, London, in *Presidential Addresses and State Papers and European Addresses*, pp. 2309-21.

[2] *Strenuous Life*, p. 29; see also *Public Addresses of Theodore Roosevelt, Governor*, p. 305.

[3] *Roosevelt-Lodge Correspondence*, I, 437; see also pp. 422 f., and *Letters to Anna Roosevelt Cowles*, p. 241.

way that will redound to the advantage of the people of the islands."[1] Two months later he declares:

> We must see to it that the islands are administered with absolute honesty and with good judgment. If we let the public service of the islands be turned into the prey of the spoils politician we shall have begun to tread the path which Spain trod to her own destruction. We must send out there only good and able men, chosen for their fitness, and not because of their partisan service.[2]

Later, when president, he informed certain politicians: "Absolutely no appointments in the insular possessions will be dictated or controlled by political considerations."[3] In his first message to Congress (December 3, 1901) he said:

> Our aim is high. We do not desire to do for the islanders merely what has elsewhere been done for tropic peoples by even the best foreign governments. We hope to do for them what has never before been done for any peoples of the tropics—to make them fit for self-government after the fashion of the really free nations.[4]

Although he was eager to serve as a benevolent father or a big brother, Roosevelt always denied that occupancy of the land entitled primitive peoples to delay or prevent the progress of civilization. In the *Winning of the West*, he wrote:

---

[1] *Public Papers of Theodore Roosevelt, Governor*, p. 264.

[2] *Strenuous Life*, pp. 20 f.; see also Roosevelt to Taft, August 21, 1907, *Roosevelt Papers*.

[3] Bishop, *op. cit.*, I, 153; see also New York *Times*, September 25, 1901.

[4] *Addresses and Presidential Messages*, p. 316. Roosevelt's views, as expressed above, are in striking disagreement with a remark David Starr Jordan quotes him as making in a conversation in 1899. According to Jordan, Roosevelt then said: "I wish to God we were out of the Philippines." Some time later he wrote Dr. Jordan suggesting that the remark ought not to be repeated, "it being a matter of private conversation, which if made public he [Roosevelt] would have to deny" (Jordan, *op. cit.*, p. 307). See also *Roosevelt-Lodge Correspondence*, I, 406, and *Letters of Archie Butt*, pp. 77 f.

It is indeed a warped, perverse, and silly morality which could forbid a course of conquest that has turned whole continents into the seats of mighty and flourishing civilized nations. . . . . It is as idle to apply to savages the rules of international morality which obtains between stable and cultured communities, as it would be to judge the fifth-century English conquest of Britain by the standards of today. . . . . The rude, fierce settler who drives the savage from the land lays all civilized mankind under a debt to him.[1]

In an address in Chicago, delivered less than two weeks before he became president, Roosevelt elaborated his ideas of the relation between barbarism and civilization as follows:

Barbarism has, and can have, no place in a civilized world. It is our duty toward the people living in barbarism to see that they are freed from their chains, and we can free them only by destroying barbarism itself. The missionary, the merchant, and the soldier may each have to play a part in this destruction, and in the consequent uplifting of the people. Exactly as it is the duty of a civilized power scrupulously to respect the rights of all weaker civilized powers and gladly to help those who are struggling toward civilization, so it is its duty to put down savagery and barbarism. . . . . Not only in our own land, but throughout all history, the advance of civilization has been of incalculable benefit to mankind, and those through whom it has advanced deserve the highest honor. All honor to the missionary, all honor to the soldier, all honor to the merchant who now in our own day have done so much to bring light into the world's dark places.[2]

The logical result of Roosevelt's philosophy appeared in his treatment of Colombia in the Panama affair; for the course which he followed was due in part to the anger and

[1] *Op. cit.*, III, 128–31. Elsewhere Roosevelt writes: "Nineteenth century democracy needs no more complete vindication for its existence than the fact that it has kept for the white race the best portions of the New World's surface, temperate America and Australia. . . . . Democracy, with the clear instinct of race selfishness, saw the race foe and kept out the dangerous alien" (*American Ideals*, p. 307).

[2] *Strenuous Life*, pp. 241 f.

contempt which he felt for the Colombians. Writing about his action to Rudyard Kipling (November 1, 1904), he condemns "the vague individuals of serious minds and limited imaginations who think that a corrupt pithecoid community" like Colombia "is entitled to just the treatment that I would give, say to Denmark or Switzerland."[1] Again, in a letter to W. R. Thayer (July 2, 1915), he says:

To talk of Colombia as a responsible Power to be dealt with as we would deal with Holland or Belgium or Switzerland or Denmark is a mere absurdity. The analogy is with a group of Sicilian or Calabrian bandits; with Villa and Carranza at this moment. You could no more make an agreement with the Colombian rulers than you could nail currant jelly to a wall—and the failure to nail currant jelly to a wall is not due to the nail; it is due to the currant jelly.[2]

The paternal quality in Roosevelt's imperialism appears in his treatment of Cuba, his dealings with Santo Domingo, his policy in Central America, and his forbearance toward Venezuela during the latter part of his administration. In his *Autobiography* he writes:

If any great civilized power, Russia or Germany, for instance, had behaved toward us as Venezuela under Castro behaved, this country would have gone to war at once. We did not go to war with Venezuela merely because our people declined to be irritated by the actions of a weak opponent.[3]

Few thoughtful people will deny the complexity of the problem presented by the occupancy of choice regions of the earth by tribes or peoples who have not progressed in the arts of civilization sufficiently to make adequate use of the natural resources within their grasp. But it is well to

[1] Bishop, *op. cit.*, I, 332; see also Roosevelt's letter to Spring-Rice (January 18, 1904), on p. 297. Cf. with John Marshall's statement concerning "the perfect equality of nations" (Wheaton, *Reports*, X, 66, 122).

[2] W. R. Thayer, *John Hay*, II, 327 f.

[3] *Op. cit.*, pp. 506 f.; cf. with his statement in a letter to Taft, August 21, 1907, *Roosevelt Papers*.

note that Roosevelt's justification for his treatment of Colombia is that which has usually been advanced by con-
querors—national security and the bestowal of the bless-
ings of civilization upon the conquered. At best the philosophy which underlies the policy of the strong in such
instances is akin to that of one of old time who said: "It
is expedient for us that one man die for the people and not
that the whole nation perish."

With one or two possible exceptions to be mentioned
later President Roosevelt had no ambition to annex territory in the Caribbean. "We have not the slightest desire
to secure any territory at the expense of any of our neighbors," he declared in his first annual message,[1] a declaration repeated in a variety of forms many times during his
life. Unlike his friend, General Leonard Wood, who favored the annexation of Cuba,[2] Roosevelt apparently had
no desire to retain possession of the island.[3] As soon as the
arrangements for turning over the government to the inhabitants could be completed, he withdrew the American
forces and terminated the American occupation—an act
in which he took just pride in later years.[4]

When the outbreak of revolution in 1905 threatened
life and property in Cuba, Roosevelt intervened with the
utmost reluctance and only after exhausting other alternatives. On this occasion, too, he ended the American
occupation as early as seemed feasible and again placed

[1] *House Document No. 1* (Fifty-seventh Congress, first session), I, xxxvii;
see also *ibid.* (Fifty-eighth Congress, third session), I, xli; and Roosevelt,
Strenuous Life, pp. 193 f.

[2] *Roosevelt-Lodge Correspondence*, I, 413.

[3] Roosevelt, *Strenuous Life*, p. 18; see also Hay's letter to Roosevelt, July 25,
1902, *Roosevelt Papers*.

[4] Roosevelt, *Strenuous Life*, pp. 239 f.; *Addresses and Presidential Messages*,
p. 7.

the island in control of the natives, but with the solemn warning that the insurrectionary habit could end only in measures by the United States such as would guarantee permanent peace.

Nor did Roosevelt desire territorial acquisitions on the island of Haiti. He assured the Haitian Minister at Washington

that the Government of the United States of America has no intention whatever to annex either Haiti or Santo Domingo, nor do we wish to obtain possession by force or by means of negotiations, and that even in the event that the citizens of the one or the other Republic should request incorporation or annexation with the American Union there would be no inclination on the part of the National Government, nor on the part of public opinion, to accept such a proposition.[1]

In 1904 he wrote a friend that he had about the same desire to annex Santo Domingo "as a gorged boa constrictor might have to swallow a porcupine wrong-end-to."[2]

Aside from a desire to control the canal zone and to acquire naval and coaling stations for its defense, Roosevelt then may be said to have had no interest in land-grabbing in the Caribbean, or elsewhere.[3] He would have been glad, however, to see the termination of European colonies on this side of the Atlantic. In a letter written in 1898 he said:

I should myself like to shape our foreign policy with a purpose ultimately of driving off this continent every European power. I would

[1] *Foreign Relations*, Part I (1907), p. 354.

[2] Bishop, *op. cit.*, I, 431; see also *House Document No. 1* (Fifty-ninth Congress, first session), I, 334.

[3] See Hay's letter to Roosevelt, September 26, 1901, in which Hay reports a request from Uruguay for the United States to establish a protectorate over it; also Hay's note of October 24, 1901, relating to the purchase of the Danish West Indies (*Roosevelt Papers*).

begin with Spain, and in the end would take all other European nations, including England. It is even more important to prevent any new nation from getting a foothold.[1]

Roosevelt's policy does not seem to have been influenced to any marked degree by a desire to stimulate the economic penetration of the Caribbean by American business men and American corporations. In furtherance of his political ends, it is true, he frequently pointed out the commercial advantages that would come to the United States from the measures he commended. For example, in urging the ratification of the Dominican Convention of 1905, he called the attention of the Senate to the disadvantages under which American citizens engaged in business in the island labored when unprotected by the intervention of the United States as contrasted with the advantages of their competitors from other lands who were so protected, if need arose, by the action of their governments. In a special message to the Senate (February 15, 1905) he said:

Under the accepted law of nations foreign governments are within their right, if they choose to exercise it, when they actively intervene in support of the contractual claims of their subjects. They sometimes exercise this power, and on account of commercial rivalries there is a growing tendency on the part of other governments more and more to aid diplomatically in the enforcement of the claims of their subjects. In view of the dilemma in which the United States is thus placed, it must either adhere to its usual attitude of non-intervention in such cases—an attitude proper under normal conditions, but one which in this particular kind of case results to the disadvantage of its citizens in comparison with those of other States—or else it must, in order to be consistent in its policy, actively intervene to protect the contracts and concessions of its citizens engaged in agriculture, commerce, and transportation in competition with the subjects and citizens of other States.

[1] Bishop, *op. cit.*, I, 79; see also *Roosevelt-Lodge Correspondence*, I, 494, and *Letters to Anna Roosevelt Cowles*, p. 180.

This course would render the United States the insurer of all the speculative risks of its citizens in the public securities and franchises of Santo Domingo.[1]

Attention to economic interests appears again during the latter part of Roosevelt's administration when he pressed the claims of American corporations upon Venezuela to the point of finally breaking diplomatic relations with Castro to whose overthrow the following year he seems to have contributed. It should be added also that Roosevelt numbered among his advisers and associates both in the cabinet and in the diplomatic service men like Bacon and Meyer who in days past had had close connections with powerful financial interests in New York City.

But for all the actions and relationships mentioned above political rather than economic considerations seem to have determined Roosevelt's course. Nor must it be overlooked that the policy he favored was often opposed by influential financiers and corporation heads. Especially was this the case in his persistent fight for reciprocity with Cuba when, as we have seen, he encountered the hostility of the powerful sugar interests. That Roosevelt was influenced in his Caribbean policy by the economic tendencies of his day is of course beyond question, but no evidence has been found to support the thesis that either his measures or his actions were determined by, or were the result of, economic considerations pressed upon him by American financiers, business men, and corporations.

In conclusion, then, it may be said that Roosevelt's policy in the Caribbean represents a high type of opportunism. Unaware apparently of the goal toward which his course tended, he took Panama, interceded for Venezuela, preserved order in Cuba, mediated in Central America,

[1] *House Document No. 1* (Fifty-ninth Congress, first session), I, 336.

and intervened in Santo Domingo. Launched upon the project of an interoceanic canal primarily for the purpose of strengthening American naval power, he was led from one action to another until his activities embraced the entire Caribbean, necessitating in the development of his policy a broadening of the Monroe Doctrine and an assumption of obligations by the American people undreamed of by the fathers. In his course of action Roosevelt ever held in the foreground the needs of national defense. In his relations with the backward peoples of the tropics, with the exception of Colombia, his attitude was paternalistic, his policy that of benevolent imperialism. With him the old era of isolation passes forever and the new era of world-influence comes to the full dawn.

Bibliography

I. PRIMARY SOURCES

A. CORRESPONDENCE AND WRITINGS OF THEODORE ROOSEVELT

Roosevelt Papers. Division of Manuscripts, Library of Congress. Washington, D.C.

Bishop, Joseph Bucklin. *Theodore Roosevelt and His Time Shown in His Own Letters.* 2 vols. New York: Charles Scribner's Sons, 1919, 1920.

Letters from Theodore Roosevelt to Anna Roosevelt Cowles, 1870–1918. New York: Charles Scribner's Sons, 1924.

Roosevelt, Theodore. *Addresses and Presidential Messages of Theodore Roosevelt, 1902–1904.* (With an Introduction by Henry Cabot Lodge.) New York and London: G. P. Putnam's Sons, 1904.

Roosevelt, Theodore. *American Ideals . . . . Administration—Civil Service* (Homeward Bound ed.). Review of Reviews Co., 1910.

Roosevelt, Theodore. *An Autobiography.* New York: Charles Scribner's Sons, 1913.

Roosevelt, Theodore. *Essays on Practical Politics.* New York and London: G. P. Putnam's Sons, 1888.

Roosevelt, Theodore. "How the United States Acquired the Right to Dig the Panama Canal," *Outlook,* XCIX (1911), 314–18.

Roosevelt, Theodore. *Naval War of 1812: the History of the United States Navy during the Last War with Great Britain, to Which Is Appended an Account of the Battle of New Orleans* (Homeward Bound ed.). 2 vols. New York: Review of Reviews Co., 1910.

Roosevelt, Theodore. *Public Papers of Theodore Roosevelt, Governor.* Albany, N.Y.: Brandow Printing Co., 1899.

Roosevelt, Theodore. *Presidential Addresses and State Papers* (Homeward Bound ed.). 7 vols. New York: Review of Reviews Co., 1910.

Roosevelt, Theodore. *Presidential Addresses and State Papers and European Addresses* (Homeward Bound ed.). New York: Review of Reviews Co., 1910.

Roosevelt, Theodore. *Strenuous Life* (Homeward Bound ed.). New York: Review of Reviews Co., 1910.

BIBLIOGRAPHY

Roosevelt, Theodore. *Rough Riders* (Homeward Bound ed.). New York: Review of Reviews Co., 1910.

Roosevelt, Theodore. *Winning of the West* (Homeward Bound ed.). 4 vols. New York: Review of Reviews Co., 1910.

Selections from the Correspondence of Theodore Roosevelt and Henry Cabot Lodge, 1884–1918. 2 vols. New York: Charles Scribner's Sons, 1925.

B. GOVERNMENT DOCUMENTS

British and Foreign State Papers, Vols. XCV and XCVI. London: Harrison & Sons, 1905, 1906.

Congressional Globe. Washington: Government Printing Office, 1834–73.

Congressional Record: Containing the Proceedings and Debates of . . . . Congress of the United States of America. Washington: Government Printing Office, 1874—.

Grosse Politik der Europäischen Kabinette, 1871–1914 (Sammlung der Diplomatischen Akten des Auswärtigen Amtes. Siebzehnter Band. Im Auftrage des Auswärtigen Amtes herausgegeben von Johannes Lepsius, Albrecht Mendelsohn Bartholdy, Friedrich Thimme.) Berlin: Deutsche Verlagsgesellschaft für Politik und Geschichte M. B. H.

House Document No. 2, "Annual Reports of the War Department for the Fiscal Year Ended June 30, 1901." (Report of the Secretary of War.) "Miscellaneous Reports." (Fifty-seventh Congress, first session), Vol. II. Washington: Government Printing Office, 1901.

House Document No. 2, "Report of the Secretary of War and Reports of Bureau Chiefs" (Fifty-seventh Congress, second session, for the fiscal year ended June 30, 1902), Vol. I. Washington: Government Printing Office, 1903.

House Executive Document No. 183, "American Interests in Colombia" (Forty-ninth Congress, second session), Vol. XXV. Washington: Government Printing Office, 1887.

House Report No. 224, "Interoceanic Canal and the Monroe Doctrine" (Forty-sixth Congress, third session), Vol. I. Washington: Government Printing Office, 1881.

Journal of the Senate of the United States of America. . . . . Washington: Government Printing Office, 1789—.

Malloy, William M. "Treaties, Conventions, International Acts, Protocols and Agreements between the United States of America and Other Powers, 1776–1909," *Senate Document No. 357* (Sixty-first Congress, second session). 2 vols. Washington: Government Printing Office, 1910.

Merriam, William R. (director). *Census Reports: Twelfth Census of the United States Taken in the Year 1900*, Vol. I; "Population," Part I. (Prepared under the supervision of William C. Hunt, chief statistician for population.) Washington: United States Census Office, 1901.

Mexico. *Boletin Oficial de la Secretaria de Relaciones Exteriores.* Mexico, 1906–9.

Moore, John Bassett. *Digest of International Law.* 8 vols. Washington: Government Printing Office, 1906.

North, S. N. D. (director). Department of Commerce and Labor, Bureau of the Census, *Century of Population Growth from the First Census of the United States to the Twelfth, 1790–1900.* Washington: Government Printing Office, 1909.

Olmsted, Victor H., and Gannett, Henry (compilers). *Cuba: Population, History and Resources, 1907.* Washington: U.S. Bureau of the Census, 1909.

Papers Relating to the Foreign Relations of the United States with the Annual Message of the President. (Published also as *House Document No. 1* of the various regular sessions of Congress.) Washington: Government Printing Office [1862]—.

Parliamentary Debates (4th series, 1902), Vol. CXVI. London, 1903.

Reports from the Consuls of the United States on the Commerce, Manufactures, etc., of Their Consular Districts, 1880, 1881, 1899, 1900, 1901. (Published by the Department of State, according to act of Congress.) Washington: Government Printing Office, 1880, 1881, 1899, 1900, 1901.

Richardson, James D. *Compilation of the Messages and Papers of the Presidents, 1789–1908.* 11 vols. Washington: Government Printing Office, 1908.

Senate Document No. 413, "Correspondence Relating to Wrongs Done to American Citizens by the Government of Venezuela." (Message from the President of the United States, in response to a Senate resolution of February 20, 1908, transmitting a report of the Secre-

BIBLIOGRAPHY

tary of State, submitting the correspondence with the government of Venezuela in relation to pending controversies with that government concerning wrongs done to American citizens and corporations in that country by said government; Sixtieth Congress, first session). Washington: Government Printing Office, 1908.

Senate Document No. 474, "Diplomatic History of the Panama Canal" (Sixty-third Congress, second session). Washington: Government Printing Office, 1914.

Senate Document No. 133, "Official Proceedings of the New Panama Canal Company, etc." (Fifty-eighth Congress, second session), Vol. IV. Washington: Government Printing Office, 1904.

Senate Document No. 95, "Relations of the United States with Colombia and the Republic of Panama" (Fifty-eighth Congress, second session), Vol. III. Washington: Government Printing Office, 1904.

Senate Document No. 317, "Report of Robert C. Morris" (Fifty-eighth Congress, second session), Vol. XXXVI. Washington: Government Printing Office, 1904.

Senate Document No. 123, "Report of the Isthmian Canal Commission" (Fifty-Seventh Congress, first session), Vol. XII. Washington: Government Printing Office, 1902.

Senate Document No. 54, "Report of the Isthmian Canal Commission, 1899–1901" (Fifty-seventh Congress, first session), Vol. VII. Washington: Government Printing Office, 1901.

Senate Document No. 17, "Treaty between the United States and New Granada, and Accompanying Papers" (Fifty-eighth Congress, first session), Vol. II. Washington: Government Printing Office, 1904.

Senate Document No. 143, "Use by the United States of a Military Force in the Internal Affairs of Colombia, etc." (Fifty-eighth Congress, second session), Vol. IV. Washington: Government Printing Office ,1904.

Senate Document No. 119, "Venezuelan Arbitration before the Hague Tribunal, 1903: Proceedings of the Tribunal under the Protocols between Venezuela and Great Britain, Germany, Italy, United States, Belgium, France, Mexico, the Netherlands, Spain, Sweden and Norway, Signed at Washington, May 7, 1903" (Fifty-eighth Congress, third session), Vol. VII. Washington: Government Printing Office, 1905.

ROOSEVELT AND THE CARIBBEAN

Senate Document No. 316, "Venezuelan Arbitrations of 1903, Including Protocols, Personnel and Rules of Commissions, Opinions, and Summary of Awards, with Appendix Containing Venezuelan *Yellow Book of 1903*, Bowen Pamphlet Entitled 'Venezuelan Protocols,' and 'Preferential Question' Hague Decision, with History of Recent Venezuelan Revolutions," prepared by Jackson H. Ralston and W. T. Sherman Doyle (Fifty-eighth Congress, second session), Vol. XXXV. Washington: Government Printing Office, 1904.

Senate Executive Document No. 112, "Interoceanic Canal" (Forty-sixth Congress, second session), Vol. IV. Washington: Government Printing Office, 1880.

Senate Select Committee on Haiti and Santo Domingo, "Hearings before a Select Committee on Haiti and Santo Domingo." (Printed for the use of the Select Committee.) 3 parts. Washington: Government Printing Office, 1921 and 1922.

Statutes at Large of the United States of America, Concurrent Resolutions of the Two Houses of Congress, and Recent Treaties, Conventions, and Executive Proclamations. (Edited, printed, and published by authority of the Secretary of State.) Washington: Government Printing Office, 1856–.

Story of Panama. (Hearings on the Rainey Resolution before the Committee on Foreign Affairs of the House of Representatives.) Washington: Government Printing Office, 1913.

Treaties and Conventions Concluded between the United States and Other Powers Since July 4, 1776. Washington: Government Printing Office, 1889.

C. AUTOBIOGRAPHIES, MEMOIRS, AND PERSONAL NARRATIVES

Abbott, Lawrence F. *Impressions of Theodore Roosevelt*. Garden City: Doubleday, Page & Co., 1923.

Abbott, Lawrence F. (ed.). *Letters of Archie Butt, Personal Aide to President Roosevelt*. Garden City: Doubleday, Page & Co., 1924.

Adams, Henry. *Education of Henry Adams: an Autobiography*. Boston and New York: Houghton Mifflin Co., 1918.

Alger, Russell A. *Spanish-American War*. New York and London: Harper & Bros., 1906.

Bunau-Varilla, Philippe. *Panama: The Creation, Destruction, and Resurrection*. New York: McBride, Nast & Co., 1914.

BIBLIOGRAPHY

Bunau-Varilla, Philippe. *Great Adventure of Panama Wherein Are Exposed Its Relation to the Great War and also the Luminous Traces of the German Conspiracies against France and the United States.* Garden City: Doubleday, Page & Co., 1920.

Cleveland, Grover. *Presidential Problems.* New York: Century Co., 1904.

Cullom, Shelby M. *Fifty Years of Public Service.* Chicago: A. C. McClurg & Co., 1911.

Dewey, George. *Autobiography of George Dewey Admiral of the Navy.* New York: Charles Scribner's Sons, 1913.

Foraker, Joseph Benson. *Notes of a Busy Life.* 2 vols. Cincinnati: Steward & Kidd Co., 1916.

Foster, John W. *Diplomatic Memoirs.* 2 vols. Boston: Houghton Mifflin Co., 1909.

Foulke, William Dudley. *Hoosier Autobiography.* New York: Oxford University Press, 1922.

Jordan, David Starr. *Days of a Man.* Yonkers-on-Hudson: World Book Co., 1924.

Leary, John J., Jr. *Talks with T. R.* Boston and New York: Houghton Mifflin Co., 1919.

Letters of John Hay and Extracts from Diary. 3 vols. (Printed but not published; copyright by Clara S. Hay.) Washington, 1908.

Long, John Davis. *New American Navy.* 2 vols. New York: Outlook Co., 1903.

Mayo, Lawrence Shaw (ed.). *America of Yesterday as Reflected in the Journal of John Davis Long.* Boston: Atlantic Monthly Press, 1923.

Robinson, Corinne Roosevelt. *My Brother Theodore Roosevelt.* New York: Charles Scribner's Sons, 1921.

von Eckardstein, Baron. *Ten Years at the Court of St. James, 1895–1905.* (Translated and edited by Professor George Young.) London: Thornton Butterworth, Ltd., 1921.

D. NEWSPAPERS

Chicago Daily Tribune. Chicago, Ill.
Daily News. Chicago, Ill.
Daily Tribune. New York City.
Post. Washington, D.C.
Times, New York City.
World. New York City.

ROOSEVELT AND THE CARIBBEAN

II. SECONDARY SOURCES

A. HISTORIES AND BIOGRAPHIES

Adams, Randolph Greenfield. *History of the Foreign Policy of the United States*, New York: Macmillan Co., 1924.

Clark, William J. *Commercial Cuba: a Book for Business Men.* (With an Introduction by E. Sherman Gould.) New York: Charles Scribner's Sons, 1898.

Coolidge, Louis Arthur. *Old-Fashioned Senator: Orville H. Platt, of Connecticut: the Story of a Life Unselfishly Devoted to the Public Service.* New York and London: G. P. Putnam's Sons, 1910.

Croly, Herbert David. *Marcus Alonzo Hanna: His Life and Work.* New York: Macmillan Co., 1912.

Davis, Oscar King. *Released for Publication.* Boston and New York: Houghton Mifflin Co., 1925.

Dennett, Tyler. *Roosevelt and the Russo-Japanese War: a Critical Study of American Policy in Eastern Asia in 1902–1905, Based Primarily upon the Private Papers of Theodore Roosevelt.* Garden City: Doubleday, Page & Co., 1925.

Dunn, Arthur Wallace. *From Harrison to Harding, a Personal Narrative, Covering a Third of a Century, 1888–1921.* New York and London: G. P. Putnam's Sons, 1922.

Fish, Carl Russell. *American Diplomacy.* New York: Century Co., 1915.

Fish, Carl Russell. *Path of Empire: a Chronicle of the United States as a World Power,* "Chronicles of America Series," Vol. XLVI. (Edited by Allen Johnson.) New Haven: Yale University Press, 1919.

Foster, John Watson. *American Diplomacy in the Orient.* Boston and New York: Houghton Mifflin Co., 1903.

Hart, Albert Bushnell. *Foundations of American Foreign Policy with a Working Bibliography.* New York: Macmillan Co., 1901.

Howe, M. A. de Wolfe. *George von Lengerke Meyer: His Life and Public Services.* New York: Dodd, Mead & Co., 1919.

Howland, Harold. *Theodore Roosevelt and His Times: a Chronicle of the Progressive Movement,* "Chronicles of America Series," Vol. XLVII. (Edited by Allen Johnson.) New Haven: Yale University Press, 1921.

Johnson, Willis Fletcher. *America's Foreign Relations.* 2 vols. New York: Century Co., 1916.

BIBLIOGRAPHY

Jones, Chester Lloyd. *Caribbean Interests and the United States.* New York: D. Appleton & Co., 1916.

Kelly, Howard A. *Walter Reed and Yellow Fever.* New York: McClure, Phillips & Co., 1906.

Latané, John Holladay. *America as a World Power, 1897–1907,* "The American Nation: a History," Vol. XXV. (Edited by Albert Bushnell Hart.) New York and London: Harper & Bros., 1907.

Latané, John Holladay. *United States and Latin America.* Garden City and New York: Doubleday, Page & Co., 1920.

McElroy, Robert McNutt. *Grover Cleveland the Man and the Statesman.* 2 vols. New York and London: Harper & Bros., 1923.

Miller, Benjamin L., and Singewald, Joseph T. *Mineral Deposits of South America.* New York: McGraw-Hill Book Co., 1919.

Munro, Dana Gardner. *Five Republics of Central America: Their Political and Economic Development and Their Relations with the United States.* (Edited by David Kinley; Carnegie Endowment for International Peace.) New York: Oxford University Press, 1918.

Ogg, Frederic Austin. *National Progress, 1907–1917,* "The American Nation: a History," Vol. XXVII. (Edited by Albert Bushnell Hart.) New York and London: Harper & Bros., 1918.

Olcott, Charles Sumner. *Life of William McKinley.* 2 vols. Boston and New York: Houghton Mifflin Co., 1916.

Orcutt, William Dana. *Burrows of Michigan and the Republican Party: a Biography and a History.* New York: Longmans, Green & Co., 1917.

Rhodes, James Ford. *History of the United States from the Compromise of 1850 to the Final Restoration of Home Rule at the South in 1877.* Vols. VI and VII. New York: Macmillan Co., 1906.

Rhodes, James Ford. *History of the United States from Hayes to McKinley, 1877–1896.* New York: Macmillan Co., 1919.

Rhodes, James Ford. *McKinley and Roosevelt Administrations, 1897–1909.* New York: Macmillan Co., 1922.

Riis, Jacob A. *Theodore Roosevelt the Citizen.* New York: Macmillan, Co., 1904.

Robertson, William Spense. *Hispanic-American Relations with the United States.* (Edited by David Kinley.) New York: Oxford University Press, 1923.

Root, Elihu. *Latin America and the United States: Addresses by Elihu Root.* (Collected and edited by Robert Bacon and James Brown Scott.) Cambridge: Harvard University Press, 1917.

Schlesinger, Arthur Meier. *New Viewpoints in American History.* New York: Macmillan Co., 1922.

Scott, James Brown. *Robert Bacon, Life and Letters.* Garden City: Doubleday, Page & Co., 1923.

Seitz, Don C. *Joseph Pulitzer: His Life and Letters.* New York: Simon & Schuster, 1924.

Silvio, Selva. *United States and Central America.* No place; no date.

Sparks, Edwin Eric. *National Development,* "The American Nation: a History," Vol. XXIII. (Edited by Albert Bushnell Hart.) New York and London: Harper & Bros., 1907.

Stuart, Graham H. *Latin America and the United States.* New York: Century Co., 1922.

Sullivan, Mark. *Our Times: The United States, 1900–1925.* (Vol. I: "The Turn of the Century, 1900–1904.") New York: Charles Scribner's Sons, 1926.

Thayer, William Roscoe. *Life and Letters of John Hay.* 2 vols. Boston and New York: Houghton Mifflin Co., 1915.

Turner, Frederick Jackson. *Frontier in American History.* New York: Henry Holt & Co., 1921.

von Bülow, Prince Bernhard. *Imperial Germany.* (Translated by Marie A. Lewenz.) New York: Dodd, Mead & Co., 1914.

Weeden, William B. *Economic and Social History of New England, 1620–1789.* 2 vols. Boston and New York: Houghton Mifflin & Co., 1890.

B. ARTICLES AND MONOGRAPHS

American Business Man, "Is the Monroe Doctrine a Bar to Civilization?" *North American Review,* CLXXVI (April, 1903), 520 ff.

Anderson, Luis. "Central American Court of Justice," *American Journal of International Law,* II (January, 1908), 144–51.

Bowen, Herbert R. "Roosevelt and Venezuela," *North American Review,* CCX (September, 1919), 414–17.

Brown, Philip Marshall. "American Diplomacy in Central America," *American Political Science Review,* VI (suppl.), 151–61.

Brown, Philip Marshall. "American Intervention in Central America," *Journal of Race Development,* IV (April, 1914), 409–26.

Cochran, Mary Elizabeth. *Panama, Colombia, and the United States.* (Unpublished Master's dissertation.) Chicago, 1921.

du Bois, James T. *Colombia's Claims and Rights.* No place; no date.

BIBLIOGRAPHY

Editorial. "First Case before the Central American Court of Justice," *American Journal of International Law* (October, 1908).

Fabela, Isidro. *Los Estados Unidos contra la Libertad* (Cuba, Filipinas, Panama, Nicaragua, Republica Dominicana). Barcelona: Falleres Graficos "Lux" Diputacion, 211, no date.

Foster, John W. *Annexation of Hawaii*. (An address delivered before the National Geographic Society, at Washington, D.C., March 26, 1897.) Washington: Gibson Bros., 1897.

Grosvenor, Gilbert. "The Hawaiian Islands," *National Geographic Magazine*, XLV (February, 1924), 120 ff.

Hale, William Bayard. "Our Dangers in Central America," *World's Work*, XXIV (August, 1912), 443–51.

Hollander, Jacob H. "The Convention of 1907 between the United States and the Dominican Republic," *American Journal of International Law*, Vol. I (1907), Part I, pp. 287–97.

Hollander, Jacob H. "The Readjustment of San Domingo's Finances," *Quarterly Journal of Economics*, XXI (May, 1907), 405–26.

Hollander, Jacob H. "The Dominican Convention and Its Lessons," *Journal of Race Development*, IV (April, 1914), 398–408.

Jones, Chester Lloyd. "Bananas and Diplomacy," *North American Review*, CXCVIII (August, 1913), 188–94.

Jones, Chester Lloyd. "Banana Trade," *Independent*, LXXV (August, 1913), 77–80.

Jones, Chester Lloyd. "Oil on the Caribbean and Elsewhere," *North American Review*, CCII (October, 1915), 536–44.

Kelsey, Carl. "The American Intervention in Haiti and the Dominican Republic," *Annals of American Academy of Political and Social Science*, Vol. C (March, 1922), No. 189, pp. 109–200.

MacClintock, Samuel. "Revolutions and Interventions in Central America," *World Today*, XXI (August, 1911), 955–62.

Moore, John Bassett. "John Hay" (a review of William Roscoe Thayer's *Life and Letters of John Hay*), *Political Science Quarterly*, Vol. XXXII (March, 1917), No. 1, pp. 119–25.

Potter, Pitman Benjamin. *Myth of American Isolation: Our Policy of International Co-operation*, "League of Nations," Vol. IV, No. 6. Boston: World Peace Foundation, 1921.

Scott, James Brown. "The Central American Peace Conference of 1907," *American Journal of International Law*, II (January, 1908), 121–44.

Showalter, William Joseph. "Redeeming the Tropics," *National Geographic Magazine*, XXV (March, 1914), 344–58.

Slade, William Franklin. "Federation of Central America," *Journal of Race Development*, VII (July-October, 1917), 79–150, 204–75.

Spinden, Herbert Joseph. "Yellow Fever—First and Last," *World's Work*, XLIII (December, 1921), 169–81.

Thayer, William Roscoe. "Bowen versus Roosevelt," *North American Review*, CCX (September, 1919), 250–54.

Travis, Ira Dudley. "History of the Clayton-Bulwer Treaty," "Michigan Political Science Association Publications," Vol. III, No. 8.

Urena, Max Henriquez. *Los Estados Unidos y la Republica Dominicana la Verdad de los hechos comprobada por datos y documentos oficiales*. Habana: Teniente Rey, 1919.

Urrutia, Francisco Jose. *Commentary on the Declaration of the Rights of Nations Adopted by the American Institute of International Law*. Washington, 1916.

C. PERIODICALS

American Journal of International Law. New York: Baker, Voorhis & Co.

Annals of the American Academy of Political and Social Science. Philadelphia: American Academy of Political and Social Science.

Independent. (Devoted to the consideration of politics, of social and economic tendencies, of history, literature, and the arts. . . . .) New York.

Monthly Bulletin of the International Bureau of American Republics. Washington, D.C.

National Geographic Magazine. (An illustrated monthly.) Washington: National Geographic Society.

North American Review. New York: D. Appleton & Co.

Outlook. New York: Outlook Co.

Political Science Quarterly. (A review devoted to the historical, statistical, and comparative study of politics, economics, and public law. Edited for the Academy of Political Science in the City of New York by the Faculty of Political Science of Columbia University . . . . .). New York: Ginn & Co.

Public Opinion. New York: Public Opinion Co.

World's Work. Garden City: Doubleday, Page & Co.

INDEX

Adams, Brooks, letter to, 21

Adams, John, 2

Adee, Alvey A.: mentioned, 102 n.; statement on the purpose of the *modus vivendi* in Santo Domingo, 164; author of protocol for Washington Conference, 186

"Adler," at Samoa, 7.

Alaska: annexation, 4, 13; boundary dispute, 145

Amador, Dr. Manuel, and Panama insurrection, 55, 56, 59, 60

Amapala: capture of, 184; Treaty of, 185; agreement of, 186, 187.

American Sugar Refining Co., 80 n.

Anderson, Señor, on causes of conflict in Central America, 188

Andrade, General Freyre, and Cuban election (1905), 88–90

Arbitration: proposal, by Lord Salisbury, 12; Venezuelan debts case, 110, 118, 120 ff., 132 n., 134–36, 137. n., 146, 147; difficulties in Central America, 181–85, 187 n., 191, 192, 194–96

Argentine, mentioned, 33, 139, 140

Bacon, Robert: and intervention in Cuba, 94, 95, 97–99, 102 n., 103; mediation in Central America, 177; mentioned, 212

Bahia Honda, naval station, 76

Balfour, Arthur J.: quoted on war with the United States, 12 n.; on Venezuelan blockade, 117 n., 119

Bayard, Secretary T. F., quoted on contractual claims, 171 n.

Beaupré, A. M., on Colombia and canal treaty, 51–53

Beers, Captain, and Panama insurrection, 56

Belgium: and Venezuelan debts, 110, 142 n.; Dominican claims, 154 f.; mentioned, 208

Bennett, J. G., on population of Cuba, 89 n.

Berkeley, quotation from Roosevelt's address at, 67

Bibliography, 214

Bidlack, Benjamin A., and treaty with New Granada, 40–41

Bishop, J. B., letter to, 157

Bismarck, Chancellor Otto von, invitation to joint commission (Samoan crisis), 7

Blaine, James G.: Pan-American Conference, 4, 5 and n., 9; supported for presidency by Roosevelt, 18; attitude on collections of French claims against Venezuela (1881), 159 n.; views on union of Central America, 174 n.

Blockade, Venezuelan, 116–19, 128–31, 137 n.

Blue Book, inaccuracy of British, 117 n.

Bonilla (president of Honduras), revolution against government of, 183–85

Bowen, H. W., and Venezuelan debts case, 120, 141–44

Boxer Insurrection, 147

Bradford, Admiral, and *modus vivendi* in Santo Domingo, 164, 165

Brazil, German foothold in, 145

Brown, Philip, and control of Tegucigalpa, 184, 185

Bryan-Chamorro Treaty, 196

[225]

INDEX

Cromwell, William Nelson, and Panama insurrection, 55, 56

Cuba: and Spanish-American War, 20 f., 69; during first American occupation, 70, 77-78, 83, 85; work of Constitutional Convention, 70-76; trade with United States, 78-79, 79 n., 212; investments in, 79 n., 91; sanitation in, 83-86; political parties, 87-88; population, 89 and n.; insurrection (1905-6), 91-93; American intervention (1906), 102-3, 197, 199-200; second American occupation, 103-5

Dakota Bad Lands, Roosevelt in, 18, 203

Danish West Indies: annexation rejected by Senate, 13; mentioned, 204

Dávila, President: secures presidency of Honduras by insurrection, 185; recognized by Roosevelt, 186

Dawson, T. C.: and Santo Domingo, directed to propose receivership for Santo Domingo, 158-59; suggests *modus vivendi*, 161; reports activity of American naval vessels at Dominican ports, 165 n.

Debts: collection of, in Venezuela, 109-11, 120, 139-40, 171-72; in Santo Domingo, 154-63, 168, 170; policy of United States, 172-73

De Lesseps, Ferdinand, 64 n.

Denmark, mentioned, 208

Dewey, George: appointment to command of Asiatic squadron, 24 and n., 25 n.; Venezuelan crisis (1902), 124-26, 128, 132-34, 144 f.; at Manila, 145; mentioned, 32

Diaz, President: mediation in Central America, 177-80, 186, 197

Diederich, Admiral, at Manila, 145

Dillingham-Sanchez protocol: terms of, 159-60; objections to, 166 and n.

Dingley Tariff Act, and Cuban reciprocity, 79, 82

Diplomacy, spirit of Rooseveltian, 52-53, 200 n., 201

Drago Doctrine: quoted, 139 f.; mentioned, 173

Du Bois (minister to Colombia), quoted, 68

Eckardstein, Baron von, 114

Ecuador: mediation, 4; history, 37

Edward VII, King, attitude toward Venezuelan crisis (1902), 129 n., 130

Egypt, Roosevelt's praise of British rule in, 204-5

Ehrman, Felix, and Panama insurrection, 61

Fish, Hamilton: on expansion, 13; quoted on American obligations under treaty with New Granada (1846), 42

Foraker, Senator: letter from Roosevelt to, 101; consulted on collection of debts in Santo Domingo, 161

Foster, John W.: draws up treaty of annexation with Hawaii, 9; suggests objection to "pacific blockade" in Venezuelan crisis (1902), 118 n.

France: Venezuelan debt case, 110, 159 n.; establishes "pacific blockade" against Siam (1893), 119 n.; Dominican claims, 154-55; mentioned, 5, 64 and n., 79 n., 205

Frelinghuysen, Theodore, opposes Pan-American Conference, 5

French Alliance, mentioned, 2

French Revolution, mentioned, 2, 153

Geneva, Treaty of, ratified by the United States, 3

George, Henry, candidate for mayor of New York, 18

Germany: and Samoa, 6-9; isthmian canal, 33, 123-24; alleged influence in defeat of Hay-Herran Convention, 50 n.; action against Venezuela (1902-3), 109, 110, 113-14, 115-18, 120-38, 141-44; Dominican debt case, 155; mentioned, 208

Gil, Alejandro Wos y, 152

INDEX

India, Roosevelt's praise of British rule in, 204–5

Industrialism, development and effect of, on expansion, 14–15

International police power, Roosevelt's idea of, 149

Isle of Pines, 73, 91

Isolation, national, disappearance of, 1–16, 213

Isthmian canal: routes for, 35, 36 and n., 47, 53; early interest in, 38 f., 65 n.; defense of, 31–33, 123–24, 133 n.

Italy: and Venezuelan debt case, 109, 116, 118, 137 n., 142; and claims in Santo Domingo, 155, 156, 160

Jackson, Andrew, and interoceanic canal, 38, 39

Japan, and commercial relations, 5

Jefferson, Thomas: quoted, 2, criticized by Roosevelt, 202

Jimenes, 151, 152

Jimenistas, 152, 153

Jordan, David Starr, quoted, 201, 206 n.

Kermit, Edith Carow, marriage to Roosevelt, 18

Kiauchau, German control of, 123, 124

Kipling, Rudyard: quoted, 204; letter to, 208

Knox, Secretary P. C.: consulted on Dominican debt collection, 161; policy in Central America, 170 and n.; mentioned, 68

Krüger telegram, and Venezuelan crisis (1895), 12

La Guaira, 112, 142

Lansdowne, Lord, and Venezuelan crisis (1902), 115, 117 and n., 121–22, 134, 135 n.

Latin America, effect of Roosevelt's Panama policy on, 68; political and financial conditions in, 106–9

Lee, Fitzhugh, delays McKinley's war message, 23

Lincoln, Abraham, mentioned, 30

Lodge, Henry Cabot: efforts of, in securing Roosevelt's appointment as assistant secretary of the navy, 19–20; opinion on value of Colombian claims in Panama, 51; mentioned, 12, 31, 161, 204 n., 205

Loomis, F. B.: connection with Panama revolution, 54, 60–61; conversation with J. B. Moore on Panama situation, 57–58; relations with Bunau-Varilla, 54, 56 n., 59, 60; quoted on conditions in Venezuela, 108

Long, Secretary John D.: inaccuracy of 19 n., 25 n.; comments on Roosevelt's conduct as secretary of navy, 22, 24 ff.; praise of Roosevelt, 28

Louisiana Purchase, comparison with Panama Canal, 30 n.

Lowden, Frank O., and vice-presidency, 29 n.

McKinley, President William: and annexation of Hawaii, 9; appointment of Roosevelt as assistant secretary of the navy, 19–20; Spanish-American War, 21, 23 and n.; attitude toward Roosevelt as candidate for vice-presidency, 22; war message, 22–23; death, 29, 33; reliance on cabinet members, 19 n., 24 n., 34; Platt Amendment, 73, 75; mentioned, 69

Magoon, Charles E., provisional governor of Cuba, 103–5

Mahan, A. T., letter to, 203

"Maine," sinking of, as cause for war, 21

"Marblehead," mentioned, 60, 63; conference, 178–79, 182, 197

Marcy, William L., and Hawaii, 8

Marroquin, President J. M.: coup d'état in Colombia, 49; and Hay-Herran Treaty, 51

Matanzas, 84

Metternich, Count, and Venezuelan debt case, 115, 121, 122, 135 n., 143

INDEX

Rio de Janeiro Conference, 172–73, 180

Roosevelt, T.: favors national expansion, 1, 31, 213; advocates isthmian canal, 1; governor of New York, 1, 2 n., 29, 32, 204; favors annexation of Hawaii, 9 n., 31; praise of Cleveland's Venezuelan policy, 11–12; physical weakness, in early life, 17, 202 f.; education, 17; first book, 17–18, 202; member of New York Legislature, 18; delegate to Republican National Convention (1884), 18; defeated in campaign for mayor of New York City, 18; marriage, 18; member of Civil Service Commission, 18–19; police commissioner, 19; assistant secretary of the navy, 19 ff., 31; urges war with Spain, 20–21, 25 n.; joins the Rough Riders, 28–29; elected to vice-presidency, 29 and n.; becomes president, 29, 198; pride in Panama policy, 30–31, 68; early interest in isthmian canal, 31–32, 36, 68, 203; opposition to first Hay-Pauncefote Treaty, 31–33, 203; attitude on Monroe Doctrine, 2, 33, 112, 131, 141 n., 149, 199, 200, 213; opposition to European territorial possessions in America, 33, 210–11; opinion on abrogation of treaties, 33; control of foreign relations, 33–34; attitude toward terms of Hay-Herran Convention, 47 n.; criticism of Colombia, 48 n., 51 n., 63, 67, 207–8; relation to Panama revolt, 54 and n., 55, 67; action in Panama, 56–63; 212; justification of Panama policy, 30–31, 58 n., 63–68, 203, 208; opinion of first American occupation of Cuba, 78; urges Cuban reciprocity, 80–82, 212; Platt Amendment, 81, 86, 96, 97, 204; intervention in Cuba, 93–105, 197, 199–200, 208–10; attitude toward laws and constitutions, 97, 100–101; regard for public opinion, 99–100; mentioned, 114, 119, 191, 196; action in Venezuelan crisis (1902), 119, 122–38, 141, 143–47, 198–99, 208, 212; national defense, 123, 133 n., 196, 200–204,

213; position on collection of debts, 140, 148, 158, 159, 161–63, 171–73, 211–12; policy in Santo Domingo, 148–49, 157, 164, 197, 199, 200, 203, 208, 210, 211, 213; annexation of territory, 157 and n., 209–11; influence of debt-collecting policy, 169–73; mediation in Central America, 176–80, 184–86, 197, 208, 212; opportunism, 198–200, 212, 213; characterization of own foreign policy, 200 n.; attitude toward backward races, 204–9, 213

Roosevelt Papers, ix, 127, 130

Root, Elihu: and Panama revolution, 54, 58 n., 63; Platt Amendment, 73 and n., 75; quoted on American administration in Cuba, 77–78; quoted on sugar industry in Cuba, 79; advocates Cuban reciprocity, 80; urges sanitation in Cuba, 85; trip to South America, 94, 102 n.; *modus vivendi* in Santo Domingo, 165–66; mediation in Central America, 186; Central American Peace Conference, 187–88, 191–92

Rosebery, Lord, quoted on war with the United States, 12 n.

Rough Riders, 29

Russia: and Alaska, 13; Roosevelt's view of expansion of, 205; mentioned, 208

St. John, annexation of, 13, 204

St. Thomas, annexation of, 13, 204

Salisbury, Lord, and Venezuelan boundary dispute (1895), 11–12

Salvador: war with Guatemala, 176, 177; "Marblehead" conference, 178–80; Corinto Treaty, 182; San José Treaty, 182

Samoan Islands, controversy over, 6–9

San Carlos, Fort, bombardment of, by Germany, 143, 145–46

San José Treaty (1906), 180–83, 185, 190, 193, 197

Santiago, mentioned, 84

INDEX